"Witty and whimsical, this book is a deep meditation on the divine feminine, a love letter to lovers of movies and memories. It's a stirring, poetic memoir of a life remarkably lived and still living."

—Margaret Cho

"The artistry of Charles Busch has no equal in the modern theater, with his genuine reverence for the women who inspire him. This memoir left me doubled over with laughter and choking back tears—sometimes on the same page."

—Armistead Maupin

Praise for *Leading Lady*

"If, like me, you already know what a major influence Charles Busch has had on your life and career, you will not be able to sleep until you finish this book. *Leading Lady* is both a page-turner with name-drops and a book depicting the thrill of creation. It is profound in Charles's stories of the relationships that formed his life. If you aren't sure of his influence on your own world, you will still be spellbound, and you will also come away with a new mentor for living an unafraid life true to who you are."

—Jim Parsons

"Fascinating, elegant, frank, and unputdownable. I devoured this book with a glee that could only be surpassed by watching Charles Busch perform live!"

—Alan Cumming

"I have loved Charles Busch since I first clapped eyes on him—he's an ac[tor,] an actress, a writer, a director, a peerless raconteur and wit, and a sentime[ntal] gentleman from my favorite school, the old school."

—Bette Midler

"I'll read, watch, and listen to anything Charles does. Drag and Holly[wood] royalty combined in one Grande Dame. *Leading Lady* indeed!"

—Jinkx Monsoon

"A long time ago in a galaxy far, far away, Turner Classic Movi[es met] *RuPaul's Drag Race* and they conceived an adorable little one w[ho grew] up to be the lady in question: Charles Busch. Saddle up for a [ ] hilarity-soaked ride."

—Bruce Vilanch

Leading Lady

LEADING LADY

A Memoir of a Most Unusual Boy

Charles Busch

Smart Pop Books

An Imprint of BenBella Books, Inc.

Dallas, TX

BenBella Books, Inc.
10440 N. Central Expressway
Suite 800
Dallas, TX 75231
benbellabooks.com
Send feedback to feedback@benbellabooks.com

BenBella is a federally registered trademark.

Printed in the United States of America
10 9 8 7 6 5 4 3 2 1

Library of Congress Control Number: 2023003246
ISBN 9781637744147 (hardcover)
ISBN 9781637744154 (electronic)

Editing by Robb Pearlman and Alexa Stevenson
Copyediting by Michael Fedison
Proofreading by Madeline Grigg and Cape Cod Compositors, Inc.
Text design and composition by Aaron Edmiston
Cover design by Brigid Pearson
Cover photograph by David Rodgers
Printed by Lake Book Manufacturing

To Katherine Carr. What would my past have been like without you? The present certainly would be impossible and the future unimaginable.

The Opening Act

It was 2013, and I was meeting Joan Rivers outside the Richard Rodgers Theatre to attend a production of *Romeo and Juliet*. I was expecting her to arrive in a taxi or limousine—instead I saw her running down the street, her nearly ankle-length fur coat flapping in the wind. She was struggling with a large cardboard sign, a comedy prop to take backstage for a photo with Orlando Bloom, the play's star. The Joan racing down 46th Street was not an elderly show business legend but her earliest self, the young hopeful, fighting the naysayers who scoffed that she'd ever make it.

Joan worshipped the theater. She tried to see everything on Broadway, Off-Broadway, and Off-Off Broadway.

"Charles, I'm telling you, I go to plays in rat-infested basements where I'm the only one who's shown up. I can see the actors peeking through the curtain and groaning, 'Oh God, that old bitch in the fur coat is here. Does that mean we've gotta go on?'"

I reminded her that she first saw *me* perform in a rat-infested basement.

With her insane schedule of flying back and forth to LA and making a weekly trip to QVC's television studio in West Chester, Pennsylvania, Joan did most of her sleeping at the theater. I once accompanied her to a critically acclaimed production of Schiller's classic play *Mary Stuart* starring the British actress Janet McTeer. Five minutes after the play began, Joan was resting her head on my shoulder fast asleep. She woke up two minutes before the end of the first act just in time to whisper in my ear, "This play . . . it's *awful*. How could they put her in those unflattering tight sleeves?"

Once I was Joan's date for producer/director Hal Prince's annual Christmas party, held at his dazzling Fifth Avenue duplex apartment. Downstairs, people gathered around the piano. The composer Jason Robert Brown was playing. Stephen Sondheim was seated in an easy chair in front, and he urged Barbara Cook to sing. Barbara moved over to the piano and delivered an exquisite performance of "In Buddy's Eyes." Joan whispered in my ear, "Can you believe we're *here*?"

Another time, dining with a group of friends at Joe Allen, Joan expressed wistfully, "I wish I had a gay son I could phone at midnight and discuss whatever movie was on TCM." Everyone laughed. I fell silent, but inside I was pleading, *Take me. I'll be your gay son.*

Joan was the most prominent in a long line of smart, bigger-than-life mother figures I've attached myself to. All my life, I've been in a search for a maternal woman whose lap I could rest my head on.

The Longest Day of the Year

June 21, 1962. Hartsdale, New York. I hadn't yet turned eight years old. Mommy, so shy around people, had mustered the courage to go down the street to complain to the LaRosa family that their unleashed dog, Rhonda, was pausing every day to take a humongous dump on our front lawn.

She had been gone only a short while when Mr. LaRosa ran into our yard shouting something incomprehensible. Seated on my father's lap, I fell hard on the ground as he leaped out of the lawn chair. Daddy and Mr. LaRosa jumped over the low log fence separating our home from the neighbors next door. We lived at the top of a hill, and we could view all the neighbors' backyards from ours. A few older boys came into our yard to check out what was going on down the hill. With only a vague notion of who they were, I heard one of them say, "Somebody's mom dropped dead in the LaRosas' yard."

I was both a spectator and a participant in this drama, which I suppose set the pattern for the rest of my life.

My mother had a damaged heart from a childhood bout of rheumatic fever and at twenty was warned never to have children. Instead, she had three—my two older sisters, Margaret and Betsy, and me. Many years later, Margaret told me that earlier that day as she was going upstairs, Mommy had suddenly pulled her aside and, apropos of nothing, said in a voice that seemed almost angry in its urgency, "Margaret, if anything should happen to me, you must promise that you'll be best friends with your brother. You have to take care of him."

Hours later, the sun was now beginning to disappear. Daddy came home and told us: "Mommy's dead."

She'd had a heart attack in the LaRosas' backyard and died on the spot. It was all over before the ambulance even arrived. Margaret and Betsy were sobbing and clinging to Daddy.

I didn't cry. I watched the characters in the movie. Daddy pulled me over to him and wrapped his arms around all of us. Crushed in that tight embrace, I wondered, *What happens to us now?*

Was that the first time I came up with that question? It's what I wonder after any moment of tragedy or joy. An opening night and a rave review is read aloud; everyone cheers and embraces each other with abandon. I stand apart, watching the others and silently wondering, *What happens to us now?*

A few days later, alone in my parents' bedroom with my mother's older sister, Lil, I observed my aunt performing the grim task of choosing a dress for my mother to be cremated in. With her suburban lifestyle, Mommy was almost always in slacks and shorts and sweaters. My father, proud of her classic beauty, once told me that in a room full of beautiful women, my mother could stand out in just a simple skirt and white blouse. I sat on the bed and watched Aunt Lil go through Mommy's closet. She took out several dresses and laid them on the bed. One was a grey and black floral chiffon cocktail dress with a full skirt, clearly the most appropriate choice.

Toward the back of the closet, Aunt Lil came across the poplin jacket that my mother had enjoyed wearing with dungarees when the fall weather grew chilly. It could almost have been a boy's jacket. Aunt Lil finally spoke. "You should have this to remember Mommy. She loved you so much. I'm going to take it home with me to New York, where it will be safe. And it will always be there for you."

She kept the jacket in a storage box underneath her bed, easily accessible, and over the next few years, every so often I would take it out and hold it close to my nose, trying to keep my mother's memory alive as she was hurled backwards into the mist of the past.

Redheaded Woman

The same year as my mother's death, I attended my first professional production, and at its center was an extraordinary Titian-tressed diva whose image would be forever imprinted in my creative consciousness. My father took me to the old Metropolitan Opera House in New York City to hear the celebrated Australian coloratura Joan Sutherland sing the role of Amina in Bellini's *La Sonnambula*.

Opera was my father's lifelong passion. Daddy possessed a rich baritone, but lacked the gargantuan drive, discipline, and exceptional talent essential to a career on the operatic stage. He had to settle for selling opera recordings at his music store in Yonkers and playing roles in summer stock and community theater. Daddy performed occasionally with the Westchester Opera Guild, and their production of *La Traviata* the previous spring made a huge impression on me, particularly the soprano playing the tragic Violetta.

After the performance I was taken backstage, where my father introduced me to the principals in the cast. The romantic doomed courtesan Violetta was revealed to be a dowdy suburban music teacher. Not in the least disappointed, I was fascinated that she could be so utterly transformed under the stage lights. Perhaps, then, a young boy from Hartsdale could be transformed into Holly Golightly from *Breakfast at Tiffany's*, which my father had recently taken us to see at the RKO Proctor's.

Now, arriving at the Met, I held tightly onto my father's hand as we passed through the dark sooty entrance on West 40th Street. We were thrust into a nineteenth-century opera house of pure gold, with four tiers of horseshoe balconies and so much gilded Beaux-Arts detail that your eyes had to give up taking it all in. It was as though I'd been miniaturized and tossed into Aunt Lil's jewelry box.

The lights dimmed. Each side of the gold damask curtain was pulled diagonally up, up, up, as the first act opened on an exterior of a village square with glimpses of winding streets.

Then Joan Sutherland made her entrance. Tumultuous, deafening applause greeted the diva known worldwide as "La Stupenda." She had thick auburn-red hair that was parted in the center and swooped down over her ears. A pale green gown exposed magnificent goddess-like bare shoulders; she dominated the stage filled with choristers and supporting players. This entire world was centered on one solitary figure.

Even at eight years old, I knew the difference between this great star and the leading lady of the Westchester Opera Guild. I was oblivious to the music, soaring as it might be. It was the theatricality, the gloriously fake theatricality, fooling no one, but allowing us to revel in the depiction of a romantic world, and a triumphant artist transporting several thousand spectators to a state of ecstasy.

I can forgive my father's failings—his foolishness, his lack of genuine interest in my welfare. I can forgive him everything because he gave me the theater.

A Trip to Hartsdale

In the early sixties, when my mother was still alive, Aunt Lil would take the train from Grand Central to visit us in Hartsdale at least once a week. The taxi brought her from the train station and up Secor Road past Ferncliff Cemetery to reach our house at 4 Eastway. My image of Aunt Lil in the early years of my youth was of a slim, angular Glinda the Good Witch in a Bill Blass suit.

Twelve years older than my mother, Aunt Lil was devoted to making Mommy's life easier. My mother, Gertie, was her sister, best friend, and in some ways, due to the vast age difference, her daughter. For years, Aunt Lil struggled as a nurse, then as a teacher. Then at the age of forty she married Uncle Lou, an older man with a flourishing accounting firm, and was able to relax in the role of a Park Avenue lady of leisure. With Uncle Lou's money, she could even buy my mother a house in the suburbs, which my father could not afford.

When Aunt Lil made her weekly visits to Hartsdale, she usually had with her a large, round, pink candy-striped hatbox. The interior of the hatbox, overflowing with crumpled pink tissue paper, was suffused with the luxurious scent of Chanel No. 5, and inside would be something she had chosen for me with her intuitive insight and flair.

Aunt Lil derived great satisfaction in searching out appropriate gifts for everyone close to her, but I suspect my interests, fully developed at an early age, especially fueled her imagination. On one of these visits, nestled within the fluff of pink paper, were the citizens of a miniature Neapolitan village.

Extracting them one by one, I counted a dozen perfectly proportioned five-inch puppets. Their realistic faces were modeled from plaster of paris, and they were garbed in meticulously detailed nineteenth-century cloth costumes. All the figures were fully jointed, with a wire that sprang from the top of their heads so that you could dangle them into movement. Everyone was there: the baker, the fisherman, the cobbler, the commedia dell'arte traveling players and their wives. I'd spend hours alone in my room inventing narratives for these tiny peasant figures. Sometimes they remained in their rustic Italian village, but often the cobbler's wife was an ambitious young singer from Brooklyn, belting out "Happy Days Are Here Again."

To take some of the pressure off my mother, Aunt Lil often had me spend weekends with her in New York City. When I think of us during my childhood, we are always walking. Aunt Lil knew every underground passage in Manhattan. On a rainy day, we could walk from Radio City Music Hall on 50th Street and Sixth Avenue all the way to her apartment at 37th and Park without getting wet. While we walked, we sang. Aunt Lil loved to sing, but I've never met anyone who was quite as tone deaf. We'd be strolling hand in hand belting out "The Battle Hymn of the Republic" and I'd be wondering, *What melody could she possibly be hearing in her head?*

The January before my mother died, Aunt Lil took me to see the 1962 film version of *Gypsy* starring Rosalind Russell and Natalie Wood during its opening week at Radio City Music Hall. Before the movie, we'd gone fabric shopping on 38th Street. Aunt Lil was planning to sew new dining room curtains for her apartment, and she bought yards of heavy ecru-colored nubby raw silk.

While she was paying for the fabric, my eyes were drawn to a wicker basket full of scraps and remnants. One piece of glittery bronze stretch fabric fascinated me. I was intrigued that there was both a sparkly side and a matte side. Aunt Lil asked a salesman if he could cut off a swatch for me to take home. I've only recently come to appreciate how magical it must've been for her to be in the company of a child who found enchantment in such odd things. She knew that a two-by-four-inch piece of glittery fabric could keep me occupied for several hours. We left the fabric store with two large shopping bags full of drapery fabric and then took the bus up the twelve blocks to Radio City Music Hall.

The cavernous theater was underpopulated, with rows of empty seats all around us. It was also freezing. We grew so cold that Aunt Lil removed a length of raw silk from one of the shopping bags and draped it around us. The fabric spilled over the seats on the sides and in front of us like a tent, with just our heads popping out. The movie's saturated colors dazzled me; the yellow of Rosalind Russell's Orry-Kelly-designed satin coat, the Christmas lights on Miss Electra's costume, and most of all the cobalt blue of Natalie Wood's "Let Me Entertain You" gown. At home in Hartsdale, my father had the Broadway original cast album, and I was stirred by Ethel Merman's bright trumpet sound, but there was something about the throbbing low velvet resonance of Lisa Kirk's dubbed voice emerging out of Rosalind Russell that was even more enveloping.

On our way back to the apartment after leaving the theater, Aunt Lil and I took a detour into the Waldorf Astoria, where we had the opportunity to sneak into a corporate convention. With Aunt Lil looking stylish and respectable, no one noticed that she'd found a discarded ID and pinned it to her coat, allowing us to sample the food on the buffet table and watch the presentations revealing the wave of the future.

The MGM Gals

1990. Las Vegas. A friend of mine, an executive at Turner Home Video, was able to bring me along as an unofficial guest to a corporate video convention, giving me the chance to hang out at the Desert Inn with legendary MGM stars Ann Miller, Debbie Reynolds, June Allyson, and Esther Williams. The evening began with a cocktail reception for the ladies. They each got up at the podium to say a few words of tribute to their old alma mater. Debbie, Ann, and June were bubbly and endearing, perfectly pitched to their corporate duties. When it was Esther's turn at the podium, she raised one eyebrow about three inches and growled into the microphone, "Of course, I don't see a dime out of any of this. But I figure if you can't kill Ted Turner, you might as well join him." Nervous laughter percolated throughout the room.

When the cocktail party drew to a close, it was decided that we'd all go down to the restaurant and have dinner. As Debbie, Annie, Junie, and the rest of our group were waiting for the elevator to take us downstairs, I looked around and asked, "Where's Esther? Shouldn't we wait for Esther?" With perfect synchronization, the three musical sweethearts turned and gave me a chilly MGM look that could have made L. B. Mayer himself wither and die. When we arrived at the restaurant, June explained, "I adore Esther, but when she drinks, she gets so bitter about MGM." Ann added, "It was our home. They took care of *everything*. I have no complaints."

It was fascinating watching these longtime friends interact and remain so true to their screen personas. Ann was like a good-natured Texas waitress, insisting on organizing our food "ah-duzs" (she had a unique way of pronouncing things). June was adorable, her crinkly-eyed charm intact and I suspect deliberately forgetful about pesky dates and career details. Debbie, a consummate entertainer, kept switching characters. She'd drape a napkin over her arm and become a fawning French waiter, then slip into her Marlon Brando and Zsa Zsa impersonations. She gently ribbed June, who for years had been a TV spokeswoman for a urinary incontinence product, by serenading her with, "It All *Depends* on You." Then, with a sudden switch of gears, she transformed into a no-nonsense old pro dispensing advice to her sweetly incompetent friends on how to promote their various memoirs, getting on the lecture circuit for senior citizen groups, and more. None of the ladies were at all interested in me, but that was perfectly fine. This fly on the wall was having a grand time.

While we were waiting for our food to arrive, Esther entered the restaurant, mink coat draped over her arm like a safari trophy and accompanied by a pair of handsome gay men. Debbie, June, and Ann, embarrassed and flustered, all began apologizing at once. "Oh, Esther, we couldn't find you! We waited and waited. Where were you, darling?" Esther, from my view the most intelligent and self-aware of the lot, tossed them a wry look that said she was on to all of 'em, and was going to have a much more amusing evening anyway swigging tequila with her matching pair of gay hunks. I heard the MGM lion roar.

G10 and G11 in the Mezzanine

1962. My father was miscast as the brave widower running a household and devoting all his energies toward his motherless children. Instead he saw our new circumstances as an opportunity for greater freedom. He threw himself into the dating pool and quixotic financial schemes such as investing in a farm to raise chinchillas and producing a rock and roll record by his personal discovery, a three-hundred-pound soul singer named Little Lamar. My aunt did her best to camouflage her vexation over my father's lack of paternal responsibility, feeling that it was important for us to have the illusion of a strong male figure in our lives. One hot summer day, she suggested that my sister Margaret and I take advantage of the swimming club membership she'd bought for us. Margaret informed her, "Oh, we don't belong there anymore." Aunt Lil did some research and discovered that, behind her back, my father had sold the membership she'd paid for to finance a vacation for himself in Las Vegas.

I was nine years old when Aunt Lil began taking me to Broadway shows. Some, like the talky and sexually explicit John Osborne British drama *Inadmissible Evidence,* were a bit of an intellectual stretch for a third grader, but Aunt Lil never explained anything to me. There was the assumption that I'd either figure it out or let it pass over my head.

She belonged to the Macy's Theatre Club, through which we'd pick the shows we wished to see before the season started, guessing at which would be hits or flops. Our ESP wasn't too keen. We tended to choose flops (*Baker Street, The Girl Who Came to Supper*) and miss the smash hits (*Fiddler on the Roof, Man of La Mancha*). The first Broadway show I attended was the musical *Tovarich,* a semi-hit starring Vivien Leigh. I'd already seen *Gone with the Wind* in its 1961 reissue and was obsessed with Scarlett O'Hara. Aunt Lil also worshipped Vivien Leigh and filled me in on how Vivien's husband Laurence Olivier broke her heart by leaving her for the younger Joan Plowright. Giving me the dish on the Olivier/Leigh/Plowright triangle is an example of a recurring theme of Aunt Lil's conversation: that women were morally, intellectually, even physiologically superior to men.

We did manage to see a few genuine hits, such as Carol Channing in *Hello Dolly*. Many years later, I spent a memorable hour with Miss Channing when we both performed at the 1995 Broadway Cares/Equity Fights AIDS Gypsy of the Year fundraiser. My friend Carl Andress went with me to the New Amsterdam Theatre, where a production staffer escorted us upstairs to a large communal dressing room. We were the first to arrive. While Carl and I began laying out my makeup and costume, Mario Cantone, one of the hosts, poked his head in the door to say hello. After checking the list of names on the door he said, "You know, you've been assigned to the women's dressing room." I shook my head and said, "That can't be." Mario insisted, "I'm telling you, I'm downstairs with Patrick Stewart, Brian Stokes Mitchell, and Nathan Lane. You're with Audra McDonald, Carol Burnett, Betty Buckley, and—"

Before Mario could finish his sentence, Carol Channing walked in, accompanied by her husband, Charles Lowe. After a pleasant but perfunctory hello, they became immersed in unpacking her costume and makeup. Once Carol was set up in the spot next to me, Charles Lowe left the room to check up on the lighting, the sound, the front of the house, and all the sundry things a husband/manager must concern himself with. Mario, Carl, and I didn't utter a word. We were rapt by the spectacle of watching Carol Channing—sans makeup—begin to paint on her "Carol Channing" face. She rouged not only her cheeks but the bridge of her nose, which together gave the appearance of a candy pink stripe stretched across the center of her face.

Time was moving on, and I had to proceed with my own makeup. As I was gluing on my false eyelashes, Carol's and my eyes met in the mirror. In that fabulous low voice of hers, a gift to generations of impressionists, Carol explained slowly and in a measured cadence that she was suffering from a permanent eye infection and could no longer glue on false eyelashes. She'd learned to create a semblance of her trademark look with just a black eyebrow pencil. Mario, Carl, and I were spellbound watching her draw thick black stripes on her eyelids. The makeup artist in me wasn't sure she was gonna pull this off.

Gradually, the room began to fill with female luminaries. An event organizer had taken my drag persona at face value and thought of me as one of these women of the theater. It was flattering—I suppose. While it might've been sexy fun catching Brian Stokes Mitchell and Patrick Stewart in their briefs, would it be half as riveting as observing Carol Channing drawing black stripes on her eyelids? When Carol finished her makeup, she turned to me at the dressing table, her face perhaps three inches from mine, and she asked with childlike vulnerability, "How do I look?"

I pulled back to take in the entire picture. "You look like her!"

That's what she needed to hear. She promptly raised herself from the chair and was ready to greet the other stars in the room.

Stagestruck

I can't remember not wanting to be on the stage. I was desperate to be a child star, but my ambitions were forever being foiled. Only a few years after my mother's death, my father told me that St. Mary's Players, a community theater group in Yonkers, was doing the musical *Oliver!*. I was perfect casting for the title role of the orphaned waif and I insisted that he take me to audition. Five times they called me back and made me sing Oliver's plaintive ballad, "Where Is Love." But no, in the end they cast some dreadful butch child without a shred of sensitivity.

Not long afterwards, I found out that a British film company was making a movie of the show. I'd be the Vivien Leigh Scarlett O'Hara dark horse and nab the coveted screen role! I had Aunt Lil take me to a photo booth in a 42nd Street penny arcade where I could make wistful Oliver faces. St. Mary's Players—look at what you cavalierly turned down! Aunt Lil helped me mail in the photos, and we waited. Several months later I received a letter from Romulus Films in London, thanking me for my interest in the production but informing me that, unfortunately, they were committed to casting a British boy in the role. When the movie came out, I snickered at Mark Lester's one-note performance. That should have been me on that screen! I might've won a special Academy Award for Best Juvenile Performance. The *fools*!

Aunt Lil encouraged my theatrical yearnings by sending me to Saturday acting classes at the Neighborhood Playhouse in Manhattan. At the first class, the teacher, a rather grand veteran stage actress, taught us how to make an entrance down a staircase wearing a gown with a long train without ever looking down at our feet—a skill that has proved invaluable in my career in the theater.

There's a large volume on my bookshelf, Daniel Blum's *Great Stars of the American Stage*, that's now seventy years old. The spine is crumbling. I should've been more protective, as it has been of such importance throughout my life. Published in 1952, the book, which Aunt Lil found in a thrift shop, was already battered and worn by the time it reached me. The first and earliest star profiled was Lillian Russell and the most current, the then-young and promising Maureen Stapleton.

Each portrait and biographical essay became another door for me to enter. Most of these stars were never or only rarely captured on film. Their performances were therefore alive only in my imagination. Eva Le Gallienne, Katharine Cornell, Jeanne Eagels, and Laurette Taylor became as fully realized to me as any film actress. After my Saturday afternoon acting classes,

I'd head over to the Library of Performing Arts at Lincoln Center and spend the rest of the afternoon in the research room, combing through scrapbooks devoted to these extraordinary women.

The figure who made the greatest impact on me was the nearly mythical Sarah Bernhardt. For hours I'd be bent over the research table, sifting through newspaper clippings documenting the French actress's frequent American tours. This was a woman who was the herculean force behind her own sixty-year career, who was the first international celebrity, who demanded that the public regard her slender, boyish body and Semitic features as a new kind of beauty. She wrote and directed her own plays and was an accomplished painter and sculptor. She played not only empresses and courtesans but numerous male roles, including Hamlet. Her personal motto was *quand même*, a phrase translated roughly as "in spite of everything." It was easy to take that defiant battle cry for my own. Without question, the life and career of Sarah Bernhardt has been my driving inspiration.

Women of the Theater

1995. I wore a knock-off of a classic black-and-white Chanel suit to the annual Women of the Theatre luncheon at the Rainbow Room. It was something of an honor to be the only male invited, and I'd been asked to deliver a short speech. Twenty minutes before the car service arrived to carry me forth to the Rainbow Room, bewigged and made up to a glossy finish, it was time to slip into the skirt. It didn't slip on as easily as it had two years ago, no doubt due to my consuming boxes of Entenmann's chocolate-glazed donuts over the last twenty-four months with nary a thought of the consequences. In fact, I couldn't zip up the back, and my panty girdle was exposed. The matching jacket would have to cover my derriere.

When I arrived at the Rainbow Room, I swiftly found my table, where I was seated among an elite group of women producers, publicists, and ad executives. After about a half hour of speeches, it was my turn at the podium. Everyone seemed to get a kick out of my retro ladies' luncheon ensemble. I spoke of how my love for actresses had shaped my life—actresses from the past and present whom I admired and emulated, actresses I'd written roles for, and actresses who've been my intimate friends. After I concluded, I made a dash back to my table, adroitly hiding the back of my skirt. But before I could reach my destination, I was accosted by the audacious, always-uncensored Broadway star Elaine Stritch, whom I'd never met. She barked, "Charles Busch, whose brilliant idea was it to have you speak? That was genius. In fact, I think I may be in love with you. And I'm the only dame here who's gonna tell you that your ass is hanging out."

Two Sisters

My older sister has been called Meg by all her friends since she was twelve, but to our family, she's always remained Margaret. Three years older than me, she and I shared skills in acting, writing, and painting. For me, those interests took over every moment of my existence and both separated and protected me from a harsh world. Perhaps because Margaret's irrepressible charm has always made her the center of a group of devoted friends and it wasn't deemed as vital, her talents weren't encouraged by our family with the same zeal as mine were. She has never for a moment begrudged me that attention.

Margaret is a skilled painter whose subject matter is most often her favorite star, James Cagney: self-portraits of her with James Cagney, portraits of her son, Jimmy, with James Cagney, and so on. (Yes. She named her son after James Cagney.) She can also pick up any musical instrument and play a tune. Animals not only flock to Margaret but are eager to please her. Without ever bribing the dog with a treat, I've seen my sister teach a friend's mercurial Labrador to perform practically a full vaudeville act. She can teach a parakeet to sing Cohan's "Over There."

Our aunt Belle had the most awful cat, Rocky. When we'd go to her apartment for Thanksgiving, we'd sometimes get a fleeting glimpse of this bloated, greasy, mean-faced animal poking his head out of the closet and then quickly retreating to the dark recesses of its cave.

In the mid-nineties, when Aunt Belle broke her hip and was in the hospital for over a month, Margaret took Rocky to live with her. One day I went over to my sister's apartment and this gorgeous, silky feline suddenly leaped into my lap and sat there preening, waiting for me to stroke him. "Whose cat is this?" I asked. "That's Rocky," Margaret replied. I couldn't believe it. This cat was like Bette Davis as Charlotte Vale in *Now, Voyager* after the cruise. With a diet and a few weeks' vacation in my sister's apartment, listening to her playing the recorder and watching her paint yet another portrait of James Cagney, Rocky was transformed.

When we were children, our three-year age difference was a vast gulf, but Margaret and I seemed to become the same age in 1971, when she was twenty and I was seventeen. That year, I auditioned for apprentice positions in non-union summer stock theaters along with two friends from my Saturday afternoon acting class in Manhattan, Andy Halliday and Jane Barish. Amazingly, all three of us were accepted at the Lake Placid Playhouse. It was a small theater that produced a different play or musical every week. On the bill that summer were *Camelot*; *Cabaret*; *Do I Hear a Waltz?*; *Fiddler on the Roof*; *Play It Again, Sam*; *Blithe Spirit*; *Dracula*; and *Plaza Suite*.

Halfway through the season, Jane decided she'd had enough and gave her notice. On my weekly phone call home to Aunt Lil, I apprised her of the Jane situation. I was vaguely aware that Margaret, on summer vacation from the University of Cincinnati, was back in Aunt Lil's apartment, devastated by a breakup with her college boyfriend. Aunt Lil had been up all night worrying about her.

"Margaret's so unhappy," she said. "She needs something to do for the rest of the summer. She should take Jane's place. I can get her on the next Greyhound bus to Lake Placid."

Being as grand as only a seventeen-year-old apprentice can be, I replied, "This is a real theater, Aunt Lil. You have to audition. They won't just take anyone." I couldn't believe that Aunt Lil thought she could simply cast the apprentice position from her aerie on the fifteenth floor at 50 Park Avenue!

"You tell them that your sister is pretty and cute as can be and a wonderful actress. And let them know that she has a lovely singing voice. Go right now, before they make other plans."

Everything she'd said was true. Margaret *was* a good actress and she had a very pretty singing voice. She'd been the best thing in her high school production of *The Lady's Not for Burning* and wore the most splendid medieval costumes in the play courtesy of Aunt Lil's expert skills as a seamstress. I got off the phone and immediately went to the office. I found the producer, Joan, and recited verbatim what Aunt Lil had instructed me to say. To my surprise, Joan clapped her hands together and said, "Great! Have her come up tomorrow." Aunt Lil had saved her the hassle of casting a replacement.

That summer brought Margaret and me together as a team. "What's mine is yours and yours is mine" has been our credo since. For the past half-century we've cared and looked after each other and have never had a single argument or any disagreement.

My sister Betsy is a full ten years older than me. She was off to college when I was seven. That age gap has made a close relationship a challenge. Of the three Busch siblings, Betsy is arguably the most intelligent, definitely the best read, and possibly the wittiest. Her impassioned, hysterically funny spontaneous arias about the frustrations of urban life offered me great material for the lead character in my play *The Tale of the Allergist's Wife*. Betsy was thrilled hearing sold-out Broadway audiences laughing at her real-life tirades. She had a long career as a textile designer and has been married for nearly fifty years to a gentle, adoring Frenchman named Roger. They live half the year in New York City and the other half in a vine-covered house on the coast of Brittany.

During the first years after my mother's death, Betsy was attending the Fashion Institute of Technology and sharing an apartment with a few girls in Greenwich Village. She'd come home to our house in Hartsdale on a Sunday and regale us with tales of her experiences at bohemian coffeehouses, bookstores, and jazz clubs. Betsy is a storyteller par excellence. At ten years old, I learned, through her, of a free-spirited artistic world with street names out of a storybook: Minetta Lane, Christopher Street, Patchin Place, MacDougal Street, and Abingdon Square. Drinking in every word she spoke, I made a secret vow that someday, if I could just make it through childhood, I'd live in the Village. And I have, for over four decades now.

Grandma

The grim reaper took up residence with our family again in 1964. Aunt Lil's husband, my uncle Lou, died from heart disease. Although I spent many weekends at their apartment, my uncle had remained a kind, wryly humorous, but rather aloof figure of imposing dignity. Aunt Lil knew she was asking a lot of him by having me around so often. Fortunately, I was, and continue to be, one of the world's great self-amusers. I didn't make too many demands.

Uncle Lou's death was a terrible loss to Aunt Lil. By the time she met him in 1949, she had resigned herself to a life of lonely spinsterhood. His love provided a cocoon of financial and emotional protection, enabling her to be a pillar of support to all of us. From this point onward she would be both matriarch and patriarch.

The concept of grandparents is an unfamiliar one to me. My mother's parents, Russian Jewish immigrants, died in the 1940s. I never think of them as my grandparents but as Aunt Lil's "Mama" and "Papa." I do have memories of my father's vitriolic mother, who was known as Grandma Lee, but I've never thought of her as my grandmother. She was rather like a colorful character I encountered in a book or a movie. Her second husband had been a powerful steel magnate, but my only recollection of him is as a silent, defeated old man. In 1960, financially ruined by speculating on the stock market and squandering their fortune, he moved to Miami with my grandmother where they could live cheaply. When I was eleven years old, three years after my mother's death, Grandma Lee, debilitated from a stroke, chose to abandon her aged, broken-down husband in Florida and move in with us. Aunt Lil had bought our house in Hartsdale for my mother, with my father paying the utilities. My father cottoned to the idea of his mother's monthly social security check helping pay those expenses.

My bedroom was given to Grandma, and the bed in my parents' bedroom was replaced with twin beds—one for my father and one for me. It made sense, since my father was at work all day and out most nights working his way through the ranks of attractive widows and divorcées he met through Parents Without Partners.

Grandma arrived in Hartsdale, displayed a quick flurry of flamboyant affection, and then replaced it with perpetual rage. Walking was painful for her, even with the aid of a cane, and one arm was partially paralyzed. Her voice was a hoarse, raspy croak. She still retained an air of late Bette Davis–like hauteur and set about remaking her new environment without any regard for the other inhabitants. Although she was now impoverished, she insisted that our housekeeper, Beulah, conform to the standards set by her previous lifestyle. Grandma, with her feeble arm, would impatiently demonstrate the proper way to wash glassware or scrub a kitchen floor. She had Beulah running up and down the stairs with her incessant demands for cups of tea. Huffing and puffing, Beulah would sigh to me, "Your grandmother is the tea-drinkin'est lady I ever did see."

The moment my father came home from work, Grandma would have her claw of an aged arthritic hand latched onto his arm like an ancient parrot. She didn't have a clue how to relate to a new generation of children or, in my sister Margaret's case, a '60s teenager. Our mammoth snow-white German shepherd, Wolfie, tried to break through her hard shell by hovering close to her. Grandma was convinced she was going to be knocked down by "that goddamn animal." Her latest nonnegotiable demand: "Ben, I want you to get rid of that dog."

My father didn't fight for Wolfie. He wanted to appease his domineering mother so he could continue receiving her monthly social security checks. Margaret and I were devastated. Our lives were constantly being shaken up. Wolfie had arrived as a puppy three years before. Our previous dog, Nicky, a black toy poodle, was bereft after my mother died and passed away barely a month later. Very soon after, my father brought home Wolfie, who seemingly overnight grew to bearlike proportions. Wolfie was my protector against a world dismissive of a nonconformist little boy. When I'd take Wolfie for a walk, any stranger who dared approach me would provoke my furry guardian to bare his fangs and snarl. To my sister, Wolfie was all cuddly comfort, and when they weren't roughhousing, eager to learn whatever tricks Margaret wished to teach him. Now, with Grandma's ultimatum, Margaret was part Dorothy in *The Wizard of Oz* threatened with the loss of Toto, and a fourteen-year-old Lizzie Borden. Her eyes blazed with undiluted hatred as she sat silent opposite Grandma at the dinner table.

Aunt Lil came up to Hartsdale for her weekly visit. She was concerned about the Wolfie situation and Margaret's and my emotional state. When my sister was at school, Aunt Lil went into her bedroom and found Margaret's diary. Ordinarily she would have respected my sister's privacy, but she needed to know what was going on in Margaret's mind. She grew alarmed when she read the most recent diary entry meticulously detailing Margaret's plan to poison Grandma's tea. Fantasy or not, Aunt Lil took action. Wolfie would stay, but Grandma had to go.

Grandma's younger sister, my great-aunt Clara, was a feverishly high-strung elderly widow with no children. She lived in the respectable Hotel Alden on Central Park West. Aunt Lil phoned Aunt Clara and laid out her perfect plan—offering to pay for Grandma to reside in a small studio apartment at the Alden, where the two elderly ladies could look after each other. Aunt Clara was apoplectic. "No way I'll have that horrible smelly old woman hanging around here! If she moves in, I'll move the fuck out!!" She hung up on Aunt Lil.

Aunt Lil tried to make me understand the pain of my grandmother's fall from her formerly high status. I was confused. "Aunt Lil, I thought you hated Grandma. You told me that when Daddy first told Grandma he wanted to marry Mommy, she said, 'They come from the black hole of Calcutta! Chickens crap on their kitchen table.'" Aunt Lil replied, "Well, later on Grandma came to appreciate Mommy for her shy, quiet ways. You should think of Grandma as Norma Shearer at the end of *Marie Antoinette*. It's most painful when you lose everything and have only yourself to blame."

None of Grandma's extended family would have anything to do with her, and she was shipped back to Miami and her ailing husband. Within the year, she suffered another stroke and died. There lay two important life lessons for me: You reap what you sow, and don't play fast and loose with your stock portfolio.

The Women in Palm Springs

2012. A role I always had a yen to play was Mary Haines in Clare Boothe Luce's play *The Women*, the role Norma Shearer played in the film. I'd had the opportunity in several staged readings produced by the group TWEED in New York in the 1990s, alongside Lisa Kron and drag legend Joey Arias, among others. It was a very different but especially memorable experience to appear in the play for a one-night benefit performance for the Coyote

Stageworks in Palm Springs, with an all-star cast including Lucie Arnaz, Lorna Luft, Michele Lee, Florence Henderson, and Kaye Ballard.

I shared a dressing room with Lorna, Michele, and Lucie. Garbed in a chic, form-fitting black cocktail dress, I was straightening my seams when Michele complained that it wasn't fair that I was the only one in the cast to be mic'd. "What are you talking about?" I asked her. "I'm not mic'd." Michele, in all seriousness, pointed to an area below my waist and said, "I see the mic pack." It was necessary to diplomatically inform the lady, "Michele, um . . . that's my dick."

The Replacement Cast

My mother's other older sister, Belle, was two years younger than Aunt Lil. A warm-hearted gal with a great sense of humor and a no-nonsense approach to life, Aunt Belle reminded me of Vivian Vance as Ethel Mertz on *I Love Lucy*, right down to the cap-sleeved housedresses. After serving as an army dietitian in the Second World War, Belle married a good-looking German Jewish refugee named Arnold Grohs, who ran a five-and-ten-cent store in Long Island City. Belle maintained a career as the head dietitian at Children's Center, a city-run home for children in need.

A year after Uncle Lou's death, Uncle Arnold died of a sudden heart attack while working in his store. Between 1962 and 1965, we lost my mother, my father's parents, and both Aunt Lil's and Aunt Belle's husbands. In the pit of my stomach, I was convinced that I'd be the next to suddenly disappear. I was in a perpetual state of nausea and addicted to Tums by the age of ten. My nose was always psychosomatically stuffed up, so I was in constant need of a handy Vicks nasal inhaler. Oh, and that's when I started my lifelong ChapStick habit. I'm off the Tums and the nasal inhaler, but in full disclosure, I haven't licked my lips in fifty-seven years.

When her husband died, Aunt Belle was so bereft she couldn't spend even one night alone in her apartment in the Bronx. Aunt Lil did some quick thinking and figured that Aunt Belle residing with us in Hartsdale might be the answer to many problems and that it would be completely unlike my grandmother's havoc-wreaking stay. Aunt Belle needed a new life and a place to live, we'd benefit from her maternal presence, her salary could help with the expenses of the house, and she could keep my feckless father on track. Daddy had no objection to Aunt Belle moving in. She didn't project Aunt Lil's air of superiority or judgment. Aunt Belle was much more easygoing and she made a good living with the city.

Once again, my bedroom was taken away and I moved back into my father's room. Returning from a date after 11:00 PM, my father wanted to lie in bed and watch an old movie on *The Late Show*, and there was no way I was gonna fall asleep when *Waterloo Bridge* or *Angels with Dirty Faces* was on TV. Those late nights may have impaired my concentration in school the next day, but they provided me with rare time alone with my father—and most of my film education, which has been the basis of my career as a writer and performer.

At first, Aunt Belle and Daddy seemed to get a kick out of each other. His silly jokes lightened her grief. The situation was a bit reminiscent of a frothy early sixties romantic comedy that might star Glenn Ford and Debbie Reynolds—the newly widowed sister-in-law moving in with the widowed husband and his children. The honeymoon period ended as my father began exploiting Aunt Belle's good nature and availability. Her presence in the house allowed my father greater freedom to roam. Aunt Belle was commuting full-time to her job in the city and handling the entire household. She was gradually transformed into a bitter drudge.

As protective of Aunt Belle as she had been to my mother, Aunt Lil viewed my father's increasingly blatant irresponsibility as a threat to our welfare. When my sister Margaret had a cyst on her cheek that required immediate surgery and Aunt Lil was unable to pin my father down to sign a consent form, she could no longer mask her anger. One evening, when my father was away for a bachelor weekend, Aunt Lil took the train to Hartsdale and gathered us in the living room for a family council.

Aunt Lil painted a horrible portrait of my father. She revealed that he'd raided a savings account my mother had established for our future college educations to finance a trip to Europe. She recounted how, after my mother's death, Daddy had threatened that he'd take us away and she wouldn't see us anymore unless she "paid him off." She even implied that my father's self-absorption and negligence in allowing my mother to shovel the winter snow in her frail condition contributed to her sudden death. Aunt Lil laid it on the line: From now on, we were either with him or with her. Margaret sobbed that Aunt Lil was destroying her father. At the age of eleven, I knew that my only recourse was to ally myself with Aunt Lil. She was trustworthy, and she had the means to protect me.

It was difficult to see my affectionate, movie-loving father as a Dickensian villain, but I began the process of shutting down any feelings of love for him. He wasn't that bright. He could be fooled. I conditioned myself to sustain a warm, fuzzy exterior while inside being cold as Barbara Stanwyck in *Double Indemnity*. If I allowed myself to feel warmth toward my father, I was betraying Aunt Lil. It's a technique I've perfected that I'm not terribly proud of. Cute as a kitten, I can emotionally cut someone off and they'll never know.

By exposing her hatred for my father, Aunt Lil revealed herself as a far more complex figure. My stylish, gift-bearing Glinda was capable of unforgiving rage. Over the next decade, any mention of my father could set her off. I learned that one person could have within her qualities of both a good witch and a bad witch.

The following year, when I was twelve, Daddy began dating a woman named Joan, a divorcée with four children who lived not far from us, in Parkchester. Before I met Joan, Daddy described her as looking like a cross between Marlene Dietrich and Marjorie Main as Ma Kettle. A unique combination to be sure, and yet someone I wasn't especially eager to meet. When he finally brought her around, she was nice and didn't push herself on me. My father had dated many women since my mother died and I never took any of them seriously. No point in wasting my personality on someone who wouldn't be around long.

One night, Daddy, Margaret, and I were in the room I shared with my father. Aunt Belle was in her room watching TV. Daddy and Margaret and I were lounging on his bed, gabbing about some movie star who'd recently been married. With his head resting on a mountain of pillows, Daddy said offhandedly, "Speaking of marriage, I'm marrying Joan tomorrow." His tone was no different than if he had said, "Speaking of engagements, I have a dentist's appointment tomorrow." There was no indication that he expected us to skip school and join them. The absurdity of his casual statement caused Margaret and me to burst out laughing. We fell back onto the bed holding our sides. Daddy began laughing as well. What were we laughing at? Perhaps it was his complete insensitivity and lack of feeling. What else could you do but laugh?

Shortly after he and Joan were married, Daddy sat me down on the couch as if we were going to play out some tender MGM father/son scene. "If you'd like to come live with us in Parkchester, you're absolutely welcome."

He knew that I wouldn't take him up on that offer in a million years. Honestly! I was going to leave our house to move into an apartment with a woman I hardly knew and her four troubled kids? He was compelled to make the gesture, and he acted his part with a certain degree of dramatic earnestness. I could've played the scene with a bit more childlike Jackie Cooper tenderness. I wasn't giving my father much to work with, and a performance is only as good as one's costar. "That's all right," I said. "I think it's best that I stay in Hartsdale." End of discussion—and, for the most part, the end of our relationship for the next twenty-five years. Without him, I still stayed up watching television till 2:00 AM, escaping into a much more emotionally satisfying world full of gallant music hall soubrettes, rebellious society debs, and feisty gal reporters.

It Happened One Night

In the late eighties, Claudette Colbert attended a show of mine on Fire Island. The following day, my partner Eric and I were invited to an afternoon cocktail party in her honor. She was everything you'd hope Claudette Colbert would be: elegant, worldly, with that beguiling catch in her voice and a seductive air of confidentiality. She dangled names in front of us like diamond drop earrings—including Edward, the Duke of Windsor, a chum of hers before his abdication. She dismissed one of her contemporaries with the blithe statement, "I suppose one could say that Bette Davis was the first ugly star." She told us that she'd recently been waiting for a flight at JFK when she was approached by a woman who gushed, "Oh, Miss Colbert, what a thrill it is to meet you. I wish my husband were here. He loves trivia."

Perhaps a year later, Claudette's good friend Claire Trevor attended a performance of my play *The Lady in Question* and we had supper afterwards. Claire was a memorable figure in some of the best examples of film noir: *Murder, My Sweet*; *Raw Deal*; and an Oscar-winning turn in *Key Largo*.

Sitting in a restaurant after the show, Claire confided, "I rarely got a part I wanted. I was typecast as a dame with a drink in one hand and a cigarette in the other." (She told me this with a drink in one hand and a cigarette in the other.) "Sure, I'd like to have worked more, but when the roles stopped coming, it wasn't a tragedy. I have a full artistic life as a painter. I have a marvelous relationship with my son. Women like Bette Davis who had only the career—they're the ones that suffered the most when they got older." I brought up how her friend Claudette was originally signed to play Bette Davis's iconic role of Margo Channing in the film *All About Eve* but had to drop out when she broke her back. "Jesus, Claudette could never have played that role. She has great style. She could do comedy, but a dramatic actress? No. Bette Davis was a wonderful actress. I suppose one could say that Bette was the first ugly star."

I thought I was experiencing déjà vu, then I recalled that Claudette had said the very same thing about Miss D. Well, at least Bette had two Oscars and a slew of Lifetime Achievement Awards to console her when she looked in the mirror.

Camp Summer Camp

Few children can say that their parental figure's every choice on their behalf was the best one, but Aunt Lil's success rate was due to her adroit understanding of her "kid." She sent me to a series of summer sleepaway camps that were devoid of athletic competition, instead catering to sensitive lads with recherché tastes.

At Camp Catawba for boys in Blowing Rock, North Carolina, the remarkable owner and director, Dr. Vera Lachmann, a Holocaust survivor and professor of classics at Columbia, directed a full-length production of Molière's *Le Bourgeois Gentilhomme*. She assigned me at the age of eleven years old the role of the soignée and much-desired Countess Dorimène. I saw the character as embodied by Audrey Hepburn and improvised a costume out of white veiled netting that to me evoked the Cecil Beaton gown Eliza Doolittle wore to the Embassy Ball in *My Fair Lady*. Had Dr. Lachmann, with her worldly European insight, perceived the romantic feminine creature residing within me?

It was in upstate New York at Camp Lexington for the Performing Arts that I wrote my first full-length play at twelve years old. The play was titled *Lovely Lace* and was highly praised. Surprisingly, no one seemed to notice that the plot was a perfect melding of *The Heiress* and *The Barretts of Wimpole Street*. The story may have been appropriated, but the female lead, a lonely invalid, could be interpreted as something of an emotional portrait of my mother and an indication of the artistic direction I was headed in.

It was bewildering to be lauded for my writing at camp while at my suburban junior high school I was dismissed as unexceptional. These summer camps were artificially constructed societies where toxic masculinity was discouraged. Because of my rather effeminate nature and lack of athletic skill, I'd experienced some homophobic bullying in grade school. It wasn't that extreme. There was always some other defenseless kid whose mere existence inflamed the viciousness in others more than mine did. I wonder if the essential remoteness of my character, and my lack of interest in being part of "the group," made me an unsatisfying target for cruelty. Perhaps this detachment also kept me safe from untoward sexual advances from older men in positions of authority. At all my summer camps, there were rumors of adolescent boys having sexual experiences with counselors or artistic staff. None of that happened to me. The staff's awareness of a very involved Park Avenue aunt may have also helped keep the wolves at bay.

The summer I was fourteen, at another theater camp, Beginner's Showcase in Lake Sunapee, New Hampshire, the competition for roles was fierce in productions ranging from *Gypsy* and *Mame* to *The Prime of Miss Jean Brodie* and even *Marat/Sade*. I never progressed beyond the chorus. That summer, however, I was introduced to someone who would remain a constant in my life, a fellow camper named Andy Halliday. Whereas I immersed myself in the classic women's pictures of the thirties and forties, Andy was bewitched by the musicals of that period. I worshipped at the shrine of Norma Shearer, Andy at the temple of Betty Grable. Though we shared a similar sense of humor, Andy had an innate sadness and level of anxiety that brought out in me a protective tenderness. Less than a year older than me, Andy had begun the painful process of becoming comfortable with his homosexuality. It didn't help when a Lake Sunapee theater reviewer criticized his performance as Og the leprechaun in *Finian's Rainbow* as being overly effeminate. Andy was devastated. I found myself in the position of consoling and counseling my friend though I was more sexually innocent than he was.

We continued our friendship into the fall and winter when we both attended Saturday acting classes in Manhattan conducted by the artistic director of Beginner's Showcase, an intense and charismatic Cuban named Jack Romano. We remained in his class for several years.

One Saturday afternoon, Jack spent part of the class conducting private interviews with each of us and offering an honest assessment of our abilities. When it was my turn to face the inquisition, Jack peered at me with a jeweler's squint and declared in his thick Cuban accent, "You're self-conscious and inhibited and you must learn to speak more clearly. However, you have an innately theatrical personality, which may prove useful." At fourteen I wasn't sure exactly what he meant by my "theatrical personality," but again, as with Dr. Lachmann at Camp Catawba, I wonder if Jack had an uncanny insight into my future as a performer.

The Summer of '68

The suburban public school I attended included both junior and senior high. To me it was a sprawling red-bricked prison, and by the eighth grade, it seemed as if I would never be paroled. Four long years lay ahead.

It was early that spring when Aunt Lil came to a Parents' Day at my school. She received quite an education. Each of my teachers reported that I was a complete nonentity in their class, failing every exam, and that they had no recourse but to recommend that I repeat the grade. My math teacher, Mrs. Brewer, was particularly vituperative. Most of my teachers made no impression on me at all, but I loathed Mrs. Brewer. She fancied herself some-thing of a wisecracking comedienne with a captive student audience. My look of blank incomprehension at her snappy explanation of algebraic log-arithms triggered a nasty response akin to the reaction of a bitter stand-up who lays an egg at an open mic night.

Aunt Lil confronted me with my teachers' harsh verdicts. I had no answers for her. She asked to see my notebook. If I couldn't understand what the teacher was saying, didn't I at least write things down? I was curiously placid, almost relieved, as I surrendered my loose-leaf notebook. When she opened it, instead of notes on math, biology, or social studies, she found the pages almost solid blue with complex Escher-like ink doodles. Within the intricate paisley patterns were portraits of the great mod beauties of the day: Jean Shrimpton, Penelope Tree, and Julie Christie.

In those final weeks, I had gone beyond mere doodling: During class, I'd occupied myself by taking the sharp tip of my pen and cutting out small pieces of the drawings to create elaborate lacework. Aunt Lil turned page after page of these rococo works of art. Her face remained admirably calm, but I could sense her shock. She had no idea that it had come to this. She had dropped the ball by assuming that her sister Belle was monitoring my progress in school. To be fair to both ladies, I'd played a clever game with my report cards. In a performance worthy of Duse, I convinced Aunt Lil that Aunt Belle had seen my report card and convinced Aunt Belle that Aunt Lil had seen it.

Aunt Lil made an appointment to speak to the principal. One of her key axioms was "Eliminate the middleman." She proposed to the man at the top that I spend the summer break with her in Manhattan and attend summer school. She would supervise me and if I passed my exams, I should be allowed to proceed to the ninth grade with the rest of my class. Aunt Lil was not the type who came on like gangbusters, but she could summon up a pragmatic intelligence coupled with an emotional tug that left opponents stuttering and acquiescent. The school agreed to her plan.

Perhaps because I had deteriorated under her watch, Aunt Belle became defensive and was of the stern opinion that I should repeat the grade, take responsibility for my failure, and learn a harsh life lesson. I never quite forgave Aunt Belle for that misguided notion of tough love.

My sister Margaret was likewise having a difficult emotional time, but she had only a year left before graduation. (Plus, her mediocre scholastic performance wasn't quite at the disaster level mine was.) She would stay in Hartsdale with Aunt Belle for another year until she left for college. We packed up my clothes and prepared for my move to 50 Park Avenue. I hated where I was, but I was terrified of what lay ahead.

Wolfie had died a few years before. He developed epilepsy, and when his seizures began occurring every five minutes, he had to be put to sleep. I'm forever haunted by the memory of cuddling with him on the floor, feeling safe with my face buried in his white fur, when his body suddenly began violently shaking and his eyes rolled up in his head. When the seizure stopped, he looked so bewildered and powerless.

After Wolfie's death, my father brought home another dog, a German shepherd we named Hansy. When my father moved out, Hansy really became Aunt Belle's dog. She doted on him. He was the perfect dog for our house of melancholy survivors, quietly affectionate and with a remarkable sensitivity and soulfulness. But I still mourned Wolfie. I kissed Hansy goodbye and fled to New York City.

Aunt Lil's small apartment wasn't conducive to houseguests. She gave me the bedroom and turned a dining alcove into her room. She came to be so comfortable with this setup that she never again slept in her bedroom, even after I moved out. ("I like being near the kitchen in case I can't sleep and need a shot of Uncle Lou's whiskey. And I have my sewing projects spread out on the beds, and I don't think it's really any of your business.")

The classroom where I attended summer school was in an office building next door to Ohrbach's department store on West 36th Street. I have no recollection of those classes. They were merely a warm-up for the important studying that took place in apartment 15C with my real teacher, Aunt Lillian.

We sat side by side at a table off the living room with my books opened before us. We had several courses to work on: algebra, biology, and English. Aunt Lil began by reading aloud to me; within minutes I'd slump over, fast asleep. Each subject elicited the same physical reaction. Though she had left the medical profession over thirty years earlier, in her spine she remained a nurse and was proud of her skill at improvisation. She went into the kitchen and returned with a cold compress. Holding the ice pack to my forehead, she would have me read the text aloud. She watched as I wrote down notes detailing what we had studied.

Together we read each work of fiction on my assigned summer reading list. It was impossible for me to concentrate—the words on the page tended to blur. 1968 was the summer of *Rosemary's Baby*, and a few weeks before the movie opened in July, I devoured the novel. "You don't have any trouble concentrating on that," Aunt Lil quipped.

It helped to discuss with her the psychology of the characters in *The Old Curiosity Shop* and *The Adventures of Huckleberry Finn*. Discussing psychology with Aunt Lil was always compelling. She was unerring in her understanding of human behavior. In our studies, wedged between facts on photosynthesis and quadratic equations, were essential Aunt Lillianisms such as "From the moment we're born, we must stretch our necks and pull ourselves upward. Gravity is the enemy." And "You can learn everything you need to know about a woman by how she applies her lipstick." I am convinced that with her intellect, her powers of concentration, and her implacable hatred of any who did wrong to my mother, sisters, or me, Aunt Lil would be eminently capable of pulling off the perfect murder. And she could always rely on her prized nurse's powers of improvisation to switch plans if confronted with a particularly meddlesome detective.

My aunt had a passion for growing African violets and kept a dozen of them in small pots on a large marble-topped table at one end of the living room. It wasn't difficult for me to see myself as the thirteenth African violet—the one that required the most nurturing to survive. She insisted that I water and feed the delicate plants. Aunt Lil explained that even the tiniest seedling or insect, the smallest cell in the human body, played a role in the great scheme of things. That included me.

Aunt Lil had us read together the front page of the *New York Times* every morning. This was the summer of the assassinations of Martin Luther King Jr. and Robert Kennedy, the March on Washington, the violence at the Democratic National Convention in Chicago, and of course the ongoing war in Vietnam. Aunt Lil took me with her to a large anti-war march down Fifth Avenue. Being the only kid in our immediate group, I felt like the teen star of an MGM musical parade number. That exultation came to an abrupt end when a red-faced male bystander bellowed at Aunt Lil, "Commie bitch, get your brat outta here!"

It would be untrue to give you the impression that I was a willing participant in my aunt's attempt at my intellectual and emotional rehabilitation. I'd run from the dining room/classroom sobbing in self-accusatory, profanity-strewn rage: "I'm such a fucking moron! Any asshole can understand this crap! Why can't I?" Aunt Lil would pull me back, stroke my hair, then pick up where we'd left off, with the properties of a parallelogram.

What to Do About Chuck

Looming ahead like an army transport to Vietnam was my eventual return to Hartsdale and my old school. Aunt Lil knew she had to keep me in New York. Any progress we'd made would fall apart if I returned home. It was now late July and school began in September. I needed to be enrolled somewhere that would have a degree of sensitivity to an academically traumatized kid. Aunt Lil thought the best place would be the High School of Music & Art, a school for gifted children that was part of the New York City public school system.

I was born with a talent for drawing people. Art was never an overwhelming interest but rather a visual manifestation of my passion for the theater. The only subjects I drew were portraits of my favorite actresses or scenes that reminded me of moments from period films, Norma Shearer as Marie Antoinette being a frequent source of inspiration. In fact, when I was eleven years old, I sent Miss Shearer one of my portraits, mailing it courtesy of MGM, Culver City, California, ignoring one small detail; she'd left the studio in 1942. This prompted Aunt Lil to conclude, "Your recurring problem in every aspect of your life is your inability to anticipate."

My aunt encouraged my drawing, and instead of sending me to an afternoon sketch class for children, she enrolled me in a nude life drawing class for adults. I wasn't at all fazed the day I saw my first female nude model. I took in her pendulous breasts and wild and wooly thatch of black pubic hair with mature objectivity. I was more tantalized by the well-built male models, naked except for their posing straps, but I was born with the cool eye of a professional.

The High School of Music & Art was the sister school of the High School of Performing Arts, but Aunt Lil felt that, since I'd been taking acting classes on Saturday afternoons for several years, developing my gift for drawing and painting would make me more "well-rounded." Besides, I would never have been able to pass the audition process at the High School of Performing Arts.

In acting class, I didn't make much of an impression. Incapable of imitating how a "normal" fourteen-year-old boy might act, I was something like an alien from another planet observing incomprehensible human behavior. My desire to be on the stage far outweighed my ability. Admission to the High School of Music & Art seemed more realistic. Applicants were required to take a drawing test and present a portfolio of art. It was highly competitive, but this hardly mattered, since the entrance exam had been almost a year before. Enrollment for 1968–1969 had long passed. Aunt Lil's lawyer, Dan Sugrue, insisted we should not accept this as fact.

Dan Sugrue was Aunt Lil's great consigliere. He assisted her in all her various financial and legal projects. After she had laid out some complex-but-legitimate tax shelter, I'd see him bow to her untrained brilliance. Dan was from Ireland, looked like a Kennedy brother, spoke with a brogue heavier than Barry Fitzgerald's, and counted in Gaelic. He had been with the high-powered law office that handled my uncle's accounting firm. When Uncle Lou died, Aunt Lil discovered that his business partner was unscrupulously trying to diminish her part of the estate and that the law firm that was supposed to protect her was exploiting her with inflated legal fees. Disgusted by this, Dan left the firm to begin his own private practice, and Aunt Lil became his first client.

To his family Dan was a devoted husband and father, but he and Aunt Lil had a kind of platonic intellectual love relationship that lasted decades and only ended with her death. He'd come to the apartment to go over her legal affairs and would always stay another few hours to discuss the latest novel by Robertson Davies. He never charged Aunt Lil for his services, but she left him a quarter of her estate in her will.

Mr. Sugrue wouldn't accept a "no" from the High School of Music & Art. I honestly have no idea how he pulled this off, but in mid-August, he gave us the news that a special test was being offered to a handful of kids. A few weeks later, the day arrived for my examination at the school, all the way uptown at 135th Street and Convent Avenue. A dozen boys and girls were given this special opportunity. We each had a private interview and displayed our portfolio to a panel of teachers.

I had thrown together a selection of drawings of dissolute 1920s flappers, 1940s tough tootsies, and a sampling of turn-of-the-century Parisian courtesans. One of the male teachers muttered "theatrical." Was that good or bad? Then it was time for the drawing test. The twelve of us sat at easels in a large classroom and were put through our paces. First, we had to draw from life a pretty girl seated in a chair before us. After that, she left the room, and we were instructed to draw the empty chair. We also had to draw a bowl of overripe fruit. The final test was a quick sketch from our imagination. I believe I drew a depressing portrait of a bedraggled older woman with her cloche hat askew, sipping her fourth cocktail at the Gypsy Tea Kettle. It was an emotionally spot-on self-portrait. The examination ended. Everything now depended on the opinion of the judges. I'd passed my summer school classes, but it was impossible to tell how much I'd truly absorbed. Unfortunately, the High School of Music & Art started a week later than my old school in Hartsdale. I'd have to go back there until I got the results of my evaluation from Music & Art.

The first day of school in Hartsdale arrived, and as I entered my math class my face took on a look of horror rivaling that of Mia Farrow first seeing the devil eyes of her newborn baby. My teacher was once again Mrs. Brewer.

I could sense her disappointment and irritation as I took a seat in the back of the classroom.

Three days passed, and while I was no longer drawing my phantasmagoric doodles, I could feel myself slipping into despondent apathy. I was sitting in the back of Mrs. Brewer's math class and about to begin a drawing of Jean Shrimpton when a hall monitor entered the room. The monitor whispered something to Mrs. Brewer, who announced that I had received a message. The monitor found me in the back and handed me a folded note. Mrs. Brewer and the rest of the class stared at me. Had someone died? I opened the note. There were only four words: *You're in. Aunt Lil.*

I got up from my seat, leaving my books on the desk, and without saying a word to anyone, least of all Mrs. Brewer, simply exited the classroom. I heard her shout, "Excuse me!" I walked down the hall and straight out the front door of Ardsley High. I felt as light as the autumn leaves swirling about me.

Vertigo

In 2014, to celebrate their twentieth year on the air, Turner Classic Movies commissioned twenty celebrities who were also known as visual artists to create original works of art inspired by classic film. It was a wide-ranging group, including Kim Novak, Jane Seymour, Joel Grey, Tony Bennett, Manolo Blahnik, Jules Feiffer, Burt Young, Todd Oldham, and yours truly. I did a pastel drawing of a Busby Berkeley line of chorus girls, with one ambitious chorine looking directly into the camera.

They flew me out to Los Angeles for the TCM Film Festival, where the artwork was to be displayed at the Hollywood Roosevelt Hotel. The first evening of the festival would be the big unveiling. I brought with me my friend Ashley Morris, a young actress/comedienne from Texas with the camp frame of reference of an old queen. Out of the twenty celebrity artists, only three showed up: Kim Novak, Jane Seymour, and me. TCM invited us to a private viewing before the public was allowed into the gallery.

Ashley and I arrived at the Hollywood Roosevelt and were ushered into the greenroom. Kim Novak was the next to arrive. She appeared a good twenty years younger than her age and was vital and energetic. I was just coming off . . . well, not exactly a depression—that would be too strong—but let's say four months of a merciless, lacerating self-assessment of my creative life, past, present, and future. Not long before, TCM host Robert Osborne had conducted a moving on-camera interview with Kim in which she was painfully honest about her emotional swings and career disappointments.

Ashley and I approached Kim, and I was compelled to let her know how much that interview had resonated with me. Right on the spot, in this greenroom at the Hollywood Roosevelt, everything around us disappeared, and Kim Novak and I began conversing intimately about our emotional lives. She'd lived for many years on a ranch in Oregon with her veterinarian husband and has had nothing to do with Hollywood in decades.

I think the best word to describe Kim would be "cosmic." Her speech was dotted with references to my "radiant spirit" and "life's journey." She may have left Hollywood behind, but she's still blazing with charisma, and having those sultry green eyes fixed on me with such empathy was hypnotic.

We were ushered into the gallery where our artwork was exhibited. Kim is a gifted visual artist and her painting, based on imagery from her classic film *Vertigo*, hung next to mine. Unfortunately, the pin spot intended to illuminate her painting was out of focus, leaving half of the work in shadow.

Firmly, but not in any way nastily, Kim requested that the light be refocused. Before you could say *Bell, Book and Candle*, a young man was up on a ladder fixing the problem. While we watched him adjust the light, Kim and I resumed our spiritual discussion. A few minutes later, I gestured upwards. "Kim, it looks like he's fixed it."

Suddenly, the face on my serene, mystical Kim Novak turned hard as that of a lifer in a women's prison movie. Her voice dropped an octave. "I took a lot of shit from Columbia. I'm not takin' any more shit today." Then, as quickly as if I'd changed the channel, she reverted to her gentle, otherworldly self.

A few minutes later she asked me what I was doing the rest of the evening. I told her that TCM was sending me across the street to Grauman's Chinese Theatre to introduce a screening of *What Ever Happened to Baby Jane?*. I said, "I think it's a complex and underrated film and Robert Aldrich's best work." Again, Kim's mellow voice turned abruptly harsh. "Bob directed me in *The Legend of Lylah Clare*. He wanted me to use a German accent and I refused. *He ended up dubbing me! I could have done it!*" Her swift changes in personae were borderline disturbing, but also a gay man's campy wet dream of classic movie star volatility.

At the end of the night, Ashley and I arrived at an after-party held by TCM at another hotel. In the back of the room, we caught a glimpse of our new best friend, Kim Novak. I wondered aloud if it would be uncool to ask Kim to record a happy birthday greeting on my phone for my Kim Novak–obsessed hairdresser, Brad. Ashley shook her head. "We are soooo beyond that now." We sallied over to Kim, who seemed elated to see us, and we took up exactly where we'd left off. Amidst the revelers, we were immersed in a serious discourse on our deepest feelings of inadequacy and the need to let go of such futile dark rumination. A crowd began gathering around us, all hoping to meet Kim Novak. I began "cheating out," which in stage parlance means that I was subtly turning my body away from Kim to assist her in gracefully ending our conversation.

Refusing to take my cue, she kept her eyes glued to mine as she continued speaking. A TCM publicist came over and said politely, "Miss Novak, there are many people who'd love to have a moment with you." It didn't take a seer to pick up the subtext that TCM was paying all her expenses and being accessible to the fans was why she was here. Kim looked the publicist square in the face, deadpan but expressive in her deadpan, rather like the majority of her movie close-ups. She then returned her attention to me and resumed her philosophical discourse without losing a beat. I was becoming increasingly uncomfortable. I didn't want to be blamed for monopolizing her time.

At last, when Kim had absolutely—and I do mean absolutely—concluded what she had to say to me, she turned and opened herself up to the fans surrounding us. With her movie studio training, she gave every single one of them her undivided attention, treating each as if they were the most important person in the world.

Lesson: Miss Novak will do what you ask with grace, but only when she's damn well ready. She had taken a lot of shit from Columbia and wasn't taking any more shit today!

Midnight in the Kitchenette

The High School of Music & Art could not have been more different from Ardsley High School. It embraced the 1968 hippie aesthetic in every way. Nearly every teacher—black and white, male and female—sported a full Afro. It was political, geared to the outsider gifted child, and there was no gym class. It was heaven.

Every day when I got home, Aunt Lil would ask, "What happened today?" "Well, everyone's getting ready for tomorrow, which is 'Fuck School Day.'" She was laughing about that one for the next thirty years. What she couldn't understand was the uncharitable spirit of my fellow art majors.

Having been involved in six of the seven arts, I'm here to tell you that visual artists are the absolute worst about sharing trade secrets. Actors will help you in a scene, musicians will guide you, writers will mentor you, but visual artists will never let you in on the secrets they use to create their work. To be fair, an artist's technique, his innovative manner of using his tools and medium, is intrinsically linked to his unique vision.

My closest friend in school was a chic and witty young girl named Shelli Segal. She was from a loving show business family who seemed ideal to me. With her parents' energy and guidance behind him, her younger brother Robin became the movie star Robby Benson. Shelli went on to be a high-profile fashion designer. As close as we were, Shelli, like so many visual artists, kept her techniques to herself.

One day I arrived home after school, frustrated that my woodcut project was a disaster and no one would tell me what I was doing wrong, neither the teacher nor my fellow students. Aunt Lil studied my woodblock trying to figure out the fatal error. Not only wasn't the ink spreading evenly, but I couldn't find a tool that would give me the width of cut I needed to produce the image I had in mind. Long after I went to bed, Aunt Lil was in her kitchenette, experimenting with various household tools. When I got up in the morning, she laid out the problem: My woodblock was almost imperceptibly warped, causing the ink to spread unevenly. She'd also found a sharp blade in her pantry closet that was precisely the thickness I needed. Aunt Lil took pride in being the behind-the-scenes project manager on my woodcut, lithograph, multimedia collage, and many other assignments.

Aunt Lil rhapsodized over any work of visual art that I produced. The summer I turned sixteen, she was planning to wallpaper the small entrance foyer of our apartment. My summer plans had fallen through, and I was restless and bored. I asked her if I could try painting a mural on the wall before she had it papered. She gave me the go-ahead and then was enthralled as the mural emerged full of decadent imagery that evoked the posters of Alphonse Mucha and Toulouse-Lautrec and the paintings of Florine Stettheimer. When it was completed, Aunt Lil declared it the most beautiful thing she'd ever seen. It stayed there for the next thirty years, gradually fading and chipping like a Renaissance fresco.

A Glimpse of the Unicorn

1970. Did I actually *meet* Greta Garbo? I was on my way home from school one day and there was Garbo with her inimitably glum Nordic stride heading toward 38th Street. She was wearing a khaki-colored pantsuit with a high standing Mao collar. In the strong late afternoon sunlight, her hair, cut with blunt bangs and pulled back into a low ponytail, glimmered, a natural mix of blonde, red, brown, and white strands. How did I, at the age of sixteen, recognize Garbo, who'd been out of the public eye since her retirement in 1941? I was most familiar with her from portraits and still photos from my treasured books, *A Pictorial History of the Silent Screen*, *A Pictorial History of the Talkies,* and Richard Schickel's *The Stars.* I'd been transfixed by the juxtaposition of that magnificent woman's face and her gawky, flat, mannish body. There was also the mystique of her reclusive legend, fed by paparazzi photos printed in the newspaper of her looking trapped and forbidding. If her movies ever appeared on television, I must've missed them.

In July 1968, the Museum of Modern Art held the first complete retrospective of Garbo's film career. By the time I got there to buy a ticket, every screening was sold out except for her early talkie *Romance.* It's arguably one of her weakest films, but the enchantment was still present. Hearing her voice for the first time, it was obvious why she was one of the few silent stars who became even bigger in the talkies. Her distinctive Swedish accent was marvelously at odds with the goddess's cool lunar beauty. Every sentence uttered was like a road trip along a fjord full of bumps and deep valleys and a climb up onto a smooth plateau.

Two years later, when our paths collided, I wasn't about to let her go, but I also refused to be some uncouth fan intruding on her solitude. Like a teenage sleuth, I tailed Garbo as she entered an Asian novelty store called Azuma. The store was empty except for the few employees. I stood facing her with only a display table piled with Indian print bedspreads between us. It was known that she possessed a highly developed radar for attention and was prepared to bolt like a deer when confronted with gawkers, whom she referred to as "customers."

I thumbed through the pile of bedspreads. My head bobbed up and down as I stole surreptitious looks at the Divine One's finely lined but exquisitely structured face. On my third upward glance, she caught me. There was no denying that I was staring. It seemed best to pretend I didn't recognize her but took her only for another shopper. I lifted a corner of one of the gaudy bedspreads with a subtle look that said, *So whaddya think? You like this one?* She raised her eyebrow revealing that lofty space between the brow and the crease of her lid. Was she acknowledging my presence? She looked down again, fingering the nubby texture of the bedspread. Our eyes met once more, and I detected a minute pursing of her upper lip. I read into her enigmatic visage, *Nah. Tacky. Strictly Baruch College dorm room.*

With a delicate movement worthy of Lillian Gish in Griffith's *Broken Blossoms*, I lifted the corner of a green and purple spread for her opinion. This selection seemed to register a more favorable silent response from the Swedish Sphinx. There was a slight tilt to her head. Without a word uttered, she was clearly advising me: *The green and purple is jazzier and more versatile but, hey, the sale is two for one, so use the other as a backup when you send this one to the cleaners.* I wrinkled my nose indicating it wasn't an option. Garbo checked out another bedspread, in pink and orange. She raised her eyes to see if this one was more to my liking. I nodded, *Possibly.* Not since her last silent with John Gilbert in 1929 had she such a sensitive and articulate pantomimic costar. My heart was pounding rapidly, compelling me to conclude our wordless design conference. It was too painful to continue the charade that I was ignorant of her identity. With a quick glance at my watch and a gasp expressing I was going to be late for my piano lesson, I fled the shop.

I sought refuge in the art supply store across the street. I breathlessly told the owner minding the cash register that Garbo was over at Azuma. Without a word, the guy hotfooted it right out of his store. If I hadn't been raised with such a strong moral compass, I could've walked off with a new set of high-priced Rembrandt pastels.

Tea and Empathy

During my high school years, Aunt Lil never had anyone over for dinner. Occasionally, though, we'd have an afternoon visitor. There was a small circle of neurotic older women who would individually visit our apartment for tea and a shoulder to cry on. Alone with me afterwards, Aunt Lil would sigh, "I'm everyone's port in the storm."

Still, Aunt Lil was forever trying to instill in my self-absorbed teenage self the all-important concept of empathy. I'd come home from school and my aunt would be offering sage advice to one of these lonely ladies. There was Rose, a much-married elderly heiress—picture Mary Boland as the Countess de Lave in *The Women*. From my room, I would overhear the heiress sobbing at the heartlessness of her latest fortune-hunting younger husband. Then there was the tall, attractive, strong-jawed Hilda, whom Aunt Lil thought might be suffering from thwarted lesbian feelings.

But the visitor who thoroughly captured my imagination was Carla, an alluring Viennese-born woman in her early fifties. Carla, Aunt Lil told me, was a true femme fatale. In the apogee of her youth, she was romantically involved with Tyrone Power. She had numerous lovers outside her marriage to an indulgent and stolid businessman and was having a painful time adjusting to growing older. When I asked Aunt Lil what was wrong with Carla's husband that she needed to step out so frequently with other men, Aunt Lil replied, "No imagination."

Carla usually visited Aunt Lil while I was in school. I met her only one time, when she dropped by just before dinner. She had once been famous for her lush auburn hair and was freaking out that it had grown thinner. On my way to my bedroom, I passed by the open bathroom and saw Carla fluffing the ends of her pageboy hairdo in the mirror. In her lightly Viennese-accented purr she asked, "Darling, tell me, what should I do about my hair? Should I have it cut? What do you think?"

This established an almost sensual intimacy between us. I was fifteen years old, but like generations of other men, gay and straight, I was hooked. I said, "No, it's beautiful. Don't do anything." I wasn't merely being empathetic as Aunt Lil had instructed me, but I meant it. Carla smiled gratefully but was hardly convinced. We both continued to study her image in the mirror. She fussed with her hair and contemplated her perfect bone structure, while I provided the silent worship she required to breathe.

Charles Confidential

Occasionally, there's a season saturated with movies and plays on the same subject. This happened with drag in 1995. Within a few months the Broadway musical adaptation of *Victor/Victoria* opened and then the films *The Adventures of Priscilla, Queen of the Desert*, and *To Wong Foo, Thanks for Everything! Julie Newmar*. As I was known as the female impersonator with the literary pedigree, this led major publications to offer me journalistic assignments. Besides interviewing Julie Andrews for the *New York Times*, I wrote a cover story on the current drag scene for *New York* magazine, and *The Advocate* had me do cover story interviews with Terence Stamp and Patrick Swayze.

I was to chat with Patrick Swayze about the upcoming film *To Wong Foo*, in which he played a wise and nurturing drag queen. I already had something of a history with the film, having been asked to do a screen test for the role that Swayze ended up playing. It was lovely to be considered but I knew that such a commercially risky project would require big-name movie stars for the leads. I had to admit that Patrick Swayze did a good job. Despite his lean, muscular physique, his performance was believably feminine and devoid of any "We both know I'm a straight macho dude, but ain't I a good sport?" winking.

We met in a small office room in LA, and I found him refreshingly modest and self-deprecating. In his eagerness to appear totally cool in his role of gay ally, he pushed it a bit too far by repeatedly calling me "girlfriend." The unspoken truth in the room was that the heat of his career had substantially cooled over the past few years. Even so, he told me that due to his status as a film action hero, strangers often felt the need to engage him in a physical scuffle so they could brag that they "took down" Swayze. He found it impossible to walk down a city street alone.

During our conversation, he mentioned that his sister had taken her own life. A career journalist would've asked a follow-up question; I didn't want to intrude and changed the subject. When I turned in the tape of our interview, my editor couldn't believe that I hadn't drawn him out on the subject. She insisted that I call him on the phone and inquire further about his sister's suicide. I begged her to let it go. What did that have to do with his new movie? She said it was a matter of conscientious reporting.

Feeling like the most exploitive of tabloid hacks, I phoned him at his ranch in Montana. I reminded him that I was a fellow performer and not a real journalist and explained that because of this I'd avoided asking him additional questions about his sister's suicide. I was mortified that my editor was insisting I make this follow-up call. "Oh, man, it's no problem. My sister suffered all her life from serious depression, and it seemed almost inevitable that her life would end this way."

After he'd finished what he had to say on the subject, I thanked him and was bidding him goodbye when he stopped me. "You know, we can keep talking. I'm just here by myself." This was so unexpected. Punctuated by a series of awkward pauses, Patrick continued reflecting about mortality. "On a ranch, we're so aware of the cycle of life. Animals are born and die and it's such a part of our daily life. And yet sometimes it just . . . gets to you." Only fourteen years later, he would die of pancreatic cancer at the age of fifty-seven.

We spoke for almost another hour. That entire time, I felt from him a profound sense of loneliness and isolation. The meter wasn't running, so I was free to tell him about my own life and work. He seemed interested and asked questions. My career couldn't have been more different from his. He may have been intrigued by my path as an Off-Broadway playwright and drag performer, but I think he just didn't want to get off the phone.

Flesh and Fantasy

1970. Aunt Lil was concerned that I was "too cerebral" and would develop heart trouble as a result. She lectured me ad infinitum that every muscle should be exercised, the heart included. Not only had my mother died from a heart ailment at forty-one, but Lil's late husband, Uncle Lou, had also suffered from heart trouble—she blamed his hardened arteries on his spending so much time seated behind a desk. I can't say she set a good example. I never knew her to engage in any form of athletic activity or spend even a minute doing calisthenics. She claimed, though, that her every move was an isometric exercise, and she certainly had the perfectly straight posture to prove it.

When I was sixteen, she presented me with a membership to go swimming at the McBurney YMCA on West 63rd Street. I was very annoyed. I could barely swim. Gyms and locker rooms were to me synonymous with being made to feel like an outcast and with keeping one's gaze averted from naked straight boys, who might ridicule or even possibly hurt you. Exhibiting a lot of epic eye-rolling and a surly attitude, I stuffed my bathing suit into my school bag.

After school, I took the subway over to the Y to face my punishment. I'd never been there, and it was a magnificent 1920s building, full of grand arches and Moroccan tiles. I walked up the stairs to the health club, showed the attendant my membership card, and was handed a towel. It was late afternoon and not crowded. Women weren't allowed in the health club, and I was the only person there under the age of forty. While I was fumbling with the key to my locker, I overheard the conversation around me: Three men were passionately comparing the musical abilities of Katharine Hepburn in the musical *Coco* to those of Lauren Bacall in *Applause*. It was apparent to even this virginal sixteen-year-old that all the men in this locker room were not only gay, gay, gay but, to my delight, *showbiz* gay! This might not be so tiresome after all.

I slipped into my bathing suit and, carrying my towel, moved to the pool area. It was a large, magnificently tiled 1920s pool, and all the men in and around it were naked! I can't say that every eye was on me, but it certainly *felt* that way, and that's more important. I found a place to put down my towel and dipped my foot in the water. It was the perfect warm temperature. I climbed in and paddled around. It was odd being the only teenager surrounded by these older men, but I liked it. Worn out after swimming two and a half laps, I moved closer to the group of men relaxing by the shallow end of the pool. They were congenial, mildly interested that a teenager was in their midst, but not especially flirty, being deeply immersed in their theater gossip. It was fun listening to the fast-paced witty badinage. For the first time, I was witnessing the camaraderie of gay men. The element of threatening macho posturing that I'd experienced in a heterosexual gym was nowhere present.

I couldn't wait to return, and I did the next day and the day after that. Aunt Lil was delighted that I had taken so enthusiastically to swimming: "I'd say this was a great success."

Seeing Charles for the First Time

A copy of *Vogue* magazine was often to be found on my aunt's Chinese lacquered desk. The prose engrossed me more than the fashion photos. Within its pages I learned of such early twentieth century ladies of fashion as Mrs. Rita de Acosta Lydig and the Marchesa Luisa Casati. There was also a section called "People Are Talking About," which featured currently newsworthy figures in the worlds of the arts and fashion. This is where I first came across the name Charles Ludlam in 1969 when I was fifteen.

I absorbed every word describing this Off-Off Broadway actor/playwright/director with his own troupe, the "Ridiculous Theatrical Company." The column was accompanied by a macabre yet strangely beautiful image of Charles Ludlam as he appeared in his play *The Grand Tarot*. I wanted badly to see it, but by the time the magazine came out, the play's run had long ended.

It would be a few years later, in 1971, that I read in the *Village Voice* that the Ridiculous Theatrical Company was performing their new play, *Eunuchs of the Forbidden City*. I took Margaret with me so that together we might find our way to the obscure location in the Village. The play, and Ludlam's performance as the Empress Tsu Tsi's chief eunuch, Li Li Ahn, were every bit as extraordinary as I'd imagined. Produced on a shoestring, the play was a decadent epic tale of the life of the courtesan-turned-empress. It was both bawdy and literate, a cornucopia of high and low cultural references.

Sitting among a nearly entirely gay male audience, I was hit by a delirious tidal wave of identification with the spectators—but most importantly with Charles Ludlam. I was only seventeen, but Charles and I shared the same frame of reference of classic Hollywood films, theater history, and opera. A few of the female roles were played by men in a comic style that was outrageous, yet always true to the story. Although I wasn't ready to abandon a dream of a traditional acting career, a seed was planted that perhaps within this grand theatrical artist's aesthetic lay a key to my future.

Ludlam once wrote, "When all the doors were closed to me, I built my own door and walked through it." At seventeen, I possessed neither the blueprint nor the tools for any sort of self-constructed entranceway.

Barging Down the Nile

Every few years, when I've felt battered and bruised by show business, I return to the raffish, maddening, funky, noble Theater for the New

City in the East Village at First Avenue and 10th Street. Founded in 1971 and still run with an iron fist by diminutive powerhouse Crystal Field, I've taken up refuge there time and time again to rekindle my love of the stage by putting on plays to which critics are cordially not invited. These off-the-radar extravaganzas have allowed me and my dear friend and director Carl Andress to form an unofficial, unnamed theater ensemble. Among these adventurous, good-natured thespians is Jennifer Van Dyck, whose elegant androgynous beauty and classical training inspired me to explore writing male roles for women in the tradition of Bernhardt playing Hamlet.

In 2016, I wrote a version of *Cleopatra* with myself in the title role and Jennifer had the unique opportunity of playing both the ruthless Octavian and his virginal sister, Octavia. Also in the cast was my friend Larry Bullock, a big, handsome, darling fellow with a bodybuilder's physique. In *Cleopatra* he played Apollodorus, who in my adaptation is Cleopatra's major domo and gay best friend. Out of affection, she calls him "Doris."

At the penultimate scene, Cleopatra is ready to face death, surrounded by her handmaidens, Iris and Charmaine, and a trusted soothsayer. Apollodorus enters carrying a small basket of figs containing a poisonous asp. The first time we rehearsed the scene, Larry, offstage, had worked himself up into an intense Method-like state of emotion. He entered carrying the basket of figs, sobbing, tears and snot dripping onto the figs. Barely able to contain himself, Larry gasped out his line, "All is ... as you ... requested, Sovereign." I couldn't help but think, *Um ... this is supposed to be* my *big scene*. Carl stopped the action and said gently, "Larry, perhaps you shouldn't be quite so overwrought." At which, Larry, still sobbing, pointed to me, for at that moment my identities as the Queen of the Nile and his friend/mentor collapsed into one: "But it's ... *her*."

Now, Voyager

In the early fall of 1972, Aunt Lil accompanied me to Evanston, Illinois, where I'd been accepted into Northwestern University as a theater major. Four years earlier, we'd never have imagined that I'd be accepted to such a prestigious school. We both wondered how in hell they had let me in. Even with Aunt Lil's constant monitoring, my high school grades never exceeded the mediocre.

We'd disagreed on what sort of college would serve me best. I wanted an acting conservatory, but she was adamant that I receive a liberal arts education. I applied to several schools that provided both: NYU, Boston University, and the brand-new state college at Purchase. All required an acting audition, and though I prepared diligently, my contemporary and classical monologues of sensitive, yearning young men resulted in three rejection notices.

The summer before, I'd been an apprentice in summer stock, and a few of the other apprentices were applying to Northwestern, which had a renowned acting program, yet surprisingly required no audition. Given my grades and blah SAT scores, it seemed a long shot. Aunt Lil and I were stunned when I was admitted on early admission. The only answer we could come up with was that perhaps, on paper, my multiple interests in acting, writing, and visual arts seemed impressive.

I was glad to leave New York. As much as I adored my aunt, I often felt like the Creature to her female Dr. Frankenstein, with no thoughts or opinions save for the ones she had programmed into my head on politics (Roosevelt/Kennedy Democrat), religion (atheist), fashion (One must never dress casually north of 34th Street), and the mechanics of living (Don't leave the air conditioner on the entire day. It'll get metal fatigue). Aunt Lil also felt it was important for me to get out from under her influence. She had a great need to be needed, but my independence was always meant to be the end result.

We dragged my monumental suitcase from taxi to sidewalk and on through the campus. When we arrived at my dorm room in Willard Hall, we were gasping for breath. My roommate, Ed Taussig, was already there. He was taller than me, sort of shapeless, with the skeptical eyes of a 1930s chorine peering out of a beardless adolescent face. And, oh, the hair on his head! He had the worst hair, blow dried to the point of conceptual sculpture. He introduced himself, and the next words out of his mouth were sarcastic; I believe it was something to do with the size of my suitcase. He didn't make a good first impression. (Years later, he told me his acerbic attitude stemmed from a lack of confidence—and he certainly hadn't expected to encounter David Copperfield and Aunt Betsey Trotwood.)

Aunt Lil always knew her place. Once she saw that I was established in the dorm, she left me to figure out my next move. This was the end of a road for us. Aunt Lil had achieved her goal. I was in college. She spent the night at the Orrington Hotel and left early the following morning. When the airport bus arrived, our farewell at the hotel's driveway was sentimental but not excessively emotional. No tears. It was more like an old vaudeville team amicably breaking up to tour as singles. I told her I'd check in by phone once a week. She reminded me to let it ring twice and then hang up. She'd call me back so I could avoid an expensive long-distance charge. As Aunt Lil's bus pulled away, I remember feeling an old shiver of abandonment. A levelheaded inner voice posed the question, *Well, what happens to me now?*

I was determined to make a clean start. Make lots of friends. Be a force to be reckoned with in the Theatre Department. There was a meet and greet in the Student Union and Ed assumed we'd go together. I didn't want us to be viewed as a team, but I didn't know how to politely shake him.

As we walked to the Student Union, we dissected the current Broadway season. Ed was from Mount Vernon, not far from Hartsdale. We'd both recently seen Stephen Sondheim's polarizing musical *Follies*. I was bowled over by the gorgeous theatricality of the production; Ed was far more critical. He had an abrasive, know-it-all attitude that rubbed me the wrong way, but I was not about to get into a debate over something as picayune as whether Alexis Smith deserved the Tony for her performance as Phyllis Stone. Several times at the meet and greet I tried to give Ed the brush-off and each time he stuck to me like flypaper.

I'd never seen so many blond blue-eyed kids. I overheard bits of conversations and was shocked to hear my contemporaries expressing conservative points of view. I couldn't believe there were girls who were against the ERA. Growing up in Westchester and New York City, everyone I'd ever known was a liberal Democrat. I didn't meet anyone that evening whom I found remotely intriguing. Ed's bitchy but apt wisecracks, à la Eve Arden, at the expense of every student we met were amusing. I assumed he was gay, but I took him for a repressed virgin.

During my senior year in high school, I'd had a variety of satisfying sexual experiences: a fellow apprentice in summer stock, gentlemen I met while swimming at the Y, and the exuberant erotic shenanigans in the second-floor men's room at the Lincoln Center Library for the Performing Arts. My teenage sexual history allowed me to regard Ed with a sophisticated, knowing air. Perhaps he could be a friend.

Ed signed up for nearly every class I chose. After an initial tight-lipped annoyance, I ceased to care. By the third day, we were inseparable. Ed was a paradox of awkward insecurity and brash, uncensored wit. At our first speech class, the twelve students sat in a circle. We were instructed to give our name and say one thing about ourselves. When it was Ed's turn, he announced, "I'm Ed Taussig, and you may think of me as Myra Breckinridge." The reference to Gore Vidal's transgender dominatrix heroine went over everyone's head but left me shaking with laughter.

Our acting teacher was a handsome young man named David Downs. We were his first acting class at Northwestern. The plays of Chekhov were key to David's teaching, so much so that Ed and I began to refer to him as "Masha Downs."

The theories of Stanislavsky were the standard of acting classes. It was necessary for actors to "use" themselves, that is to identify similar experiences from their own lives and relate them to the scene. One day in class, David had each student choose a character from a play, go onstage alone and without dialogue, and just *be* the character. The point was to explore the character through invented behavior. I checked out the printed list of characters to choose from. This was before the time of *Torch Song Trilogy*, *The Normal Heart*, *Angels in America*, or *The Inheritance*, and there was no male character on that list that I could remotely identify with.

At a loss, I chose Archie Rice, the aging vaudevillian in John Osborne's *The Entertainer*. I wore a belted silk kimono and sat at a dressing table fiddling with makeup and seeming not at all like Osborne's womanizing loser, but rather a quivering Blanche DuBois—the character I should have chosen for myself. David did his best to encourage and coach me, but I was reluctant to reveal to the class the impossibility of my employing my teenage gay experience in exploring this completely foreign aggressively heterosexual man. Gay actors have always had to make a psychological adjustment in playing heterosexual roles and substitute their own experiences to those of a straight character. In 1972, I was unable to make those substitutions. My attempts onstage in acting class that year were fugitive, frustrating, and fake.

I felt like a complete failure and sat in the back of the theater observing but rarely participating.

I was impressed that Ed wasn't in any way intimidated by older people. His critical faculties were highly developed and his judgments often superior to those of our professors. Ed was taken by my ability at eighteen to evoke the voices and mannerisms of famous actresses. My pièce de résistance was recreating Blanche Yurka's ferocious performance as Madame Defarge at the revolutionary tribunal in the 1935 film of *A Tale of Two Cities*. Ed even had the foresight to suggest, "This is what you should be doing onstage." But nothing in my experience at Northwestern suggested that there was a viable place for my queer talents in the professional theater.

During freshman and sophomore year, I continually auditioned for university plays but was never cast. One play I auditioned for was *The Magistrate*, a nineteenth-century British comedy by Pinero in which one of the leading roles was a teenage boy whose aging beauty of a mother forces him to dress up as much younger to conceal her true age. Finally, I thought, this was a role for which I was appropriate casting. I auditioned and did well. I had an instinctive flair for period farce from all my years of watching classic film comedies.

I was deeply disappointed when a preppy straight boy got the part instead, but my pragmatic nature asserted itself and I could see why this young man was cast instead of me. The role required a believably heterosexual young man forced into this undignified impersonation. I would've brought qualities to the character that were incompatible with the plot. How could I pursue a career in the theater if there were no roles suited to me? Even more disturbing was the fact that there were no roles I longed to play. Toward the end of the term, when I spoke to Aunt Lil on the phone, she picked up on my air of confusion and then wrote me this insightful letter.

May 21, 1973 (en route to the Metropolitan Museum)

Dear Chuck,

Writing a letter on a moving bus is not easy—nor will it be exactly legible. Je m'excuse. I called you last night because all week I worried about you in a vague sort of way. What troubles me is not that you are depressed and discouraged at times (even deeply), but how you cope with the problem. Most everybody—probably creative people more than others—has to struggle with emotional ups and downs. A parent probably is least able to help when help is most needed. There is too much emotional involvement and sensitive privacies. Of course, I am concerned, and no doubt always will be. But that is not too important, and you mustn't be under pressure about me, and how I feel. This seems to be a pivotal year for you, Chuck, but it does not have to be crucial. If part of the problem that has you down is that you are at crossroads of careers—why does anything have to be so decisive? There has always been a drive in you to write—you always will write. Isn't it conceivable that you will write and perform—or that you can combine the two. You have time! It's hard for anybody—even you—to diagnose your problems—so I am kind of making suggestions hit or miss. Maybe none of the above is relevant—but I'm trying.

    Soi content—Cheri.

Je t'aime,
Aunt L

If I couldn't change the Northwestern Theatre Department or the portrayal of gay people on the American stage, I could at least change Ed. I took it on myself to give my roommate a complete makeover. There was an undeniable beauty in his face. He possessed a perfectly straight nose, sensual lips, and large dark eyes with long thick eyelashes. Since we ate three meals a day together in the dorm cafeteria, the plan was simple: Ed would eat exactly what I ate. Within six months, he'd lost thirty pounds. My next project was the hair. Shortly after we'd met, I'd asked him why he tortured his naturally curly hair with a blow dryer. He replied, "I'm afraid I'll look too pretty." I kept silent, but inside I wondered, *And what's wrong with that?*

I'd seen a coupon in the *Chicago Reader* for a half-price haircut at a unisex hair salon. Ed was surprisingly malleable. I presented him to the beautician assigned to us and helpfully requested that she "do something" with Ed's hair. The first thing, she explained after examining him, was that it desperately needed conditioning. Ed changed into a smock and off he went to be conditioned. I sat in the waiting area for what seemed an eternity. At long last, Ed emerged—with a lovely aureole of ringlets, looking like a porn Botticelli angel. We were both astonished by the metamorphosis.

Within a year, the boy with the hideous hair was being photographed as a model for hairstylist trade publications. Pleased with my role of Svengali, I was also perturbed by the shifting balance of power. I had always been the good-looking one, with Ed my pudgy sidekick. It had been established right off that he was Rhoda to my Mary. Now we were two Marys, and that took some adjusting on my part. Ed reveled in his new attractiveness. He flung open the closet door and fell into bed with a dizzying parade of boys. I handled it with admirable equanimity until one evening I caught him necking with a boy I was dating. We thrashed it out, and I think he learned an important lesson, that lovers come and go, but a best friend who helped you get your look together is irreplaceable.

During our Christmas break sophomore year, a spurned boyfriend of Ed's wrote a vindictive letter to Ed's parents outing him. His mother was hysterical. In my bedroom in Aunt Lil's apartment, I consoled Ed on the phone. When I returned to the living room, Aunt Lil, unaware of this unfolding drama, asked me how Ed was doing. I decided to tell her the truth. I filled her in on the boyfriend, the letter, and Ed's mother's emotional reaction. By telling her all this, I knew that I'd be getting Aunt Lil's Miss Marple–like curiosity going. Perhaps I was ready to come out to her. She picked up on it immediately. "So, are *you* gay?" "Um . . . yeah."

I could understand Ed's mother in suburban Mount Vernon dissolving into hysteria, but one might hope an intellectual, liberal Manhattanite like Aunt Lil would react in a more rational manner. Not so. She launched into a tearful rant about the lonely, loveless life I'd be committing myself to; an outsider to society, reduced to furtive and meaningless sexual encounters. I'll cut her some slack given that it was 1973 and gay imagery in the media was horrific. Like most misinformed people, she seemed to think I had a choice in the matter. Sex was not high on Aunt Lil's list of priorities. After her husband died, to my knowledge she never went on a date; during the time I lived with her, she never left the apartment after 6:00 PM unless it was with me. I guess sublimating one's physical passions didn't seem such a tall order.

Still, I was disappointed in her ignorance and uncharacteristically conservative point of view, and I couldn't wait to return to school. Aunt Lil never spoke of my homosexuality again. I occasionally brought a boyfriend over to meet her and she was always welcoming to them, even lending one money when he was in trouble, but she and I never discussed the romantic or sexual elements of these relationships. I accepted her terms because she kept her own emotional life so close to the vest. Hadn't she repeatedly told me over the years, "There are things I don't discuss, even with myself"? Okay, I thought; if she wished to live blindfolded, I would explore this fascinating new gay world with no fear of her disapproval.

Danish Delight

By the end of sophomore year, I'd given up auditioning for roles in university productions. Occasionally, I'd be asked to appear in a grad student project as a dissolute nobleman, in keeping with my image on campus as a notorious queen. What should I have expected? My everyday look was modeled after Maria Schneider's in *Last Tango in Paris*: shoulder-length dark curly hair, tight jeans, boots, and a woman's 1940s mink coat casually tossed over my shoulders.

Ed and I were ready for a change. We agreed it might be a good time to ditch Evanston and do a junior year abroad. In the spring of our sophomore year, we both applied for a theater program in Manchester, England. Ed was accepted; I wasn't. There was a notice on the Theatre Department bulletin board for an arts study program in Copenhagen. It sounded a lot livelier than Manchester. I was accepted into that program.

Part of the experience was supposed to be living with a Danish family. No, thank you. I sought greater freedom than I'd known at Northwestern; I had no intention of explaining my comings and goings to any family, Danish or otherwise. Consequently, I was one of only five American students who chose to reside in the international dormitory. I can't say I learned much from the program's classes on Kierkegaardian philosophy or the traditions of Bournonville ballet, but I certainly received an education on Copenhagen gay nightlife.

I became best buddies with another American student living in the dorm, an imperious black New Yorker named Garrett who referred to himself in the third person as "The Diva." We made quite a pair when we appeared at the top of the grand staircase at Madame Arthur's discotheque. Within a few weeks of my arrival, one of the bartenders informed me, "Everyone is talking about the new American bitch." Wow. That was me? Very cool. It sounded like someone with power, temperament, and pizzazz.

A common nightmare involves being forced to take an exam for a course you've never attended. That was my reality. I was having such a wild time exploring the gay netherworld of Copenhagen that I could only occasionally drag myself to a dull class taught in English by dry-as-dust Danish instructors. The worst was the large lecture on the history of Scandinavian painting. Nearly the entire class of American students failed the midterm exam. The next day the stone-faced Danish professor revealed the answers to the test questions: "And if you left out the umlaut on Düsseldorf, I took off five points." From the back of the lecture hall, a female student from New York loudly exclaimed, "Gimme a break!"

An average day for me began with 4:00 PM cocktails with my Danish buddies at the intimate Masken bar, flirting with some pleasant older gentleman to get him to pick up the tab for dinner, perhaps proceeding to a brief genial dalliance at his place to reciprocate, then off to Madame Arthur's to dance, leaving there at 2:00 AM with seventeen admirers for a private apartment and a Scandinavian bacchanalian orgy, and then at 4:00 AM rounding out the night with a raw egg yolk, anchovies, and a whiskey at the Why Not Club. I hung out with the most dazzling group of girly male whores, leather daddies, corrupt noblemen, and debonair thieves. I'm not kidding about the latter two categories, except that both were embodied by one person—a sexy and thoroughly sinister Swiss count, who unbeknownst to me was the ringleader of an antique thieving ring. And to think that in my guileless innocence we made love on a purloined sixteenth-century papal bed!

Shortly after I returned to Northwestern, I received word that Count Armando had been apprehended and sentenced to hard time in a Danish prison. I'm glad the story broke after I left town, as I'd once naively been coerced into purchasing a crowbar as a birthday gift for his henchman. I returned to Northwestern worldlier and wiser, having miraculously flunked only two of my five courses.

Cruising Cousin Itt

1992. Paramount Studios, Los Angeles. A mammoth sound stage houses the set for the rear half of the Addams Family mansion, the grounds leading to a cemetery where a wedding scene is to take place. About a hundred seats have been set up for the extended family and friends of the bride and groom. One of these seats was for me. *Addams Family Values* was my first experience being on a film set or on a Hollywood studio lot. The screenwriter, Paul Rudnick, was an old friend and generously wrote me a small female role as the Countess Aphasia Addams Du Barry. The Countess Aphasia had only three scenes, but I was costumed in the height of glamour by the multi-award-winning Theoni V. Aldredge: a confection of trailing purple lace and ostrich feathers. Add to this a large face-framing picture hat with veiling atop a cascade of red curls.

I figured out quickly that the caste system on a Hollywood set is quite different from that in the theater. Actors in a play or musical are together eight shows a week for an indefinite amount of time. The backstage at even a Broadway theater is cramped and crowded, which encourages camaraderie and equality among the stars, supporting cast, and ensemble. On a movie set, on the other hand, a star is sequestered and equipped with an invisible shield that protects them from being approached by an actor with a small role. Unless, my dear, that actor is in drag and has mild delusions of grandeur as the legendary star of Off-Broadway's long-running *Vampire Lesbians of Sodom*. On the set of *Addams Family Values*, I thought, *Hey, I'll go talk to Anjelica Huston if I feel like it*. And I did.

"Anjelica, I was thinking: A great role for you would be Miss Madrigal in the play *The Chalk Garden*. Deborah Kerr played the role in the movie."

Her face lit up at the mention of Deborah Kerr. "She was a great friend of my father's. I have wonderful memories of spending time with her during my childhood."

I'd felt the simmer of envy from the other supporting players: *Who told Charles Busch he could just go up and talk to Anjelica?*

Now, the crew was setting the lights for the big wedding scene. All the other actors, all the extras were gone, except for a few people I didn't recognize. I sat in my assigned chair on the aisle, about ten rows from the altar. Standing on the far side of the set was a lovely woman I had noticed when we were filming my other scenes. She was draped in a tacky purple lace shawl and sported a ratty red wig.

The only other person seated in my row was a small guy, and cute as can be. Tom "The Dukes of Hazzard" Wopat in miniature. He was so diminutive that his legs dangled above the floor. I moved a bit closer and whispered to him, "Who's that girl with the red wig? She's always hanging around me."

"That's your stand-in."

"I have a stand-in?"

He looked at me as if I were some rube who'd wandered in from a studio tour. "All of the principals have stand-ins."

"I'm a principal?"

"Yeah, you're a principal. You know, you don't have to be here. I'm the stand-in for Cousin Itt."

"You are?"

"I was on the first picture as well. The stand-ins are called the second team."

"Ohhhh. I wondered why everyone came running out of their dressing rooms when they called 'first team.'"

"No point in you sitting here while they focus the lights."

What else was I going to do? I was sharing a dressing room with a respected New York stage actress with a fixed sour pickle expression. She'd recently won a slew of awards for her performance in a highly acclaimed Off-Broadway drama and resented having an even smaller role in this picture than me. No thank you—I'd rather stay and watch a team of experts ply their craft. The director of photography was Don Peterman, the veteran Oscar-nominated cinematographer of such films as *Cocoon*, *Splash*, and *Flashdance*. Perched on a periously tall ladder, adjusting the lights, he looked down and noticed me. I gave him a jaunty wave. He smiled and shouted, "You know, you don't have to be here." I slipped on the glacial mask of Gloria Swanson and exclaimed grandly, "There's only one person with Charles Busch's face and that's Charles Busch!"

He laughed. "Well, then let's see what we can do about that."

I decided to take this gambit further. "Mr. Peterman, if you hit me with a nice von Sternberg/Dietrich key light, it would work wonders."

Even high up on the ladder, I could see that I was amusing him.

"Von Sternberg, eh?" He began refocusing a light directly on me. I hadn't thought he was going to take my camp suggestion seriously. Since, evidently, he was, I sucked in my cheeks, raised my eyebrows, and tilted my face upward. I held still as a statue. I could feel the heat of the light on my cheekbones. Was this how Dietrich felt? I bet *she* didn't let a stand-in take her place. The cinematographer appeared to be enjoying himself. I guess it had been a while since he'd met up with a character like me. The lights were focused. The extras were called in and finally the first team. Shortly, all the seats around me were filled and the filming began.

About six months later, the film opened, and my role had been almost entirely cut out. It was a big disappointment, though I should've expected it. If you have a small role and your dialogue doesn't include "The butler did it," chances are you're gonna be cut. I had one moment that remained. When the bride, played by Joan Cusack, tosses the wedding bouquet, the young Wednesday Addams catches it. I'm standing behind her, and I mutter, "Tramp." That was it. My only line after three weeks of filming.

That said, in the long shot of the audience at the wedding, one person pops out of the screen. A glamorous lady with a big hat in the tenth row on the aisle is lit as carefully as any actress from the golden age of Hollywood. Who is she? She must be someone very important.

I'm a Pretty Girl, Mama

During the years I attended Northwestern, from 1972 to 1976, the Theatre Department had a full acting curriculum but no playwriting program, only a playwriting class one could take for a single semester. There was also at that time no system in place for a student to put on an original play. I'd written several plays during my adolescence, though none had been performed since my time at summer camp. Returning from my louche semester abroad, and again failing to find a place for myself as an actor in the Northwestern University theater world, I turned once more to writing as a creative outlet. I worked diligently on a full-length naturalistic play heavily influenced by Lanford Wilson, about the sad denizens of a thrift shop. The English Department was holding a literary contest with a five-hundred-dollar cash prize. I submitted the play—titled *Out-Takes of a B-Movie*—and won. My celebratory glee was dashed when it was discovered that I was a theater major, not in the English Department, and they were forced to rescind the prize.

Bitter but not defeated, in my senior year I penned a one-act comedy in the Ludlam vein called *Sister Act*, about a traveling freak show. I wrote the starring roles of a squabbling pair of conjoined Siamese twins, Hester and Esther, for Ed and me. The central conflict of the play was that one of the sisters, my role, wants the pair to undergo surgical separation, despite the risk of death. The other sister has succeeded in having a full and satisfactory life, complete with a lesbian lover, and views their conjoined physicality as a political statement of otherness.

I see now that the play is a representation of my desire for independence both from Aunt Lil and from Ed himself. *Sister Act* was the first of numerous plays of mine that have used twins as a metaphor for an intense symbiotic relationship. I don't even realize I'm doing it until it's pointed out to me. *Myrtle Pope, Psycho Beach Party, Pardon My Inquisition, Die Mommie Die!, The Third Story,* and *The Tribute Artist* come to mind. I suppose my theatrical persona—*the actress*—could be perceived as my twin, a comforting role that at times has felt suffocating.

Sister Act would be my first shot at writing, directing, and starring in a play—and at performing in drag. The original, far from ambitious, plan was to present the play in the dorm lounge for our friends on a Sunday afternoon, but I knew a student, Scott Blakeman, who organized a weekend cult film series called Midnight Madness in the Student Union auditorium. When he lost the rights to the film scheduled for a few weeks ahead, he made me an offer: "How about doing your play for two nights on a real stage?" He could give us the funds that had been allocated for the film rental. We'd have a modest budget. We'd have a theater. We would have wigs!

What a relief when I first saw myself in the mirror in full drag. I had small features, no discernible Adam's apple, was only 5'7", and had been blessed with the same great legs as the women in my family. The point is that although I may not have been as stunning as Ann Sheridan (few are so fortunate), I could realistically look like the female character I'd written for myself. Never was there a thought that performing in drag could have any negative repercussions or even be considered an act of bravery. The question "What will people think?" has put the brakes on so many creative aspirants and it's something that's simply never occurred to me.

The campus newspaper, the *Daily Northwestern*, chose to do a story on our show. My first interview! Ed and I met with the journalism major assigned to the task in the Student Union cafeteria. A young man with a blank, expressionless face, he didn't ask a single question. What sort of celebrity profile was this? Without any prompting, I launched into a vivid description of the plot, the tradition of the Ridiculous Theater, and my defiant pursuit of my theatrical destiny. After a half hour orgy of nonstop self-promotion, the student journalist, still mute, appeared satisfied. A photo shoot was arranged with a staff photographer, and the following day Ed and I got into costume and had a lot of fun pretending to be fashion models along the lines of Suzy Parker and Dovima.

A few days later, the morning of the show, we woke to find a large, grotesque, coarsely lit photo of Ed and me splashed across the front page of the campus newspaper, under the lurid headline "Degeneracy Reigns at

Midnight Madness."The upcoming campus visit of President Ford's son Jack was relegated to the lower half of the page. I worried that every homophobic jock would show up that night to jeer and disturb the performance.

The auditorium was jam-packed. Ed and I were strapped into a red sequined Siamese twin costume with matching curly red wigs, fishnet stockings, and platform shoes. When the curtain opened and the student audience got their first glimpse of us, there was a whoop of laughter and applause. We sensed instantly that it didn't smack of ridicule but giddy shock. (Later I came to learn that I was to many in that student audience what Ludlam had been to me.)

For the first time—not counting my definitive and imperishable turn as Countess Dorimène at Camp Catawba, aged eleven—I felt comfortable onstage. Up till then, forced to eliminate any effeminate mannerisms, my stage presence had been about as lively as the animatronic Abe Lincoln at Disneyland. Playing a female role gave me a freedom of movement and vocal variety I had never known. Drag for me was not an expression of outrage or even satire, but rather a passageway to channel the feminine in my nature, which turned out to be a place of authority.

From the beginning, I had a naturalistic approach to my female characterizations. Okay, not exactly naturalistic—naturalism as taught by the studio dramatic coaches at MGM circa 1939. Still, pathos was as important as getting a laugh. Years of performances have allowed me to refine my style, visually and dramatically, but the essential core of who I am as an actor was fully born that night performing *Sister Act*.

Berle, Bea, and Charles (Not Me)

In 1994, as part of the twenty-fifth anniversary of the Stonewall uprising, Ken Elliott produced and directed an event I headlined at New York's Town Hall called *Charles Busch's Dressing Up! The Ultimate Dragfest*. In his book *Drag*, Frank DeCaro calls it "one of the greatest nights in the history of modern drag." So many wonderful artists performed, including the luminous female impersonator/comedian Charles Pierce, who'd been living in retirement in California.

All drag performers owe a debt to Charles, who brought his satiric impressions of Bette Davis, Joan Collins, Mae West, and other female icons to a wide-ranging audience over several decades. Insecure about his ability to remember lines, he was nervous about returning to the stage and brought along his best friend, Bea Arthur, for moral support. She even consented to make a cameo appearance in the finale, costumed as a tough lesbian biker in a black leather motorcycle jacket.

There was another show business legend on the bill known for his drag appearances: Milton Berle. His approach to drag was part of the vaudeville tradition of the nance. It could be viewed as the gay equivalent of blackface, appropriating gay humor in a manner that both celebrated and ridiculed the nelly homosexual stereotype. Berle had eliminated the drag element of his act many years before, but to our surprise, he agreed not only to appear en travesti, but—for the first time ever in his long career—at a gay event.

Milton Berle was known to be "difficult," so we demanded as little of him as possible. The afternoon of the show, I was sent to Berle's dressing room to go over his introduction and our few lines of banter. I found him seated in a classic silk dressing gown and cravat, smoking a cigar, and appearing quite vigorous for a man well into his eighties. Berle was legendary not only as a comedian but for the enormous size of his penis. Perhaps because he knew I was gay, he repeated the oft-told story of how, in a contest with another well-endowed celebrity, Forrest Tucker, he took out only enough to win. He perused the program, which listed the performers and the women they were impersonating—including Marilyn Monroe, Judy Garland, and Edith Piaf. Running down the list, he murmured, "Banged her. Banged her. Banged her."

For a one-night production involving nearly a hundred people onstage, things ran surprisingly smoothly until the start of Act Two when Mr. Berle made his appearance. I gave the 100 percent laugh-free introduction that Berle had worked out with me and gestured stage left, whereupon he entered. The sold-out audience leapt to their feet. This was the first I had seen him in costume. With only vague memories of old kinescopes of Milton Berle in drag, I wasn't prepared for the George Grosz Weimar Republic–like image before me. He wore a straight auburn wig styled somewhere between twenties Louise Brooks and early sixties Barbra Streisand. The heavy makeup made him appear much older, the pale flesh-colored foundation and poppy pink rouge settling into every line and crevice. Red lipstick smeared all over his large yellow teeth gave the carnivorous impression that he'd just come from munching on the flesh of an inept production assistant. A wardrobe supervisor on staff had costumed him in a shapeless red beaded gown that accentuated his rounded geriatric spine. As the applause grew even louder, he moved slowly across the expansive Town Hall stage until he met me center stage. His trembling hand grasped mine in a death grip.

As the waves of applause washed over us, something eerie took place—Milton Berle began to grow younger. His neck extended, his back straightened, the extra folds of skin on his face tightened. It was as if he were draining the youth out of me to restore him to his former self. His transformation complete, I was left a dried husk of a female impersonator and relinquished the vast Town Hall stage to this ageless vampire. Berle was undeniably brilliant that night, his timing impeccably precise. His corny material may have been from another era, but that night it all worked. He was in his element, reborn—and he refused to let the enchantment end.

Scheduled to do twenty minutes, he was still going strong after forty. There was a lot more show to go, but we had to end at exactly 11:00 PM or risk paying exorbitant overtime fees to the stagehand and electrician unions.

Charles Pierce, Bea Arthur, and I were watching from the wings. I voluntarily cut my last number and a duet with another performer. It looked like Berle might have it in him to go on for a full hour. What more of the second act could we cut? In his comeback appearance in the first act, Charles Pierce had stopped the show and received two standing ovations. Would he be willing to cut his second act Bette Davis routine? It was an awful thing to ask. His Davis characterization was his trademark—it would be akin to asking Judy Garland to cut "Over the Rainbow."

Bea Arthur, standing by the stage curtain ropes, forbidding in her butch black leather jacket, was spitting fire. "I told the producers they should have a contingency plan. The man is a monster. He's never going to get off that stage unless he's dragged off." Bea wanted to send me out there to give him the hook. Ohhhhh no. Berle would make mincemeat of me. Perhaps he'd have some respect for a veteran artist such as Charles Pierce.

Before he could protest, Bea and I pushed Charles onto the stage. The audience began laughing, aware that he was there to give Berle the signal to wind things up. Berle refused to take the hint. He continued to ad-lib and left poor Charles Pierce standing helpless stage left until, after a few extremely awkward minutes, Charles comically threw up his hands in defeat and returned to Bea and me in the wings. Eventually, Berle ran out of material or steam and made a triumphant exit to yet another ovation. Thirty drag queens from the Imperial Court of New York quickly made their entrance. Berle passed me on the stairs, his face aglow, the applause and laughter still ringing in his ears. His assistant had a lit cigar ready for him. Inhaling a deep puff and speaking to no one in particular, he intoned, "They loved me. They loved me. It's not even my audience, and they loved me."

Back offstage himself, Charles Pierce was in a highly emotional state, distraught over having his Bette Davis routine cut. "I shouldn't have come back. A dreadful mistake. I'll never appear on the stage again. Never! *Never!*"

At the after party at an Italian restaurant, my partner, Eric, and I sat at a table with Charles and Bea Arthur. After a few cocktails, Charles had calmed down to the point where he was able to relive his undisputed first act triumph. Two standing ovations! Sipping his martini, Charles conceded that, yes, perhaps he *would* perform again, if the perfect situation presented itself.

I was seated on Bea's left. Eric nudged me and whispered, "You haven't introduced me to Bea Arthur." I turned to her. "Bea, I'd like you to meet my partner, Eric." She sat impassive, like a Madame Tussaud figure in a *Golden Girls* tableau. She refused to even look at me. I assumed that while the supremely good-natured Charles Pierce had perhaps already forgiven the Act Two Berle debacle, his loyal best friend, Bea, was still fuming—and evidently placed the blame squarely on me.

Over the next few years, if Bea Arthur's name came up in conversation, I'd usually add my two cents, namely that she was an A number one bitch. Until 1999, when I was appearing in the Los Angeles stage production of *Die Mommie Die!*. Bea came to the show and stayed afterwards to say hello. She enveloped me in a warm embrace and was wonderfully complimentary. When I began to thank her, she stopped me from going further: "What did you say, honey? I'm stone deaf in my left ear."

Rubbing Shoulders in Chicago

It was 1976. Charles Ludlam and the Ridiculous Theatrical Company were appearing at the University of Chicago, presenting two plays in repertory, *Camille* and *Stage Blood*, as well as conducting a Saturday afternoon workshop. Ed and I, wrapping up our senior year at Northwestern, snapped up tickets to both performances. The university campus on the South Side of Chicago was a big schlep from Evanston where we were living. Neither of us had ever been to the South Side, but we weren't going to let a mere thing like geography deter us from seeing both plays and attending the workshop.

Friday night was *Camille,* with Ludlam playing Marguerite Gautier in his comic adaptation of the Dumas classic. The play stayed true to the structure of the original and managed to be both parody and infinitely moving. Charles worked several miracles. He had thick masculine features and yet his eyes were beautiful for any gender, luminous and dark. A black wig of nineteenth-century corkscrew curls and full drag makeup couldn't make him pretty, but his acting skills and charisma made you believe he was a great beauty. His art was not about trickery and illusion—he was quite simply an incomparable Lady of the Camellias with a hairy chest.

The following day, Ed and I took the L back to the University of Chicago to attend the workshop. We didn't know what to expect. Would we be participating in some sort of improvisation or working on scenes? It turned out to be a conventional question-and-answer format. With about a dozen people present, a dismally pedantic moderator conducted the interview.

To be fair to the interviewer, Charles was not a lighthearted subject. He was a serious and articulate theorist on his unique style of anarchic theatrical parody and resisted all attempts by the moderator to place him within the context of drag queen entertainment. At one point, the moderator referred to him as a transvestite, which did not go over well. The interview was then opened to questions from the audience. The questions were either pretentiously academic or simplistic to the point of idiocy.

I raised my hand and asked Charles something specific relating to the 1936 Garbo film of *Camille*. Whatever I said went over well and Charles was able to give it a full answer. When the interview concluded, Ed and I approached Ludlam, and he thanked me for helping him out with a thoughtful question. As only someone so young and ambitious would, I'd brought with me as a gift a poster of *Sister Act*, the play Ed and I were about to perform on campus. As soon as I handed it to Ludlam, I thought, *Oh, he's going to toss this in the trash*. Several members of his company were present, among them Georg Osterman, who played the female ingénue roles. He was younger than the rest, closer in age to Ed and me. Georg was naughty fun, and after we finished dishing all the dreary attendees of the workshop, he suggested that we stick around after the performance that night and go with the company to a closing night party at the home of a wealthy philanthropist.

There was no time to return to Evanston, so Ed and I sat for hours in a coffee shop before that night's show. *Stage Blood* was a backstage comic thriller about a touring production of *Hamlet*. Much of the play took place in a theatrical dressing room. As the lights came up, Ed and I gasped—our *Sister Act* poster had been taped to the wall of the set. It was possible that I'd made a favorable impression on my idol, but more likely they simply needed something to decorate a blank wall.

Before anyone could leave for the party, the set would have to be struck and the costumes and props packed away. It was only good manners to help.

The stage manager suggested that I take the costumes off the rack and fold them into a trunk. I removed and packed several costumes and then saw that the next costume on the metal rack was Charles's first act ball gown from *Camille*. I lifted it gently off its hanger. To smooth out the costume, I had to press it against myself. I looked up to see Charles observing me. We were in the exact positions as Anne Baxter and Bette Davis in the scene in *All About Eve* where Margo Channing discovers her scheming young assistant, Eve, posing with her stage costume. There was a sizzle of electricity between us, almost as if all the lights in the Midwest blacked out for an instant. If we'd known each other, we might've laughed at the visual accuracy of our re-creation.

The closing party was held in a majestic townhouse. As the crowd was thinning, Georg ran outside and around the building until he was just below the window facing a table full of wine and whiskey bottles. When the coast was clear, Ed and I tossed the bottles to him for a late-night party back at the hotel where the company was staying. Once there, the two women in the company, Lola Pashalinski and Black-Eyed Susan, retreated to their room and Charles and his lover, Everett Quinton, in the first blush of their romance, went directly to theirs. Ed and I hung out with Georg, the tall, cadaverous character actor John Brockmeyer, and Ludlam's dissolute leading man, Bill Vehr.

Ed and I, feeling rather like genteel Miss Porter's finishing schoolgirls, found Bill and John's camp humor to be on the disgustingly scatological side. It grew late and we were anxious about getting back to Evanston on the L. Georg suggested we bunk down with them at their nearby hotel. Since Georg had only a small single room, Bill and John chivalrously offered to let us spend the night in their larger suite. There was nothing sexual in the invitation. The fellas didn't find Ed or me any more delectable than we found them, and the night I spent sharing a narrow single bed with John Brockmeyer passed with our backs to each other and both of us sound asleep.

Bill and John seemed so much older than us, yet there was most likely only about an eight-year age difference. I wondered if Ed and I were a new breed of post-Stonewall gay men—John and Bill the renegade outlaws, and we the young city dwellers about to change the tone of the frontier. Being gay in New York in the pre-Stonewall sixties couldn't have been all grim: There was Judy at Carnegie Hall and Callas at the Met. I'm sure there was some satisfaction in being part of a secret society, with its own transgressive slang and sexy inside humor. Still, one would be subjected to police raids on gay bars and being patronized, marginalized, and ridiculed as a minority not worthy of any consideration.

The Stonewall Uprising gave gay people a new identity, no longer as pathetic victims or the subject of dirty jokes but as a fierce political entity. That activist spirit made it hip to be gay. Or even gay-adjacent: Bette Midler's rise to fame performing in a gay bathhouse and Liza Minnelli's Oscar-winning performance in the film *Cabaret* took the desperation and poignancy out of the role of "fag hag." A straight woman could run with a gay male crowd and not be a sad drone but the fabulous Queen Bee. Coming of sexual age in the early post-Stonewall 1970s, Ed and I experienced none of the furtive paranoia of our recent predecessors and blossomed in the new gay chic of urban life.

Carry On, Nurse

1976. When I came home for spring break during my senior year, I arrived at the apartment and found Aunt Lil lying on her daybed. That was unusual. My aunt was nearly always immersed in some activity: hemming a skirt, practicing her French or German, studying the philosophy of Martin Buber, or repairing a broken radio. She rose to greet me, and I saw that her arm was in a white canvas sling. After I kissed her cheek, I asked, "What's wrong with your arm?" She hesitated, then responded in a small, tremulous voice, "I had . . . my breast amputated." It took me a moment to take in that odd statement. What an arcane nineteenth-century way of expressing that she'd had a mastectomy. And then she started to cry.

I held her close to me. For the first time, I was the adult in our embrace. I must've spoken to her on the phone several times over the past few weeks and yet all of this had been kept from me. How had she pulled off that smoke screen? I wasn't annoyed. I knew that any secret had been meant to protect me and was kept so as not to distract me from my work in college. Aunt Lil explained that she'd gone for a routine mammogram, and all seemed fine. Then her doctor called back to say that he'd discovered a small shadow on the X-ray, probably nothing. She'd had a second examination, and this time a tumor as miniscule as a pin prick was revealed. A biopsy was performed, and the tumor found to be malignant. This was the mid-seventies, so the doctor recommended a radical mastectomy, removing the entire breast as well as the muscle in the armpit. Aunt Lil was also advised to do a course of chemotherapy.

I was home for two weeks. Determined to prove that I could be depended on, I devoted every moment to Aunt Lil, cooking and attending to all her errands. As she had zero interest in speaking to anyone, I ran interference on the telephone. Some of the people she chose to avoid got pissed off at me. Aunt Belle, for one. After the third time I informed her that Aunt Lil couldn't come to the phone, she barked, "You can tell Lil she can go fuck herself." (*Beat.*) "I'll drop off some stuffed cabbages on Sunday." *Click.*

Aunt Lil and I spoke little during those weeks. The only time she was sharp with me was when I was attempting to express sympathy and told her that, whether you had one or two breasts removed, it was the same traumatic experience. She misinterpreted my remark and thought I was saying the opposite, that the removal of one breast wasn't as bad as losing both. "How would you like it if you had one ball cut off?" she snapped. I let it go—an important lesson that I'd learned from my aunt was to make allowances for people, set ego aside, and not take things personally from someone who's tense or unhappy. My goal was to be as perfect a caregiver as she would've been to me, and it was difficult being that perfect. Aunt Lil's standards for giving were impossibly high. It wasn't enough to put someone else's needs above your own. You had to anticipate their needs and attend to them without being asked. I'm still working on that.

The Shopworn Angel

1976. I'd managed to graduate from Northwestern. I never got around to taking the final two science requirements, but the dean seemed more than glad to waive them. The diploma was mine and I was sprung.

When you're an aspiring actor from another city, there's a point when you feel ready to hit New York. It's more confusing when you're *from* New York. If you're not ready, then what? As validating as it was, the experience of writing and performing *Sister Act* left me confused. How does one begin to pursue a career as a playwright/drag star?

Several days after graduation, I arrived back in Aunt Lil's apartment just as the city was celebrating the bicentennial weekend. When I phoned Ed at his family's suburban home, his mother told me that he'd found a job as a bartender in Chicago and stayed there. He must've landed the job within twenty-four hours of my leaving him. That did it. The day after witnessing the spectacle of the tall sailing ships in the harbor, I flew back to the Windy City and found an apartment in the gay neighborhood known as Boystown.

I promptly wrote another short theatrical vehicle for Ed and myself—a parody of the 1943 Bette Davis/Miriam Hopkins movie, *Old Acquaintance*, which Ed titled *Old Coozies*. We performed it twice at a popular New Wave club, La Mere Vipere. There was no stage except for a tiny platform high above the dance floor in the far corner of the cavernous room. The platform was so close to the vaulted corner ceiling that if we moved stage right, we had to make a dramatic point of leaning seductively against the slanted wall. It was exhilarating playing a film-inspired heroine for a gay crowd who shared my love of old movies. When you get a boffo laugh with an obscure line from the movie *Sorry, Wrong Number*, you know you're in the right place.

I began what would be a decade of searching out employment that wouldn't interfere with my theatrical ambitions. I worked for a while as assistant manager of a memorabilia shop on Clark Street, which sold old movie posters, window cards, antique toys, and artifacts from the Chicago World's Fair. Dwight, the proprietor, both paranoic and unctuously sentimental, appreciated my talent for drawing golden age movie actresses. Within weeks the store was decorated with a dozen signs featuring portraits of Myrna Loy, Jean Harlow, and Kay Francis.

I was gradually edged out of that job when Dwight became obsessed with a hyperactive ex-con named Woody, whom he installed as manager. Woody brought in his moll, a vacant-looking broad named Cookie, to work part-time. A bisexual bantam rooster, Woody would corner me in the storage room and imagine he was enticing me with a flirtation style honed in Joliet Prison, boasting of a pecker decorated with three warts that according to the ladies was akin to being screwed with a French tickler. 'Twas time to move on.

I admire people with the ability to throw themselves into any professional situation. Alas, I'm not one of them. In my various survival jobs, I was pleasant, congenial, and industrious only up to a point. Once when I was toiling as a temporary receptionist for a high-powered female executive, she castigated me for my lack of initiative in stuffing her envelopes. "Young man, you will never be successful in life unless you always give 100 percent." Her finger wagging only brought out in me a sullen Virginia-Mayo-in-*White-Heat* indifference. Ninety percent of my energy was reserved for my theatrical career. She'd have to accept the remaining ten percent or get some other sap to stuff her envelopes. No, I cannot say I was ever asked back for a return engagement as a full-time office worker. There was, however, one part-time job that I found extremely stimulating and to which I was able to give all of myself.

Picture a graceful hand balancing a long cigarette holder and lightly scanning the want ads in a gay newspaper. *Hmmmm. David's Models.*

There is a long tradition of theatrical hopefuls who have earned their beans by commercializing their personal charms. Finding herself in an early period of unemployment, the divine Sarah Bernhardt, illegitimate daughter of a courtesan, took up the family trade. Years later, when she was a great star, a resentful former actress from her company named Marie Colombier penned a scurrilous roman à clef titled *The Memoirs of Sarah Barnum*, exposing Bernhardt's sexual history. Sarah, accompanied by her current lover, burst into Marie Colombier's Parisian digs in vengeful fury. Brandishing a dagger from her recent production of *Nana-Sahib*, she chased the terrified authoress around her boudoir, slashing drapes and furnishings. To ward off such unwelcome exposure, I've chosen to come clean about my own adventures in the demimonde.

To seek a spot on the roster of David's Models, an applicant had to submit to not only an interview but a brief roll in the hay with the physically unappetizing and abrasive boss. It wasn't so bad. I flattered him, laughed at his caustic sarcasm, and brought out the "cuddly bear" in David. My favorable audition established the template for my role of rent boy.

The men who demand the services of a muscle-bound hunk want their money's worth of hard-core action. In contrast, I clued in quickly that clients who desired my type would not necessitate too much sexual activity on my part. My waiflike image tended to attract older gentlemen who were grateful for an hour's worth of gentle naked interplay, and often actual conversation. It wasn't dissimilar to my brief foray into apartment cleaning. When it became apparent to my elderly women clients that I didn't have a clue how to clean an apartment, they rather enjoyed showing me the proper way to scrub a stove or mop a hardwood floor. Most of our time was spent poring over their photo albums and talking about their late husbands. The apartments weren't spic and span, but I left the old ladies a little less lonely.

I'm a natural-born interviewer with an innate curiosity about people. Everyone has a story, and most people don't get a chance to tell it. There was the grandfather from Wilmette, a retired podiatrist whose family would never imagine the patriarch was indulging in a nude afternoon rendezvous *avec moi*. Another client was an ethereally wan high school kid, mercilessly bullied by his schoolmates, who saved up his money for an hour of me holding him tenderly and letting him know that he was beautiful and of value. There were times, however, when the job became more heated . . . and exacting.

One afternoon, I was booked for an erotic foursome. Two girls were to arrive at two forty-five, the gentleman at three. I looked around the room. I had vacuumed and dusted. There were no dishes in the sink. The apartment appeared presentable. I'd agreed to host as I'd only been working for the agency a month and wanted to impress upon management that I was a team player.

At 2:40, five minutes early, the doorbell buzzed, and the first girl arrived. Her name was Sandra, a pretty brunette in her twenties with a Farrah Fawcett shag and an intimidating take-charge demeanor. Sandra assessed the bedroom, pronounced it adequate, and filled me in on the situation. In the brusque manner of a military attaché to Patton, she explained that Bob, a regular client of hers, was a wealthy married executive with children. This was the first time he had suggested adding more personnel to their encounter. She made it emphatically clear that Bob was strictly hetero. He simply had a kinky desire to watch Sandra having intercourse with another man. "Only we're not really gonna. Get it?" "Got it," I assured her.

"Chuck, or whatever your name is, this is a onetime experiment. I can guarantee you'll never be hearing from him again." She explained that we'd be joined by another girl, an exotic dancer hired through a third agency who'd be performing an erotic dance. I was dubious. From a theatrical perspective, it seemed like a lot of show for one hour.

Bob arrived before the dancer and was not at all what I expected. A blond midwestern dad in his late thirties wearing an expensive perfectly tailored grey suit, he shook my hand as if we were about to play a game of squash at the country club. He asked what had happened to the dancer. Sandra established their close bond by embracing him around the waist, explaining that she couldn't take responsibility for some other chick's tardiness. Another buzz at the door and the dancer arrived—a gorgeous black girl named Holly, ebony dark and wearing a long wig that went all the way down her straight dancer's back. Holly explained that her agency had given her the wrong street number and she'd had to find a phone booth to call them and straighten it out.

I shared a similar experience, in which the client had then only wanted to pay me for half the session. Sandra temporarily dropped her office manager demeanor and chimed in with a funny anecdote about ringing the wrong doorbell and having sex for half an hour before she realized she was with the client's neighbor. The three of us began exchanging war stories. I'd never socialized with others in my new line of work, and it turned out that all three of us were in the arts, Holly an aspiring ballet dancer and Sandra a ceramic sculptor. Bob cleared his throat and tapped his Rolex, turning into a dad with three obstreperous teenagers. "Hey, kids. We're on my dime."

Sandra flipped her switch to "sultry." Holly and I watched her sensuously remove Bob's suit jacket and carefully lay it on the bedroom chair. She knelt and removed his expensive Italian shoes and socks. She was a pro—it's always a pleasure watching a professional at work. She then unbuckled his belt and unzipped his grey pants. Stepping out of them, he stood there in his crisp white shirt, tie, and fitted boxer shorts, awaiting her next move. She loosened and removed his tie, then unbuttoned his shirt and slid it off. He had a good body, no doubt kept trim through frequent workouts at an expensive health club.

With the swiftness of a vaudeville quick change artist, Sandra threw off her own clothes and was topless in a pair of bikini briefs. She led Bob to the bed. I took off my jeans and T-shirt and joined them. There was a genuine sense of intimacy between them so I remained a bystander and watched them make out, thinking, *This could be a very easy hundred bucks*. Holly unpacked a cassette player and put on some sexy disco lounge music. She chose a wooden straight-backed chair as a prop and began sinuously removing her clothes, getting down to a thong and a pink lace bra. Watching her undulate to the disco beat, I still didn't quite get her role in this *partouze*. It seemed a bit silly, but Bob was into her squirming and posing, occasionally suggesting a new angle in order to get a clearer view of her ass. I got the impression that Holly had never fully crossed the line into the role of sex worker. I could picture her as a regular churchgoer.

My mind began drifting back to the end of the first act of a new play I was writing. It occurred to me that perhaps, like this session, the play had one too many characters.

I was woken out of my reverie when Bob announced in a businesslike boardroom tone that it was time for me to "do it" with Sandra. My costar turned her face upstage and shot me a tight-lipped grimace, unnecessarily reminding me that we were going to fake it. I pulled off my underwear and climbed on top of her. Bob moved over to the side of the bed to get a better look at the proceedings. Sandra made a variety of orgasmic moans and sighs as I nuzzled her neck. We began grinding our hips against each other and I summoned up my mime skills and faked insertion.

Bob had to know we were pretending, but it didn't seem to matter. There's always a suspension of disbelief in any theatrical performance. I felt Bob's hand lightly caressing my arched back. *Hmmmm*, I thought. *Let's see how straight Daddy really is.* A degree of diplomacy was required here. A step too bold could make this heterosexual dad head for the hills. I pulled away from Sandra and, attempting to climb over her to get to Bob, nearly got my foot stuck in her mouth. She was not pleased. Upon my suggestion, Bob rose from the bed and I, dropping to my knees, chose to make a game-changing move, advancing on his tantalizing suburban bratwurst. With a lot invested in this guy, Sandra was not about to let my scene-stealing antics go too far. She joined me on the floor, and it became an Olympic competition of oral calisthenics, gay boy vs. straight girl. Poor Holly was left grinding away to her Barry White tape without an audience. Guaranteed her seventy-five dollars, I don't think she cared.

Deciding she'd had enough of our tournament, Sandra pushed me aside with such force I was left sprawling quite ungracefully onto the floor. Well, that did it. She was not going to have the entire finale of the show to herself! I stood up on the bed and launched a solo performance of, dare I say, virtuosic eroticism. Bob was as engrossed as if he were watching Heifetz plucking his fiddle. Holly even took a break from her gyrations out of respect for my artistry. Sandra leaned back in a chair, arms folded, impatiently checking

her watch. I was the star at last, and I employed every bit of my accumulated stage technique and theatrical know-how. One might even venture
that it was something of a breakthrough. Performing for an audience not
accustomed to my talents, I commanded the stage with a brio that left them
vanquished. A tad excessive perhaps, but it was pure theater! Greek! Eliza-
bethan! Restoration! Broadway! *Theater!*

A postscript: A week later, the service phoned to say that Bob had requested
a solo session with me. Well, well, well, well, well.

The Country Girl

It was 2009. The long, winding driveway to Joan Rivers's Connecticut
home was so baronial that my partner, Eric, and I felt like the new Mrs.
de Winter approaching Manderley for the first time in *Rebecca*. At the end
of the drive, the chauffeur opened the car doors and we were greeted by
our hostess, dressed simply in jeans and a man's untucked white shirt. After
an affectionate embrace, our gracious chatelaine had us sign releases—she
intended to film us later as part of the pilot for her new reality series.

We were awed by the attention to every detail of the grounds, the house,
and its country manor interiors. In our guest room, Godiva chocolates rested
on the pillows. Joan requested that we wait for her in the drawing room
while she made a short business phone call. Comedy Central was honoring
her with a celebrity roast and they were having trouble lining up comics.

This was most definitely during a plateau in her career. As we waited for Joan, we could hear her speaking on the phone to her producer regarding a last-minute addition to the roster. "Let's take him. At this point, I don't care if he has three jokes and two of them have *cunt* in them."

Windy City Blues

1977. My friend Michael Mitchell told me he was going to audition for the role of Orestes in a production of *The Flies*, Jean-Paul Sartre's existential take on Greek mythology, produced by a small storefront gay theater called The Drama Shelter. I decided to go along with him and, for the hell of it, audition myself. They paid the actors only a small weekly stipend, so they double cast every role, because when you're not getting paid, lots of very important things turn up that cause you to miss shows. Michael and I were cast together in both the lead male role of Orestes and the small role of Orestes's aged tutor, which we would alternate at each performance. After a few weeks, Michael grew tired of playing the arduous part of Orestes and gave me the role full-time while he continued as the tutor. That was fine with me, for even then, I was only really happy when I was the protagonist.

I'm not sure why this gay theater was producing *The Flies*—there's nothing gay about it. Well, usually. The director most definitely possessed an appreciation for the male form and had his lover, the costume designer, put us in extremely short Greek chitons. Underneath, we wore an ancient

Greek version of a thong. Whenever I'd turn my back to the audience and raise my arms dramatically in exhortation to Zeus, my miniskirt would rise, exposing my bare ass. The exclusively male audience would hoot and holler as if they were at a carnival cootch show. All too briefly, Sartre's three-hour philosophic treatise on the importance of freedom became the camp-fest this audience longed for.

I worked diligently on the role of Orestes, studying the theory of existentialism and strengthening my vocal stamina and articulation. I took it very seriously and, entre nous, I thought I was damn good. Ed came to the opening night, and after the show, I asked him what he thought of my performance as the young Prince Orestes. "Well, you were noble and aristocratic. You were very Katharine Hepburn in *Holiday*." He nailed it. I was playing Sartre's tormented hero as a Bryn Mawr–educated tomboy!

I hit it off with the cast of *The Flies*. The girls were fun, the boys good-natured. How high was the talent quotient? Not particularly, but it was a lively dressing room. One night I confided in them my ambition to have my own troupe like Charles Ludlam's Ridiculous Theatrical Company for whom I could write camp movie–inspired comedies and be the leading lady in drag. The entire cast surprised me with their enthusiasm. Jeanine, the actress playing Queen Clytemnestra, was a budding director and the most eager to bring this idea to fruition.

I've never had any desire to direct a play. I've enjoyed coaching actors, but taking full responsibility for the production and staging of a play doesn't interest me. The directors I've worked with relish being asked a million questions and instantly providing an answer to every one of them. My response would be, "Why are all of you bugging me? How the hell do I know?" (Oddly enough, I've enjoyed my few experiences directing film. There are so many department heads with specific expertise that each member of their team goes to them for an answer.)

By the end of the run, the cast of *The Flies* had become The Imitation of Life Theater. Jeanine gladly took on the role of director, and within a week I furnished us with a new play, *Myrtle Pope; the Story of a Woman Possessed.* Not surprisingly, I played the title role, and over the course of the hour-long play, Myrtle suffered agonies inspired by such tearjerkers as *Madame X*, *Now Voyager*, *A Stolen Life*, and *Blonde Venus*. With no budget, we performed on a bare stage and all of the actors improvised their costumes from their own closets. I pieced together my haute couture leading lady wardrobe from raids on the Salvation Army and Goodwill. My hair was so long and full (*Ah, those were the days. Sic transit gloria . . .*) that wigs weren't necessary. I could differentiate the phases of Myrtle's story with four well-placed bobby pins, inserted to create a variety of period hairdos.

Between Jeanine and me, we booked the show in one-night stands all over Chicago in straight saloons and gay clubs along with three weekends of midnight stage shows at a neighborhood movie theater after its final screening of the night. The response to our performance there varied according to the movie. We didn't do well after Clint Eastwood's *The Gauntlet* but drew a large appreciative crowd after a showing of the 1968 Franco Zeffirelli *Romeo and Juliet.*

It was an intoxicating period for me, playing before different kinds of audiences and adjusting my performance accordingly. I was entering into a mutually seductive relationship with the "monster"—also known as the audience. My way of playing a character whose voice and mannerisms evoked a different classic film actress in each scene drew a heady response from the crowd, and I basked in their warm approval like a baby chick in an incubator.

Several months in and just as we were beginning to get some nice mentions in the Chicago gay press, Jeanine thought it would be helpful if we all got together to explore our feelings and the future of the group. We sat in a circle to do round-robin sharing. I looked forward to telling the group how much I enjoyed their company and enjoyed writing roles for them. One of our actresses, Laura, was the first up. "Jeanine, I love you so much. I feel such incredible support. You've made me a better actress and a better person." Laura then turned to Phil. "Oh, what can I say? Phil, it's the greatest joy being onstage with you. I get such a kick out of our little pre-show improv." Laura moved on to Bob. "Oh, Bob, Bob, Bob, you are always there for me. You give me such strength." I was next in line and prepared to receive this lovely young woman's grateful words of endearment. "Charles, how do I say this? This is hard. But . . . it's always about *you*. This is your show. You're the *star*." Laura made the word "star" seem so ugly. "I don't feel I even know you. You're this . . . *thing*. It's all you, you, you, you." I'd had no idea she had such a problem with me, the *thing*.

She continued going around the circle. Everyone else she was crazy about. It seemed that they all made her a better person. Then Jeanine and another girl, Wendy, likewise went around the circle expressing their undying love, gratitude, and respect for everyone but me. Wendy sighed, "Charles, I just don't feel like you're one of us." As the encounter group progressed, it became clear that everyone in the company was nuts about each other except that all of the women had major issues with me. They revealed that they could not care less about having roles tailored to their talents and they sure didn't appreciate having me as the leading lady. They felt I was holding them back and that my insistence on being both playwright and star was going to keep them from moving forward. I'd had absolutely no idea that The Imitation of Life Theater was such a hotbed of resentment. I'd been gluing on my false eyelashes in a fool's paradise.

Not *everyone* in the group denounced me as a self-absorbed egotist. The three men—Bob, John, and Phil—had no problem with me. The girls weren't totally wrong. I had no desire to be part of an equal ensemble, acting in other writers' plays. My goal was to continue developing as a male actress and be the star of my own work, but hadn't I made that ambition clear from the beginning?

My friend Ed, an outside observer to this backstage drama, quipped in his inimitable way, "Honey, they took the goose that laid the golden eggs and made egg salad."

Alone with a Cast of Thousands

I've never quite gotten over being blindsided the way I was with the Chicago troupe; I was disappointed in my own obtuseness in not divining the group's discontent. This perceived betrayal propelled me to make a dramatic move. At twenty-four, I was at last ready to return to New York. Raising my fist heavenwards, I vowed, "As God is my witness, as God is my witness, I'll never let anyone, least of all non-union actresses, make me feel guilty for taking the final bow!"

I'd written a new play for the group, a parody of movies about Hollywood such as *A Star Is Born*, *The Bad and the Beautiful*, and *Sunset Boulevard*, which I titled *Hollywood Confidential*. No point in wasting all those good lines—why couldn't I play all the roles, male and female, myself? At Northwestern, I'd taken classes in oral interpretation of drama and prose fiction with two brilliant teachers, Dr. Robert Breen and the Tony-winning director Dr. Frank Galati. We were taught simple techniques using physical movement that made it clear to the audience when a different character was speaking. I'd turn *Hollywood Confidential* into a solo performance piece! No more sharing the dressing room *or* the applause.

Perhaps because I've viewed my life as a narrative while I was living it, I've always been aware of when a certain chapter has come to an end. There was nothing to keep me in Chicago. I'd been enjoying a free-spirited bohemian life away from Aunt Lil's penetrating eye, but now it was time to buckle down. Ed had already moved to New York to work in advertising. Being in the same city as my best friend and most astute critic was a lure. If I truly wanted a career in the theater, New York was the place to pursue it. And it was home.

Once again, I moved into Aunt Lil's Manhattan apartment, assuming I'd be there for a month at most, by which time I'd surely find an apartment in Greenwich Village, steeped in atmosphere, for a mind-bogglingly modest rent. I brought with me from Chicago a hundred or so rambling pages of *Hollywood Confidential*. Ed was dating a director named Patrick Brafford, full of enthusiasm, imagination, and patience, who helped me develop it into a tight one-hour solo performance piece.

A major influence were the recordings of the great American monologist Ruth Draper. From just after WWI to her death in 1956, she was the American theater's preeminent solo dramatist. She long resisted being recorded or filmed, but shortly before her death she conceded to go into the studio to record her most celebrated pieces, including *The Italian Lesson, Doctors and Diets*, and *Three Women and Mr. Clifford*. Among the lessons in dramaturgy and performance I gained from listening to those records were those related to Draper's ability to let her audience "see" the people her characters were addressing. These offstage figures that her characters were responding to were as vivid as the women Draper was physically embodying. From photographs, I gleaned that Ruth Draper differentiated her characterizations visually with only a change of hat or shawl.

In *Hollywood Confidential* I was introduced to the audience as a young male newspaper reporter investigating the mysterious death of a movie love goddess, Lola Lamé. The neutral costume that I wore throughout the show was a white buccaneer-styled shirt and a pair of gold lamé trousers. As the reporter, I put on a trench coat and fedora. When I switched characters and became the German motion picture director, I took off the coat and fedora and added a monocle and a beret. For the Hedda Hopper–like gossip columnist, I donned an outrageous wide-brimmed hat and a fox fur piece. When I appeared as the enigmatic Lola, I threw on a disheveled blonde wig and an ostrich feather boa.

Where was I to perform this piece? I had no connections in the theater, and any sort of theatrical production required a budget. A cabaret seemed the most realistic venue. There was a small cabaret room in the West Village called Scene One. I stopped in one afternoon and introduced myself to the manager, Bobby Kneeland. I performed a few minutes of the show and he booked me for a few random nights on the spot. I couldn't be too self-congratulatory. Honestly, only a diagnostic report from a state asylum pinned to the back of your coat stating *Do not hire. Dangerous!* would've discouraged a booking from Scene One.

On another afternoon stroll in the Village, I noticed that the fabled cabaret The Duplex on Grove Street, shuttered for years but once home to such performers as Stiller and Meara, Dick Cavett, and Rodney Dangerfield, was now open again. I stepped out of the bright sun and into the dark lower bar and met Erv Raible, the new owner.

Erv was a small dynamo. He and his lover, Rob Hoskins, had been teachers at a performing arts high school in Cincinnati. In a bold move considered deranged by their academic colleagues, they quit their jobs, moved to New York, and bought the moribund club. Erv spoke with a pronounced flat Midwestern accent and sizzled with ideas and plans. After I performed a brief fragment of my act, he immediately made me part of those plans. With his academic theater background, he was intrigued and supportive of the fact that *Hollywood Confidential* was more theater than cabaret. I became part of his stable of talented offbeat performers such as Bruce Hopkins, Ira Siff, Ruby Rims, and Julie Kurnitz, all of whom came to cabaret with a unique perspective. Their originality expanded the traditional concept of cabaret as exclusively the realm of song stylists and stand-up comedians.

I was grateful for Erv's belief in me but the person whose acknowledgment I craved most was Charles Ludlam. By now, he had his own theater at One Sheridan Square where his plays ran in repertory a few blocks away from The Duplex. I honestly don't know what I wanted from Charles. My goal was not to collaborate or to be a member of his company or even his friend. It would be enough to know that he thought I was gifted and viewed me as a kindred spirit. His work had opened my mind to the idea that I could be a playwright and create roles for myself. His artistic vision gave me license to view my ability to evoke actresses of the past as a valid theatrical tool.

Taping flyers for my act on the lampposts near his theater, I ran into an actress from his company, Black-Eyed Susan, and happened to have with me a stack of postcards for my show. She promised to place them on a table in the theater lobby. I also went a more traditional route and wrote Charles a letter inviting him to a performance. One night I looked at the reservation list: As usual there were only about ten reservations, but two were under the name Ludlam. I had much steadier nerves in those days and I didn't allow his presence to throw me. When the show was over, I was disappointed to learn that he and Everett had quickly paid their bill and left.

Shortly after that, I saw an ad for something called the Charlie Comedy Awards. It was named after Charlie Chaplin, and Charles Ludlam was to be honored. I brought Margaret to the ceremony. After the awards presentation, she and I milled about the room. I was stalking my prey. Spotting him seated at a table with Everett, I straightened my metaphoric girdle and approached. "Charles, it's Charles Busch. I understand you were at my show the other night at The Duplex. Thank you so much for coming."

He gestured for us to sit and join them and said in a soft voice, "We loved it. I'm funny about going backstage afterwards. What's up next for you?"

"Nothing really. Just trying to find places to do the show."

Charles exchanged glances with Everett. "You should do your show on weekends at my theater after our play comes down. You could go on at eleven o'clock."

This was way beyond what I'd hoped for. "*Really?*"

"When would you like to start?"

Was he always this spontaneous? I'd need some time to do press and organize myself. This was in May, so I suggested a start date in late June. He said that sounded great. And that was that. Margaret and I left Charles's table and looked at each other. "Did you hear what I heard?" I asked her, in confirmation.

Now I was in a quandary about how to get some notice in the press. I was still living with Aunt Lil, and she mulled over my dilemma. "You should contact *The Joe Franklin Show*. I bet he'd have you on." Joe Franklin was a veteran radio and TV broadcaster who for decades hosted a low-budget TV interview show, *Joe Franklin's Memory Lane*, later called *The Joe Franklin Show*. I scoffed at Aunt Lil's suggestion. "I'm not famous enough to be on that show. I wouldn't even know who to call. You need a publicist to get on a program like that."

She grabbed the large Manhattan phone directory and began flipping through the pages. "Here he is. Joe Franklin. There's his phone number." I humored her and dialed the number to prove how futile this was. Joe Franklin himself picked up. Within a few minutes, I had a date to appear on his show. Aunt Lil shook her head. "You'd save yourself a lot of time if you didn't always put up an argument and just did what I tell you."

The day I appeared on the show, the other guests included the Oscar-winning actress Joan Fontaine, who was plugging her new memoir, and Ursula, Brazil's most popular disco star, who was promoting her upcoming appearance at the dance club the Palladium. Joe brought me over to meet Miss Fontaine and introduced me as Charles Bosch. Rather than giving her the correct title of my solo show *Hollywood Confidential*, he told her I was the star of the hit Off-Broadway musical *Hollywood Canteen*. She granted me a glacial smile. "Lovely to meet you, Mr. Bosch." She gave no indication that a rejoinder was necessary or desired. It was a lesson in classic movie star noblesse oblige watching Joe Franklin introduce Miss Fontaine to "Ursula, Brazil's most popular disco sensation." "A thrill to meet you, Ursula."

I sent out a press release, which generated a few items in the weekly gay bar publications. My opening weekend was soon approaching. It was time to schedule a tech rehearsal. A little less than a week before the show, I stopped by Charles's theater just as his performance of *Camille* had ended. I poked my head in his dressing room and found him removing his makeup. I tried to get his attention. "Hi. Charles Busch?" Without looking away from the mirror, he asked, "Were you at the play tonight? A strange crowd." "No, I just stopped by. So next weekend I'll be doing my solo show here and I wanted to know when I could arrange for a tech rehearsal." He left his reflection in the mirror and looked directly at me for the first time. "Your solo show?"

I died. "We talked about this at the Charlie Awards. You very kindly offered to let me perform *Hollywood Confidential* on Friday and Saturday nights at eleven o'clock." I could see that he didn't remember making the kind offer. "Huh. Hmmm ... Gee ... I think you should call our business manager, Cathy Smith. Yeah. You should talk to her." He searched for a pen among his makeup and, finding one, wrote her number on a piece of paper for me.

The next morning, I phoned Cathy and began to tell her about Charles's offer. Interrupting, she told me to stop by her office.

"This is the first I've heard about this," she said once I'd explained in person. "I don't know what Charles promised you, but we can't do it. We've gone through all our grant money for this season. Come to me next year and maybe we can do something with you." Cathy Smith's unwashed hair and bleary eyes gave the impression of someone overtaxed, underpaid, and overwhelmed. "You don't understand, Cathy," I told her. "I've sent out a press release. I'm listed in all the free gay bar magazines. I have a photo in *Michael's Thing*. I was on *The Joe Franklin Show!*" She explained that the company was struggling and had no money to pay overtime for the box office person and lighting operator. "You won't have to pay anyone," I promised. "I'll bring in my own box office person and lighting operator. I'll do everything. Just give me the space, *please*." Faced with such an onslaught of naked desperation, she relented, and even agreed to give me a single line of advertising at the bottom of their weekly *Village Voice* ad.

Andy Halliday, my close pal since theater camp, ran all over the Village with me in the dark of night pasting flyers on every available lamppost. Ed agreed to man the box office, and he and my director, Patrick, ran the lights and sound.

The first performance that Friday went smoothly, but none of my press breaks helped. The small audience was composed solely of members of Ludlam's troupe and a few Ludlam acolytes who remained in their seats after his performance. But Charles was generous in his praise, and I felt that he was pleased to be presenting me under his aegis. After four weekends, never finding an audience, it was deemed best by all not to continue.

It had been worth doing, for my engagement at the home of the Ridiculous Theatrical Company marked the first time I was written up in the gay news magazine *The Advocate*, which for years afterwards treated me as a worthy cultural figure long before I'd done anything worth writing about.

A Limited Engagement in Hades

One afternoon shortly after I finished my run of *Hollywood Confidential*, Ludlam phoned me in a state of agitation. The girl playing Hecate, the Goddess of Hell, in his production of *Bluebeard* had to leave the show immediately due to a family emergency. Could I go on for her that night? It was a small role only appearing in one short scene toward the end of the play. Charles said I could pick up the script at the box office and rehearse it with the stage manager right before the show. I was young and fearless. Sure. Why not? I'd seen the play and had one stipulation. I didn't care for Hecate's clown-like wig and costume. "Charles, would you mind if I came up with my own costume and wig?" I asked. "Yeah, yeah, sure. Whatever you want."

I rummaged through my drag box (every boy has one) and assembled a dramatic look consisting of a bustier, a long trailing red satin skirt, five-inch patent leather platform heels, and a waist-length auburn wig with a large pouf of red tulle pinned to the top to give me stature. I showed up at the theater with my few lines memorized and went over the brief scene with the stage manager. Charles came into my dressing room to inspect my costume, hair, and makeup. I was a chic and very female Hecate. "Looks good. Give me your eyebrow pencil. You're supposed to be my spiritual twin. We need to share a feature." With that, he drew a small devilish triangular beard on my chin to match his own. It conflicted with my attempt at nineteenth-century symbolist female beauty, but I wasn't about to object. I sat in the dressing room for most of the performance.

y fine romance had its complications. Alex was in a committed rela-
p with an aspiring operatic tenor named Sean. I was prepared to
my rival, but not only did Sean and I resemble each other physically, as
ing performers of the same age we hit it off the moment Alex intro-
us. I was never quite sure if Sean was aware that there was a sexual
nent to my friendship with his partner. We certainly never discussed
ean was cognizant of that truth, perhaps he wasn't threatened. After
nutes with the two of them, it was clear that he and Alex were meant
h other. Whenever I uttered some idle, not terribly well-thought-out
n, Alex would force me to defend the statement. I'd flip my opinion on
t to please him—whereas Sean, under similar grilling, would deflate
with a crisp, "Oh, shut up and finish your drink." Upon which Alex
laugh and toss back his martini.

y being in residence at Aunt Lil's made it difficult for Alex and me
a trysting place. One afternoon, Alex sat me down and announced
e'd spoken with his attorney about setting up a bank account in my
from which he would pay the rent on an apartment for me. I gave his
ition some serious thought. It's not often that a boy gets this kind of
gly indecent offer involving real estate.

udence forced me to decline. How would I have explained to Aunt Lil
ould suddenly afford a luxury prewar Manhattan love nest? I'd also seen
h movies to know that sort of *Back Street* arrangement never ends well.
I told Alex I couldn't take him up on his offer, it began the gradual fade-
our *amour fou*. It became too much of an effort to keep up the sizzle. I
o regrets. Alex's belief in my talent and the confidence that gave me was
tely worth far more than a monthly allowance and an Upper East Side
s, even one complete with bedroom skyline views, a twenty-four-hour
an, and concierge services including on-site dry cleaning.

At last, the climax of the play was approaching: Bluebeard, played by
Charles, conjures forth the Goddess of Hell. I stood in the wing. The stage
was filled with dry ice smoke and there he was, magnificent with his blue
facial hair and those extraordinary hypnotic dark eyes. His stage voice was
masterfully vibrant and full of power. There was a sound cue of eerie music
and on I sailed. With no direction, I chose to employ a European Lotte Lenya
voice redolent of her performance as the decadent Contessa in the film *The
Roman Spring of Mrs. Stone*. I purred my lines in an evil, seductive manner.
The brief scene ended, and I returned to the dressing room. After the show,
Charles's coterie of admirers rushed backstage and a few of them, including
the artist Christopher Scott, complimented me on my performance and said
I should be a member of the company. Charles sauntered over. "You were
very good, but you need to be bigger. Much bigger."

The next night, I tried being more intense while retaining my simmer-
ing Lenya characterization. Afterwards, more people complimented me and,
again, Charles said, "I'm telling you. You gotta be bigger. Much bigger." The
third night I tried again, but as soon as I left the stage, Charles grabbed me
roughly by my bare shoulder. "Who the fuck do you think you are? I had egg
all over my face! I told you to play it bigger! Fuck you!" He spun around and
left. I hadn't meant to displease him. I thought I *was* playing it bigger. What
did "bigger" even mean?

When I got home to Aunt Lil's I related what had transpired. By this
point, I idiotically believed that Charles's ugly behavior was due to jealousy.
Aunt Lil turned down the volume of the television. "He gave you the chance
to do your show at his theater. You do exactly what he tells you."

I returned to the theater the following night, left my Lenya impersonn-
ation at the door, and proceeded to play Hecate in a loud, bombastic manner.
When the play was over, no bouquets were hurled at my feet, but Charles said,
"That's the way to go." It took me a few years to understand what Charles

had needed from me as Hecate. Experience has taught me that an actor may come up with an interpretation that's bold and original but doesn't serve the play. Ludlam's *Bluebeard* was an expertly constructed comic melodrama that accelerated throughout its two acts. Hecate appeared at the climax. I was wrong to bring down the level of intensity that Charles had been building in his writing, direction, and performance. I wish he could've taken me aside and rehearsed our brief scene and taught this young actor that important concept.

I counted the days till my commitment was over. I imagine Charles thought I was a bit full of myself. In the middle of our scene one night, at the height of Bluebeard's passion, he playfully yanked down my bustier. As we left the stage, I turned to him with indignant hauteur worthy of Dame Judith Anderson and huffed, "I hope you'll refrain from doing that again," to which my esteemed idol replied with a smirk, "I'll stick my finger up your ass if I feel like it."

Portrait of a Portrait Artist

Every few months I'd look for an apartment, but I couldn't find anything I could afford on my own. Gay Roommate services proved disappointing. How was I ever going to get out of Aunt Lil's apartment? I was growing tired of her wisecracks. "I thought you were only shacking up here for two months. It's two years now." Then, referencing the Kaufman/Hart play about a long-term houseguest from hell, she'd add, "You're the man who came to dinner."

There was one possibility that appeared out of the b Andy Halliday and I were offered a pair of comp tickets to Broadway musical, *Carmelina*. We arrived at the lobby inger Theatre, and as we were ascending the grand stair I became aware of a handsome blond gentleman at the b staring up at me with the same seductive intensity as Rh first laid eyes on Scarlett at Twelve Oaks. Throughout t think of nothing but this charismatic flirt with his dashin Intermission couldn't arrive soon enough, and I tempor on the pretext of going to the restroom.

Searching through the crowd, I collided with my Rh was Alex, and he was a thirty-five-year-old East Coas major motion picture studio. We exchanged sophistic ual innuendoes, and phone numbers (well, my phone lights dimmed for Act Two. A few nights later, Alex sho sparsely attended shows at The Duplex. Waiting for me dragging on a cigarette, he fixed me with his startling "You're very good. Do you know how good you really familiar, yes, it's a scene right out of the 1954 version of tell whether my life is unusually jam-packed with classi if I simply translate my experiences into cinematic trop hooked. Alex shimmered with manic drive and was an ulate alumnus of the Yale debating team.

I became swept up in the vortex of his enthusiasm. in love . . . with *me*. He was making a lot of money at the the great photographers of the seventies, Kenn Duncan, photos. Then he paid for posters for my act and had them city. It didn't bring in any more customers, but it was thril suggestively nude posters of myself lining the entire front

At last, more sensible good fortune appeared in the person of Ken Elliott. Ken was a freshman at Northwestern when I was a sophomore and we met in a university production of *Romeo and Juliet*. He was cast as Paris's page. I was the capricious but canny Veronese apprentice to a goldsmith—in other words, I was an anonymous townsperson. When Ken first arrived at Northwestern from Indianapolis, he was a tall, lanky boy with a Prince Valiant haircut and a languid manner that would've made him a perfect young Lord Alfred Douglas in a movie about Oscar Wilde. The most eccentric and original people I've met have all been from Indiana.

Ken spent the first few years after graduation working as a stage manager at some of the top regional theaters in the Midwest. His goal was to be a director, and he decided to try his hand in New York. In 1980, he came to the city to scout around for an apartment, and we met for coffee. He still had a delightfully mannered way of speaking that wouldn't have been out of place in a twenties Somerset Maugham play, but he'd acquired an attractive adult dignity and gravitas. I latched onto the idea that Ken was my ticket to eighty-sixing Aunt Lil's and suggested that we find an apartment together. He could go back to visit his family in Indianapolis for the holidays while I searched for a two-bedroom apartment.

I was determined to find us the perfect place. I sort of did. The neighborhood couldn't have been nicer—the picturesque West Village. The building was on a great street, West 12th, but it was a decaying old tenement. When Margaret first visited and was walking down the narrow hallway with its single stark bare light bulb, she called out preemptively to an imaginary hidden assailant, "I have a knife! I have a knife!" It also wasn't exactly a two-bedroom. It was what was known as a railroad flat, where each room ran into the next like railroad cars. But technically we each had our own room, and the price was right. Divided, the rent was a doable $250 a month for each of us.

Ken and I were the building's youngest tenants. The rest were classic old Greenwich Village bohemians. There was Reva on the first floor, stumbling about on her cane, placing pins on the large map of the world she used to chart the activities of the international peace organization she volunteered for, and which consumed most of her time and energy. There was the artist on the top floor who, at the age of 102, was engaged in cutting up her valuable art books to create intricate Surreal collages. On our floor was a witch-like Italian woman who dressed all in black, spoke no English, and cast spells on the landlord by burning chicken feathers. My favorite tenant, though, was Chubby Carrube, a plump cherub of an aging retired female impersonator, who had his wigs perched on the electric candles of his living room chandelier. Venus Castina! Today I *am* Chubby Carrube!

Ken got a job as personal assistant to the Broadway librettist Michael Stewart (*Hello Dolly, Bye Bye Birdie, Barnum*). Stewart was an intense, mercurial man, but he was encouraging and generous to Ken. I'd sometimes pick up Ken at Stewart's apartment near Carnegie Hall. It had a large, stately living room tastefully appointed with antiques, which not a soul was permitted to set foot in, not even friends and family. I preferred his office, lined with photos of Michael with Carol Channing, Chita Rivera, and Presidents Kennedy and Johnson, along with numerous caricatures by Al Hirschfeld of Michael's many productions. His was a great career in the theater. That was what I wanted.

I continued to perform my solo material at The Duplex and other small clubs in Manhattan such as SNAFU in Chelsea and the Ballroom in Soho. My style of solo performance was evolving through my collaboration with a young director named Peter Napolitano. I had recently seen the work of the downtown performance artist Jeff Weiss, who played multiple characters without any change of costume, allowing him to perform rapid-fire dialogue between two characters. This virtuosic technique created the illusion that we were witnessing an intense emotional scene and not a monologue, to the point that it seemed as if the two voices were overlapping each other. His was a violently physical style of performance, and his solo play, *And That's How the Rent Gets Paid*, was maniacally funny, terrifying, and disturbingly autobiographical.

Influenced by Jeff Weiss and encouraged by my exacting new director, I tossed away the hats and boas and pushed myself into creating more challenging solo pieces. My second show had the umbrella title of *Vagabond Vignettes*. It included a naturalistic study of several people riding an NYC bus as well as a ten-minute montage of the history of American film titled *That's Show Biz*, the pace of which grew increasingly faster and more frenzied as the rapidly changing century moved on. The show concluded with a dramatic portrait of an early-twentieth-century muse of fashion and art, the Marchesa Casati, in her impoverished twilight years.

It was impossible to earn a living doing these sporadic cabaret gigs, so I attempted to support myself with a succession of part-time jobs: receptionist in a zipper factory; selling, over the phone, office supplies that I was supposed to claim were made by IBM but weren't; and working for a sports gambling phone line where I furnished tips (fortunately provided by professionals and not generated by me) on how to bet on baseball, basketball, soccer, and hockey games.

My chief form of employment in the seventies and into the early eighties was as a quick sketch portrait artist. It began while I was still in college. In the summer of 1973, I saw an ad in the *New York Times*: A woman named Florence Holden was looking for quick sketch pastel portrait artists to work the summer season in her portrait studio on the boardwalk in Wildwood, New Jersey. Talent for achieving a likeness was more important than expert pastel technique. I submitted some drawings and got the job. My housing was the ramshackle Victorian Hotel Ruth Lynne just off the Wildwood boardwalk with a room directly above the penny arcade. The storefront portrait studio opened on to the boardwalk, with easels for eight artists and a counter in the back for Florence.

Florence was a small, agitated widow in her fifties. Although she received half of what we charged for a drawing, for her the real money was made after the portrait was finished. Then she could elevate the price through the customer's purchase of an expensive frame and a fee for the use of her supposed patented invention to preserve the fragile pastel drawing. Drawing in hand, the customer was sent to the counter, whereupon Florence launched into her act. "Oh my, this is a *gorgeous* portrait. Such a likeness. I don't say this often, but . . . it's a masterpiece. Now, with such a portrait, you must be careful. Pastels are chalk. It rubs right off." She took a dainty finger and ran it across the top of the drawing, deliberately smearing the chalk. "See how easily it's ruined? A fine work of art must be protected. For only five dollars more, I'll run it through this special laminating machine of my own invention that will preserve it in museum quality forever."

It took me only a week to clue in to the fact that an overly realistic interpretation of the customer's features wasn't preferable. But then, as I'm prone to do, I went too far. My flattering drawing of a long-haired man with a profile resembling Don Knotts wound up looking disconcertingly like Rita Hayworth. On one occasion, I did an especially good portrait of a young man, so good that I thought it transcended Boardwalk art. I accompanied Florence into the back room to watch her run the picture through the laminating machine. As the portrait emerged, across the man's hairline were the words "End of roll." I panicked. "What are we gonna do?" Florence wasn't about to have me waste valuable time redoing the portrait. She grabbed a pair of scissors and cut across the top of the man's forehead, giving the portrait an oddly modernist quality. For once she didn't prod the customer into purchasing a silver chrome, ebony black, or antique gold frame.

In New York, I worked for a while as a quick sketch portrait artist through an agency called Witches-to-Go that booked tarot card readers and palmists. You might well ask why I circled that listing in the *Village Voice* want ads when it specified an expertise in fortune-telling that I clearly didn't possess—when one is a struggling person in the arts, it's part of our survival skill set to shrug, *Hey, you never know*. At my interview the head honcho witch, Diane, artificially bronzed the shade of Brazilian teakwood, laid it on the line. "Sorry, but I have no need for a pastel portrait artist. I wish I could do something for you. You have an intriguing polarity of yin and yang."

As I was zipping up my artist's portfolio, she grabbed my forearm. "Not so fast. Charles, what if you did . . . psychic portraits?" "Um, what are those?" I asked. Diane clasped her hands with their talon-like painted fingernails. "You, my friend, can use your pastels to draw people as they were in their previous lives."

Diane soon began sending me to weddings and bar mitzvahs, where I'd set up my easel and make every effort to clue into my hitherto neglected psychic powers. Underneath her pagan/Wiccan jargon, Miss Diane was a straight shooter with a genuine concern for her stable of astrologists, palmists, tarot card readers, and assorted seers. While driving with her to a birthday party on Long Island, she complained in her New York accent as thick as a filet mignon about an ex-actress turned palm reader: "I've given this girl nothing but positive *enuhgy* and all I get back from huh are negative ions."

My psychic impulses may have been dicey, but my knowledge of period costume design was extensive. I chose not to weigh down my bar mitzvah/ wedding/anniversary/birthday party guests with the heavy mantle of having been Nefertiti or King Henry VIII in their previous lives. I drew Aunt Shakie as a warmhearted, popular lady-in-waiting to Queen Victoria. Uncle Sid I envisioned as a wise minister of finance to Louis XVI whose warnings went grievously unheeded. I enjoyed granting historic pasts to my subjects, much as I later took pleasure in creating acting roles for my friends. But invariably, halfway through the event, most of my sitters told me to cool it and draw them as they were in the present, garbed in Ralph Lauren and Perry Ellis.

Lady of Burlesque

1981. An ad in a gay paper sought male strippers for a two-week tour of Washington, DC, and Pittsburgh. It paid a whopping thousand dollars and offered a reprieve from life as an office temp, zipper factory receptionist, and psychic portrait artist. This windfall could subsidize my career as a solo performance artist for at least a few months. No more drawing someone's Cousin Steffi as Eleanor of Aquitaine's masseuse.

I circled that ad in red. It could be an illuminating experience if I stayed true to my own fanciful nature. Had there ever been a male stripper exactly like me? I employed this conceit with every non-theatrical job I did: Don't let the job alter me. Enjoy how I might affect my surroundings. It allowed me to feel as if I were the star of my own long-running situation comedy. The other reason I wanted to snap up this opportunity was that I thought it might be good to take a break from my puckish gamine persona and get in touch with my dormant testosterone-fueled masculine sexuality. From what I'd seen, you didn't have to do much as a stripper, just get naked, play with yourself, and dance butch, which means move to the rhythm in a desultory heavy-limbed manner.

The first stop was Pittsburgh. It was just me and one other "dancer," a short, dark-haired Italian boy named Danny. I can't say I saw much of

Pittsburgh. Danny and I did ten shows a day. There was a featured star on the bill, a well-known gay porn performer named Derrick Stanton. Like many headliners, he was cordial but aloof.

Joan Rivers once told me that was how Shirley MacLaine treated her when Joan was Shirley's opening act in Vegas. "She showed up at my dressing room, and without even a hello, asked what I was going to be wearing. I told her and she left." I'm not sure where our headliner was being put up, but Danny and I were stashed away in cubicles at a local gay bathhouse.

Danny's unswerving goal was to come away from these two weeks with as much cash as possible. When he wasn't onstage dancing, he was having sex with an audience member in the back room. The number of men he could service within a few hours was prodigious. I didn't pursue that activity, though not out of any prudery or moral objection—the only experience I sought was being a stripper. At first, I was enjoying the sleazy atmosphere and the theatrical challenge of removing my clothes to the disco beat of the music while sustaining an erotic mood. The novelty wore off after four days in Pittsburgh. I'd gotten the gist and was ready to come home. However, there was still half a week to go in Pittsburgh and another full week in Washington, DC. By the time I arrived in our nation's capital, I was despondent.

I phoned Ken in New York. "It's so grim and depressing. I honestly don't know how I'm gonna get through this week." My current vocation was far beyond Ken's well-bred experience. "Well, don't you get any sort of dinner break?" he asked. "About an hour and a half." Ken gave it some thought. "Call up my friend Scott Sublett. He lives in DC. Have dinner with him. Remove yourself temporarily from that ... *milieu*."

I phoned Scott, who exclaimed, "Perfect timing! I'm having a party as we speak. All sorts of neat people are here. Come on over!" I jumped into a cab and instructed the driver to hotfoot it over to Dupont Circle. Scott's place was teeming with interesting guests, many of whom were part of the

Washington theater community. After about a half hour, Scott suggested, "Why don't you do one of your solo pieces?"

I was apprehensive. To this day, I get rabbity when asked to perform at a party. (Paradoxically, I'd had no hesitancy about jumping around naked on a platform to Diana Ross singing "I'm Coming Out.") I stood near the artificial fireplace and performed a short piece from my repertoire called *That's Show Biz*. The party guests were a great audience. It was heartening being back in my own world of young aspiring theater people. When I finished, a tall, imposing man approached me and introduced himself as Bart Whiteman, the artistic director of a nonprofit called the Source Theatre Company. He proposed that I come back to DC in six months to do my show as part of his upcoming season.

A year before, I had returned to Chicago to perform the hour-long *Hollywood Confidential* at the Victory Gardens Theater. What I hoped would be a triumphant "so there" to all who had previously rejected me turned out to be a humiliating critical and commercial disaster. One critic vituperatively finished me off with, "As writer and performer, the young, wispy, unapologetically swish Mr. Busch displays no discernible talent whatsoever."

Years later, Aunt Lil would recall, "When you returned from doing your show in Chicago, you were so thin and crestfallen. Your face was absolutely green. I really was concerned." This Washington engagement would be my first time attempting a full two-act version of my new solo repertoire. I titled the evening *Charles Busch, Alone with a Cast of Thousands*. The entire first act was a piece called *A Theatrical Party*, about a posh soiree in 1912 London rich in sentimental intrigue and gauzy romance, in which I played all the guests and servants.

The Source Theatre was quite small, seating perhaps seventy people, yet it was deemed best to do my show at their even smaller "alternative theater space." This was a former bank vault, large enough to accommodate a solo performer and twenty seats. The company was producing Martin Sherman's play *Bent* on their "main stage," so I was left to fend for myself. The one piece of furniture my show required was an antique armchair. Otherwise, I was working on a bare stage. The chair I was given was scuffed, battered, with the stuffing bursting out of the seat cushion. I acknowledged the effort spent dragging it from the trash heap outside, but insisted they come up with something more appropriate. The replacement chair was at least intact, and three out of its four legs were even the same length. There was nothing in the budget to pay a lighting designer/operator, so they gave the position to a young girl who'd just begun volunteering as an usher. Together we figured out how to turn the lights on and off.

Despite these hiccups, I received glowing reviews from the alternative press, the gay press, and an out-and-out rave from the *Washington Post*. A Foggy Bottom supermarket weekly praised me as "an amazing cross between Sir John Gielgud, Helen Hayes, Glenda Jackson, and Richard Chamberlain." With my raft of glorious DC reviews, the entire engagement at the Source Theatre sold out. True, there were only twenty seats, but I did five shows a week for a month, and then the show was extended another month, and another. It was my first real validation that no, I was *not* demented to be pursuing this line of work.

I Left My Heart at the Valencia Rose

1981. My successful two-act solo show at the Source Theatre encouraged me to book myself at small nonprofit theaters all over the United States.

Having no management, I did everything myself: assembling a press kit, doing the research, sending out the mailings, making the phone calls (and the follow-up phone calls), and conducting the negotiations. I returned to the Source Theatre twice more and played Chicago, Boulder, Los Angeles, and Santa Cruz.

San Francisco became a second home. I'd devoured the first few *Tales of the City* books by Armistead Maupin and was determined to get to San Francisco and experience the glow of the city as expressed in his writing. Debra Crane, a New York friend of mine who was now in arts management in the Bay Area, came up with the idea of having me appear for one night at a gay theater called Theatre Rhinoceros as a benefit for the Golden Gate Businessman's Association. She filled the small theater with people who might be of help in bringing me back for a regular run of my show.

Among those invited was a young man named Donald Montwill, who was managing a gay arts center/cabaret in the Mission District called the Valencia Rose. He was lanky, with high cheekbones, shoulder-length blond hair, and a strong commitment to community activism, and in looks and manner reminded me of Vanessa Redgrave. Donald and his mischievous half-pint lover, Jimmy Manness, flipped over my performance and assumed that I was a big-time New York entertainer. They were dumbstruck, given my long-established and thriving career, that I'd deign to consider performing at their emerging venue. Given the circumstances, I chose not to destroy Donald and Jimmy's illusions.

I returned to San Francisco later that year for my first month-long engagement at the Valencia Rose. It was a former Spanish mortuary that the new owners had only partially renovated. The chapel was now a stylish performance space decorated with camel head sculptures as lit sconces. On the other hand, the embalming room on the third floor hadn't been touched and still reeked of formaldehyde. Donald and Jimmy fashioned a room for me to live in farther down the hall. It was still under construction with no sheet rock, just the bare wooden frame. I visited the local Goodwill store and found several pairs of voluminous gold brocade curtains to drape over the walls, creating an Arabian Nights harem effect.

For my introduction to San Francisco gay society, Donald and Jimmy brought me to a hot-tub party at an enclave of ramshackle Victorian houses in the Castro. There were about seven of us naked in the tub, and a more attractive, witty, hip, politically aware group of young men could not have been assembled. The lively discussion of gay politics and cultural pursuits eventually turned into a sexual free-for-all under the stars, and I thought, *Wow, I'm really in San Francisco!* During a brief intermission, the conversation turned to the new gay cancer scare that was being mentioned in the national press. Jimmy announced, with a touch of activist pride, that he had a tiny lump in his earlobe that he was sure was an early symptom. I remember thinking he was inventing that to seem au courant. By the decade's end, not one of those young men in the tub with me would be alive.

During my career as a solo performer, I worked with several directors, Peter Napolitano, Ron Vigneau, and my roommate Ken Elliott, each one contributing to my development as writer and performer. Ron, who later died from AIDS, was helpful in ridding me of excess gestures and an awkwardness of movement. Peter convinced me to give up the security of using costume pieces to delineate my multiple characterizations and made me see that the storytelling I was attempting to do was best achieved with simplicity. Ken, as he would prove over and over in the next years, was an excellent dramaturg who guided me through the creation of complex multi-character narratives that were never confusing to the audience. We co-wrote one of my most artistically successful pieces, a monologue titled *Après Moi, Le Deluge*, based on his Indianapolis high school drama coach. I even enlisted the aid of my former acting teacher from Northwestern, David Downs, in directing another of my solo pieces, an Irish ghost story titled *Phantom Lovers*. Our earlier relationship as teacher/student had failed due to my psychological block around performing in class. Post-graduation, David became a true mentor to me, and he continues to be my friend.

Some of the pieces in my repertoire were inspired by classic film, but as I progressed, I began drawing on my own life as well. One half-hour solo piece was about three bullied young boys at a summer camp in North Carolina who must spend the night in a self-built hut. That much was based on my own experience. What I invented was their encounter with a hermit-like old woman who frightens them with a tale about a notorious hatchet murder that had taken place in those mountain woods decades before.

Another solo piece involving a homicide was titled *After You've Gone*, in which I played a young man whose enigmatic father has been killed; though he was innocent, the son is implicated in the crime. He embarks on an odyssey to uncover the unsavory truth of his father's life. I played not only the young man but the gallery of James Purdy–like grotesques that he encounters along the way.

Entre nous, I was never at ease playing any of my solo-show male characters. My imagination only took flight when I played a woman. My enigmatic countess was far more compelling than my old Irish fisherman. Perhaps I'm too harsh on my younger self, but looking back, my straight male characters were perfunctory, bland ciphers and my gay male characters tended to be stereotypical fussy old queens. The few male characters I was proud of, such as a worn-out world-class kept boy and a vulnerable ninety-year-old Italian prince, were successful because they seemed to transcend gender. My gallery of female characters, which included a mercurial French actress, a Victorian spinster novelist, and a drug-addled jazz singer, came alive through my comforting embrace of the feminine within me.

Upon seeing one of my solo plays, Charles Ludlam, with his incisive theatrical eye, naturally picked up on this creative quandary and asked me flat out, "Why don't you just play female characters?" I had no answer. I assumed that to present a full narrative required male characters. Of course, there should be no assumptions, and there are no rules, only those that you impose on yourself out of fear.

I arrived in San Francisco two years after the assassination of Harvey Milk. Milk was already becoming a myth, and at the Valencia Rose I met several of the people connected to him, including his lover and campaign manager, Scott Smith, one of his final sexual dalliances; the adorable Steve Beery, his second-in-command; the activist Cleve Jones; and Harvey's loyal photographer/historian, Danny Nicoletta. Performing at the Valencia Rose, I felt privileged to be a part of the history of a place that I sensed would not soon be forgotten.

Among the other performers who found an early home there were Lea DeLaria, Marga Gomez, and a young woman who'd just begun calling herself Whoopi Goldberg. Five minutes into her act, you knew this person was going places fast.

My years as a solo performer were difficult because I couldn't fully earn my living. I'd be in one of these cities and treated with great respect. A sold-out fifty-seat house on a rainy Tuesday in Santa Cruz is nothing to sneeze at. However, I'd close on a Saturday night, fly home on Sunday, and show up at the temp office on Monday hoping to find a receptionist job. It wasn't easy maintaining a sense of identity. Who was I? Entertainer or temp? A temporary entertainer? Or, horror of horrors, an entertaining temp.

Journey to the Edge of the World

My salad days, the decade of my twenties, were a struggle, but unlike many young artists, I had a safety net: Aunt Lil. I was never going to be homeless. She paid for my health insurance. To my credit, I was always up to some gambit, however harebrained, to make a buck while pursuing my goal of earning a living in the theater. Yet there were times when I'd come up short at the end of the month and be forced to make the dreaded walk of shame to 50 Park Avenue.

A proud survivor of the Great Depression, Aunt Lil felt compelled to give me a tough love lecture. "I can't go on subsidizing you forever. I didn't have a rich aunt bailing me out. At some point, don't you have to be self-sufficient?" She'd offer suggestions. "I was watching *The Tonight Show*, and do you know that Johnny Carson has a line of men's sport coats on the side?" I'd gasp and sputter, "I'm having trouble getting booked Tuesday nights at The Duplex, never mind starting a men's fashion line!" Sighing like a weary Mother Cabrini, she'd get out her checkbook. And yet, when I'd sink into despair upon hearing of recent Northwestern graduates appearing on television or others dropping out of show business for well-paying careers, Aunt Lil would always tell me it was too soon to give up.

By 1983, I was pushing thirty and my theatrical career was not progressing. In fact, it appeared to be slowing down if not completely stalled. I had developed a circuit of venues around the country, but one by one they were burning down, going broke, or developing the unpleasant habit of not paying me. During the early eighties, my one constant was my work as a quick sketch portrait artist. For five summers I plied my trade at the New York Renaissance Faire in Tuxedo Park, New York. Faire personnel were divided into performers and craftspeople. The young performers broiled in the hot sun posing as villagers and sometimes acting in severely abridged Shakespeare plays, netting around thirty dollars a day. The craftspeople made a solid living selling everything from decorative candles and leather laced bodices to figurines of peasant women with faces sculpted from preserved apples. My boyfriend at the time, Jim Murphy, built me a quaint if primitive wooden booth that provided shade for my subject and me. In a good two-day weekend, I could pocket $350 in hard, cold cash. Multiply that by five weekends and I finished each summer with a tidy nest egg.

One performer stood out: an arresting Pakistani performance artist named Bina Sharif, who played an exotic gypsy fortune teller. Her job was to harass fairgoers into having a fake fortune told. She was atmosphere. I didn't see much of Bina on Saturdays. The director of the performing company kept her roaming all over the grounds. I occasionally ran into her trying to wrest a free turkey leg out of one of the food vendors.

On Sundays, I always brought along the Sunday *New York Times*. Bina, exhausted and overheated from her improvised gypsy exertions, would hide in the shade of the back of my booth and read the newspaper. Before she got to the crossword puzzle, a stage manager would usually poke his head in, find her, and yank her out into the blazing sunlight.

I remained in contact with Bina over the course of the following year. In the spring of 1984, she invited me to see her perform a new solo piece at a place called the Limbo Lounge deep in the East Village. Even though I'd lived in New York City most of my life, I'd never ventured into the area known as Alphabet City, which at that time had the reputation of being one of the most depressed, dangerous, crack-infested neighborhoods in Manhattan. I persuaded Ken to go with me, principally for company navigating the area.

Upon graduating from Northwestern, Ken's goal had been to become a theater director, but after six years of struggle he'd decided to apply to law school. He was accepted to New York Law School and was scheduled to begin classes that September. Ken's abandonment of the theater made me feel even more anxious about my own weed-strewn path.

On our way to Bina's show, Ken and I walked east from Seventh Avenue and observed the economic health of the landscape gradually deteriorating. Fifth Avenue, Broadway, Third Avenue, Second Avenue. At First Avenue, I assumed we'd meet up with a cliff and the end of the world. Who knew there was more? Avenue A . . . Avenue B . . . The blocks that composed Alphabet City were lined with burned-out shells of buildings, and the tenements still standing looked half abandoned.

In the middle of the urban rubble, there appeared an apparition. A skinny girl, perhaps twelve years old, glided down the street on roller skates, with a cloud of pink hair and wearing what looked like her father's baggy Bermuda shorts gathered around her waist by a rope. A welcoming ambassador, she weaved figure eights, and—I'm not making this up—was blowing bubbles out of a bottle with a plastic wand. On 10th Street, toward the end of the block between Avenues A and B, was a darkened storefront. This was the Limbo Lounge, an art gallery/bar/performance space run by three young people going by the monikers Michael Limbo and Jeannette and Victor Anonymous.

Entering the narrow space, I was spellbound by the garage sale opulence of the decor. The art displayed on the walls was part of an ornate installation that enveloped the viewer. A long bar that stretched along one wall and opposite that were a few torn red patent leather booths. With no stage, the audience was seated mostly on the floor. They were a mix of East Village kids, sort of goth, sort of punk, sort of gay, with an array of piercings that made some of them look as if their ears had been stuck in a typewriter. They all spoke with a slight, affected accent indigenous to the East Village that sounded vaguely Bulgarian.

Michael Limbo was a good-looking, sexy young man with an angular Irish face. With his hairline shaved back several inches, and the rest dyed a bright Bozo-the-clown red, he was the spitting image of Daniel Day Lewis portraying Elizabeth the First. Sipping a Heineken, he quieted the crowd and introduced Bina. Garbed in a sleeveless black sequined minidress, her face and mane of hair flecked with glitter, she was both innately chic and yet also ridiculing chic. I can still hear her intoning in her richly musical Pakistani accent the names of designer perfumes Opium and Obsession. Her show was intellectually provocative and politically astute, with an undercurrent of comic rage.

As charismatic and gifted as Bina was, one couldn't separate the performance from the delicious carnival ambience of the room. It was a Weimar Republic Berlin cabaret, a secret 1920s Manhattan speakeasy, and the fin de siècle Moulin Rouge. I experienced the rare feeling of not being divided into my usual roles of participant and detached observer. I was experiencing completely the pure exhilaration of being a welcomed guest at a fabulous party with Bina the glitter-bedecked hostess.

When the performance ended, I was reduced to froth and announced to Ken, "We *haaaaave* to do a show here!" Before he could respond, I darted about the club like a firefly in search of Michael Limbo and found him at the bar. With the words tumbling out of me, I gushed that I wanted more than anything to perform at the Limbo Lounge. I was accustomed to auditioning, but he simply took out a large, battered calendar, saw that a Friday and Saturday night at 8:00 PM were available a month from then, and wrote me in. No questions about what kind of show I'd be doing or whether I'd ever performed before. I returned to Ken with the news that I was booked. Ken assumed that meant that I'd perform some of my solo material. The decadent boudoir ambience and the audience garbed in the cutting edge of downtown fashion made me long to rise to their level of flamboyance. Why would I want to appear at the Limbo Lounge garbed austerely in black pants and a cotton turtleneck sweater and perform my increasingly naturalistic solo repertoire?

No. I'd have to be in drag. Except for my few performances as a red-wigged replacement Goddess of Hell with Charles Ludlam, I hadn't performed in women's attire since I'd had my ass kicked by my ill-fated, ungrateful (*yes, it's time I let go of that one*) theater company in Chicago. For too long, due to the nature of my evolving solo repertoire, I had tamped down my natural inclination toward visual extravagance. I'd had enough of twisting myself into male characterizations that other actors could do better. My female characters had greater nuance and, strangely, were more real. This time I wanted to present myself as the leading lady.

I told Ken that I'd quickly dash off some sort of a theatrical vehicle that would star me in a scintillating female role, and that he was going to direct it. I said I knew he was renouncing the theater, but he couldn't ask for a jazzier farewell. It involved little commitment and no money to be raised. Since there wasn't a stage, a set wasn't required. We could rehearse a few times at our apartment. I was sure that Ken would dismiss the idea as a silly waste of time, and that convincing him would take some arm twisting, but he surprised me with his immediate enthusiasm. "It sounds like fun," he said.

Fun? I couldn't remember the last time either of us had thought of anything to do with theater as "fun."

What Can I Do with This Wig?

At the time, I was working at Time Warner Communications as a temp receptionist for an executive who demanded little of my energy. Perfect! I needed to come up with a play that ran at least thirty minutes, required no scenery, had costumes I could easily improvise, and offered a role I could sink my teeth into.

I've always had a fascination with vampires. The blood drinking aspect doesn't grab me, but the concept of century-spanning eternal life always has. It was easy connecting the trials and tribulations of actresses of film and stage who had sustained multidecade careers with the plight of an ageless vampire. The central joke would be that my protagonists are actresses first, vampires second. Joan Crawford meets Nosferatu. As the centuries flew by, my character would be forced to conceal her ageless vampirism by periodically changing her stage name. In the 1920s, she's known as Madeleine Astarté; by the time she's headlining in 1980s Las Vegas, she goes by the name Madeleine Andrews.

Madeleine and her rival, Magda Legerdemain, have their first tumultuous encounter in ancient Sodom, when Madeleine is served up as a virgin sacrifice to the terrifying Succubus (Magda). It doesn't go well. The Succubus, for one thing, has a big chip on her shoulder.

SUCCUBUS (Magda)
You look around and see the glamorous way I live. My slaves, my riches, my dishware. True, I have caskets full of sparkling jewels, but where the fuck can I wear 'em?

VIRGIN (Madeleine)
Forgive me if I don't weep. Seek good counsel from the High Priest, and
then, hie thee hither, you blood-sucking old bag!

Through a trick of fate, the young virgin Madeleine not only survives but is transformed into a rival vampire, and she and Magda carry on their feud through the next millennium. It was imperative that I come up with historical periods that would be easy to costume on a budget of—zero. Silhouette is everything. If you get the silhouette to convey some sense of period accuracy, the audience will forgive you the details and a ten-dollar budget. That left out the Renaissance, the French Revolution, and the fin de siècle. Hollywood in the twenties? That would be easy. I could improvise the flapper look and Erté-inspired drapery of early screen sirens.

Even though it was intended as merely a sketch never to be performed after this one weekend, the play needed a title. Ed was now a top advertising executive, his sharp acerbic wit essential to his meteoric rise in his field. On the phone I gave him the lowdown on what the play was about and off the top of his head he suggested a title that evoked exploitation paperback novels of the fifties: *Vampire Lesbians of Sodom.* It certainly had a ring to it. "Thanks," I said. "That'll do."

My friend Kathie Carr would have to be involved, I decided. Ken and I had met her a little over a year before when we attempted to produce my solo show Off-Off Broadway. Kathie was the production's stage manager. A word to the wise: A one-man show starring a complete unknown with no publicity budget and presented in a seventy-five-seat theater on a dark, little-traveled side street is not a promising venture. Our lighting operator was a vivacious fellow named Vinnie with an orange-hued punk haircut. An aspiring director, he was flirtatious and flattering and made me think we were destined to be best friends for life. When the show closed prematurely, an insignificant flop, Vinnie stopped returning my phone calls.

Kathie, whose appreciation for me wasn't at all dependent on my success or failure, became an essential part of my world. She was a few years older than I and had already lived several lives before her current incarnation as an Off-Off Broadway stage manager—as a bouffant-sporting teen secretary in Brooklyn in the sixties and a professional disco-dancing competitor in the seventies. Streetwise down to the neat way she'd toss her finished cigarette butt, she could be a great asset in this off-the-wall endeavor.

As I was unknown to the East Village netherworld, Ken and I felt we needed Bina Sharif to pull in the crowd. Was it a problem that her Pakistani accent made it impossible for her to pronounce the "V" in Vampire? Hey, "Wampire" might be funny. Without seeing a script, Bina said yes.

Who besides Bina and me would be in the cast? Considering there'd be no pay, no dressing room, and almost no rehearsal time, the talent pool would have to be limited to the terminally stagestruck. There was no question that Andy Halliday would play a role. If one can be said to be both shy and insecure and still a big personality, that was Andy. His youthful hope of being a teenage tap-dancing MGM musical star aside, Andy was also one of the most down-to-earth, reliable people I knew, and I had a feeling those qualities would be essential in this freewheeling environment.

Theresa Aceves was a deliciously fuzzy five-foot kewpie doll who could, on the turn of a dime, replace her comic blankness with a hard-boiled line reading worthy of Edward G. Robinson. We'd met in Washington when I was performing my solo shows at the Source Theatre Company. She was so impossibly vague that at times it was hard to believe she wasn't faking it. Once when we were all warned to remember to set our clocks forward for daylight saving time, Theresa seriously queried, "Watches too?"

Arnie Kolodner was a handsome auburn-haired magician who had recently graduated from NYU. As was the case with Bina, I'd met him working at the New York Renaissance Faire. Although he was only twenty-three, he could affect a B-movie smarmy charm that made him the ideal leading man for my parodies. A critic once described Arnie's performance in one of our shows as "Joel McCrea on Ex-Lax." None of us could quite decide if that was meant as a compliment.

Tom Aulino was a versatile character actor who'd attended Northwestern with Ken and me. He could effortlessly play any age and gender and possessed the gift of true comic invention. It's surprisingly difficult to find an actor who can land a funny line (or at least not get in the way of a funny line), and it's exceedingly rare to find an actor who can get laughs when there's nothing funny on the page. Tom Aulino was truly funny.

Bobby Carey had never acted before and had sensibly never given a thought to going on the stage. He was a strikingly handsome boy with a smooth, muscular body and plump lips like Brigitte Bardot's, his gravelly New Jersey shore voice at odds with the perfection of his features. He was contentedly working behind the desk at the Helmsley Palace Hotel. Ken had recently begun dating him and asked if I could come up with a small role for Bobby in the play. I'd already decided to have the opening scene take place in ancient Sodom, so there was certainly room for a lad who'd elicit whistles wearing a loincloth. Ease with dialogue was not a priority.

This was our cast, and Ken and I assembled them in our tiny living room. They were all thrilled to be in a show, even if it was for two nights without pay in a bar on the Lower East Side. We read through the script that I'd Xeroxed on the sly at my temp job. The reading went well. Sort of. A bitchy naysayer might've quipped that Bina's accent made the line "I conduct myself with dignity and grandeur, whilst you roll in the gutter, parading your twat onstage and calling it acting" incomprehensible anywhere but in downtown

Karachi, but why quibble? It turned out not to matter, for the following day Bina phoned to say that her mother in Pakistan was desperately ill and she was getting on the next flight to be with her.

Decades later, Bina, despite having enjoyed a distinguished award-winning career as a downtown performer and playwright, still regretted that decision. "Charles, I should have done your play! I should have! My mother . . . she was in a coma. She didn't even know I was there! Now look at me, still in the East Village. You got out! I'm still in!"

The Director's Daughter

2010. *In the Life*, the LGBT news magazine show on PBS, asked me to interview Liza Minnelli on camera in conjunction with her being given an award from the organization PFLAG. We originally planned to do the interview on the night of the award show at the Marriott Marquis Hotel, but in the mad hubbub of the event, Liza wasn't feeling up to it. The interview was rescheduled for a few weeks later at a small studio in the West 20s. Liza was to arrive at 2:00 PM and we were on notice that she had to be out of there by 5:00 sharp.

I arrived at 1:15 and found the crew busy setting up the lights and a set with a large round table and two chairs. I've learned over time that I most definitely have a more flattering side to my face. It's my left side, and I make every attempt, both lightly humorous and deadly adamant, to be filmed so that it is toward the camera. In this case, the producers were notified in advance that Liza also preferred being photographed from her left side. I accepted with grace the crew's instructions that the chairs be set to favor her.

Everything was ready by 2:00, and we waited for Liza to arrive. We waited and we waited. At about 4:00, Liza and her small entourage arrived at the studio. We'd met several times over the years through mutual friends, and each time, including this one, she'd greet me with vivacious congeniality. Though I'm certain she'd never been to one of my shows, she always made a lovely point of telling me, with ardent sincerity, and in front of witnesses, "I'm such a fan."

As I showed her to her seat at the table, I jokingly admitted, "Liza, even though we share the same good side, I'm making the supreme sacrifice and will be photographed from my hideous Phantom of the Opera right side." She cackled, reached across the table, and grasped my hand.

"Oh, baby, you're so sweet. But hey, I can do something about that. I'm going to make sure you're fabulously lit." While I was explaining that we had to hurry, she motioned to the gaffer to move one of the lights that was creating an unflattering shadow. "Charles, it's better already. Just sit very still."

I could see from the producers' concerned faces that we needed to start the interview. But Liza was now fully inhabiting the role of lighting designer and thoroughly enjoying herself. Again, I attempted to break in, but she wouldn't hear of it.

"Baby, I'm a director's daughter. I'm a Minnelli. This is what I *do*." As the daughter of Vincente Minnelli (and, of course, Judy Garland), she'd grown up visiting her parents' film sets, and she herself had a considerable filmography working with such stylists as Bob Fosse, Stanley Donen, and Martin Scorsese, along with some of the most renowned cinematographers. I could see from my image in the monitor that she was doing a superb job. Instructing the gaffer to lower a light, raise another, turn off a lamp that interfered with the modeling of my cheekbone . . . I was looking better on camera than

I ever had before. It was now after 4:30. Ten minutes later, my face was at last lit to her satisfaction and we sped through the interview. I'd studied several of her past TV interviews and tried to offer questions that she'd never been asked before.

Not only is Liza an expert lighting designer, she's also brilliant at the politician's skill of the non-answer, responding to any question with one from her collection of stock responses, no matter how inappropriate. "Liza, you've said that your father was a great influence on how you developed your iconic look for the film *Cabaret*. What specific help did he give you?" Her large eyes gazed at me with glistening sincerity. "Charles, my father . . . my father taught me . . . how to dream."

Perhaps because I was interviewing her for a gay TV program, her guard was up that I might steer the conversation to the rumors that her late father had led a secret gay life. Her deflection of any query that might take her down a new road of revelation may also derive from seeing her mother treated disrespectfully by the press in her later years. Some of Liza's interviews in the first years after Judy's death in 1969 were surprisingly candid, but over the following decades she'd become much more protective of the legacy of those close to her.

We wrapped at exactly 5:00 and I escorted Liza outside to her waiting car. She apologized for having to rush but she'd organized a group of friends to see the singer Sam Harris perform his cabaret act. "Baby, why doncha come with us? It'll be so much fun!" I was worn out from the long day and politely begged off. Holding onto my arm, she stopped when she reached the car. She turned and spoke in a quiet, steady voice that no one else could hear. "I have lots of stories, wonderful stories, and some time we'll get together, and I'll tell them to you—but only to you."

Liza climbed into the limousine. Just before it pulled away, she thrust her arm through the open window and grasped my hand. With classic

Liza Minnelli exuberance, and again, generously in front of witnesses, she shrieked, "Baby, I want *more!*" She let go of my hand and away she went, the limousine barreling down the street rendering the perfect last long shot for this director's daughter.

Succubus Number Two

With Bina gone to Pakistan, we needed another Succubus, and in a hurry. Lola Pashalinksi was an Obie Award–winning downtown cult theater figure, and an original member of Charles Ludlam's Ridiculous Theatrical Company. She was a good fifteen years older than we were, with a formidable Gertrude Stein–like presence. In my days in the Ludlam orbit, Lola had always been sympathetic and kind; I phoned her and, to my surprise, she was game. Disaster averted.

As the play was barely forty-five minutes long, we scheduled only five rehearsals. Plus, when you're not paying people, you don't want to test their commitment by demanding too much of their time.

It was lovely witnessing Ken's enjoyment of being a director again. Lola remained a stoic, benign presence seated in the big Queen Anne chair, while the rest of us were discovering a shared sense of humor. Kathie and I improvised costumes from the collection of slips, sequined tube tops, and shawls that I'd stuffed into a box in my closet, remnants from my drag performances in Chicago and the few times I'd dressed up for Halloween. I possessed two auburn wigs, both in deplorable condition, one flowing to the waist and the other shoulder length. The first would serve well for the young virgin sacrifice in Sodom. The shorter one could be pinned up into a modified French twist when my character evolved into a silent film vamp in the twenties.

Kathie was in my apartment when I first attempted to fashion one of the wigs into a hairstyle. She was appalled at what I was considering wearing onstage. "Charles, you need to give it a good brushing. You can't go onstage with that matted thing on your head. Give it to me." Kathie's long suppressed skill at teasing hair and pinning on wiglets from the sixties all came back in a flash. She began experimenting with sewing several wigs together and wrapping the synthetic hair around Styrofoam cones to create what amounted to hair topiaries. Before we had scenery or even more than rudimentary costumes, we had Kath's elaborate wigs, which were mentioned in the press as often as any other element in the show.

For the previous eight years I'd struggled to get more than six people a night to attend my solo performances. Luckily, each of the eight cast members of *Vampire Lesbians of Sodom* invited six people, so we were sold out! Make that seven members of the cast—I doubt that Lola invited anyone.

The two shows were a lot of fun. The audience, composed mostly of our friends, responded to the unpretentious theatrical lunacy with steady laughter. Anything that gives me pleasure I'm compelled to do a second time: Surprisingly, another weekend was available only a few weeks ahead. Unsurprisingly, Lola refused to do a second weekend; she was at a different place in her life than the rest of us. She'd gone down that funky road with Charles Ludlam and the Ridiculous Theatrical Company in the late sixties. She didn't need to travel it again. At forty-six, one couldn't blame her for wanting to be paid for her work, be treated as a professional actress, and perform in a legitimate, established performance space.

In search of a Succubus once again, I was turned down not only by every actress I knew, but every woman whose path I'd crossed who seemed as if they might've possibly once worn a feather boa. The last person on my list was a blonde girl named Julie Halston whom I'd met a year or so before. She was thirty years old, divorced, and working for a Wall Street investment firm as a corporate librarian. Julie had vague notions of being a performance artist, or rather a "puh-faw-mence awtist," as she pronounced it in her Commack, Long Island, accent. I'd been a witness to her confused attempt at being a female Spalding Gray, and it wasn't promising. But I was desperate for a bloodsucking diva with comedy chops.

When I asked Julie on the phone if she'd play the Succubus, she said yes rather too swiftly. I was compelled to ask, "Um . . . have you ever been in a play?" With an indignant air, as if I'd inquired of Meryl Streep if she could do accents, Julie replied, "Dawling, I played Nina in *The Seagull* at Hofstra!" "Well . . . um . . . why don't you come over to my apartment and meet my roommate, Ken, who's directing the play? It's not an audition," I quickly added.

Julie came over and we read through her scenes. She was dreadful, without a clue as to how to play a highly theatrical style or, well, *any* style. In his gentlemanly manner, Ken asked, "Charles, could I speak to you . . . in the kitchen?" With the kitchen less than five feet from where we were standing, Julie later told me she overheard our entire conversation.

"She can't act!" Ken whispered. "She's terrible!" He wasn't wrong. But Julie was my last hope. Without a Succubus, we couldn't do the show. "Well, she played Nina in *The Seagull* at Hofstra," I told him. Julie got the role.

Again, we assembled the cast in my living room. Self-deprecating and curious about each of them, Julie won over everyone within five minutes. Her conversational style has always been that of a mid-sixties afternoon talk show hostess. "*Chawlz*, thoughts and reflections upon the death of *Mawvin* Gaye?" When we read through the play, Julie's "attack" on the character engendered puzzled looks from the rest of the cast. As we rehearsed over the next week, she only got worse. At the final rehearsal in my apartment, Julie, an intuitive person, stopped the scene and announced to the group, "Look, I know I stink, but I'm telling ya, put me in a wig in front of sixty queens . . . and I *glow!*"

Something happened when Julie got in front of the audience. She remained physically awkward, and she had some peculiar line readings that sounded like a Martian doing a cruel imitation of an earthling, but she exuded a wacky authority and, more importantly, a supreme likability. She also invited everyone she knew, and the audience was largely filled with her friends and Wall Street colleagues. She came off like the most popular girl at summer camp, with everyone pleased that she was having such a good time up on stage.

So many years later, Julie, having matured as an accomplished and inventive comic actress, still exudes a comforting warmth to an audience. She's a hand-knitted sweater that humorously doesn't quite fit, but that you'll never give away. She's an outsized amaryllis that brings a sigh of relief when it returns every year.

Backyard Royalty

I'd already written another forty-five-minute play for our troupe to do at the Limbo Lounge—a parody of a nineteenth-century Sarah Bernhardt historical melodrama that I titled *Theodora, She Bitch of Byzantium*. I managed to include a new role for Julie as the Dowager Empress Aunt Vulva.

Ken, who would play a libidinous Emperor Justinian, arranged for us to do twelve performances over the course of three weeks. With this second play, I began to figure out everyone's trip—that thing that made them special. It wasn't difficult. Each member of our company had a genuine quirkiness. Nobody was bland. Purely by happenstance, they all filled a specific role in a traditional nineteenth-century stock company. I was the leading lady, Arnie the leading man. Julie was the sidekick soubrette, Theresa the ingénue, Bobby the juvenile, Ken the silken villain, and Andy and Tom the character men and women.

Theodora, She Bitch of Byzantium was scheduled for June. That first weekend, New York City was hit with a blistering heat wave and, of course, the Limbo Lounge wasn't air-conditioned. So it was decided that we'd perform outside in the sculpture garden that they shared with the art gallery next door. That plan fell apart the afternoon of our opening night when a sudden downpour flooded the garden. The performance would have to be canceled.

My nascent career seemed to be following a pattern: a burst of encouragement followed by a kick in the ass. After the rain stopped at about 3:00 PM, Ken phoned me from the club. It seemed there was a small hole in the ground that led to the basement. Michael Limbo was willing to push the accumulated rainwater through the hole, which would flood their basement but allow us to perform in the backyard garden. My initial reaction was that this was an absurd operation and doomed to fail.

I arrived at the Limbo Lounge at 5:00 PM, my dubious expression firmly in place. I found the backyard garden abuzz. A large tarp had been unfolded to serve as the stage, folding chairs were being set up, and Michael Limbo was pushing the last of the dirty water down the hole. You couldn't help but be moved by the mad activity. I thought, well, if Michael is willing to flood his basement, I shouldn't be such a pill. Quickly assuming the role of Mother

Courage, I rolled up my jeans, got down on my knees, and began rubbing the tarp dry with rags.

At seven o'clock, it was still light out and the play was ready to begin. Kathie's chief duty as stage manager was pushing the button of the tape recorder that played the opening music cue from the soundtrack of the 1961 movie epic *El Cid*. Due to the distant location of the electrical outlet, the closest she could get to us was inside the club. One of the cast members had to give her the thumbs-up five seconds before the sound cue.

From the various windows of the tenements surrounding the courtyard, old neighborhood women were leaning on the sills watching the play, as if from balcony boxes. Our painted backdrop stretched taut between two poles; Julie found herself changing costumes behind the drop. With her bare breasts exposed to anyone watching from the third and fourth floors, Julie felt it necessary to justify herself to our leading man. "Awwnie, don't judge me on this. I'm actually an adult. I have credit cawds."

Even though we had done only a handful of performances of *Vampire Lesbians of Sodom*, word was already out that we were a group to be followed. There was an excitement about the new play and our backyard audience hooted, hollered, and cheered. The steamy city night was lit up with possibilities. And there was proof that it wasn't a hallucination: a photo of us performing *Theodora, She Bitch of Byzantium* in the sculpture garden appeared in *People* magazine, part of an article exploring the outré performance art scene springing up in this obscure neighborhood in New York City.

That night's sweaty "let's put on a show" endeavor cemented our relationship with Michael Limbo, who suggested that we become the resident theater company of the Limbo Lounge. I'd had a taste of being playwright-in-residence/star with my aborted theater company in Chicago, but those other actors and I hadn't shared the same vision, and I became an outsider.

This new collection of lovable oddballs believed in what I had to offer and, like children in a sandbox, wanted to play with me.

For his part, Ken had always dreamed of being artistic director of a company, though his goal was more along the lines of the Arena Stage in Washington, DC, or the Guthrie in Minneapolis. I knew that he didn't want to go to law school. He was too young to give up his hope of a directing career and this fateful set of circumstances threw his plans up into the air.

One evening, I had dinner with Michael Feingold, the theater critic for the *Village Voice*. I told him we were trying to come up with a name for our theater company in residence at the Limbo Lounge; on the spot, he suggested "Theater-in-Limbo." Bingo! As was the case when Ed gave my play the title *Vampire Lesbians of Sodom*, this didn't seem like a major Warner Brothers movie moment accompanied by a lush Max Steiner musical score. It was merely giving a name to something as ephemeral as a dream from which at any moment we might awaken.

Rule Number One: Have Talented Friends

Michael Limbo and his partners, Victor and Jeanette Anonymous, were doing very well as art dealers, so much so that they were photographed for Italian *Vogue*. They decided to close the Limbo Lounge for the rest of the summer and reopen in the fall in a much larger space a block south, on East 9th Street between Avenues A and B. The new space had been a garbage truck garage and required at least a modicum of renovation. The timing was perfect for me, as I had booked my most important solo engagement yet in the cabaret space at the Indiana Repertory Theatre in Indianapolis in August. The plan was for Theater-in-Limbo to do a season of plays in the fall, with three-week runs of each play.

When Ken was directing my solo pieces, he could be maddeningly detached. I once had him call a potential financial backer and heard him describe me as "really quite good." When he hung up the phone, I pleaded in exasperation, "Really quite *good*? Wouldja have gone to jail if you'd told him I was a goddam *genius*?" It was hard for any of my solo show directors to get too worked up since there was nothing much in it for them. I couldn't afford to pay them, and they were rarely mentioned in any of the reviews.

But once Ken made the decision to put off law school, he poured all his energy into Theater-in-Limbo. He called on his professional relationships, and his talented colleagues elevated our operation considerably. Vivien Leone, who was already an assistant lighting designer on Broadway, helped establish the feel of a nineteenth-century theatrical traveling troupe by lining the lip of the stage with old-fashioned footlights. Another colleague was a costume designer named John Glaser. John, already designing for television and film, was an invaluable resource for upgrading Kathie's and my improvised attempts at costuming. Kath and I had done our best, but the results were variable: Our costumes for *Theodora* were created from my old bedsheets, dyed various colors. I think we may have left out one of the steps of the dyeing process because, in the heat, Ken's royal robe began dripping streams of purple dye down his long legs.

An especially instrumental figure was Ken's friend Brian Whitehill, a graphic designer for New York City's PBS-TV station WNET, who had created logos for many of their long-running series such as *American Masters*. Brian felt that since Theater-in-Limbo was sharing the space, a functioning art gallery, with rock bands and other theater performances, we needed a trademark graphic visual image that set our productions apart. Brian created our logo: a horizontal oval holding the name Theater-in-Limbo, flanked on either side by two nude figures holding masks of tragedy and comedy. And, since the only publicity would be our mailings, he designed a series of eye-catching and mildly erotic 8 × 11-inch flyers that we hoped would be saved and taped to kitchen refrigerators throughout the city.

Brian also painted a clever backdrop for each show. For *Theodora* he came up with a subway map of Byzantium. In years to come, when Brian had a real budget to work with, his deviously clever sets for my plays were as much art installations as stage scenery. The brick walls of a convent in *The Divine Sister* were made of sponges and the statue of the Virgin Mary created from a grey ironing board. In *Shanghai Moon*, he made the priceless jade bust of the Empress Heng Lu out of a lime green plastic pitcher. Brian's 1991 set for *Red Scare on Sunset* was a Russian Constructivist nightmare of foreshortened angles with every platform and piece of furniture built at a crazy slant. I explained to him that a major plot point involved Julie grabbing a knife off the desk. Wouldn't it slide off the severely angled surface? Brian solved that one by attaching Velcro to both objects, creating several big laughs when the various characters slammed the knife down or snatched it off the desk. I had to learn to clam up and trust Brian's imagination.

One key Limbo collaborator, the Broadway dancer Jeff Veazey, was introduced to us by Andy Halliday. Jeff was one of the wittiest people I've ever known. He was hysterically funny in a classically acidic gay way, but there was an inherent sweetness in him that was always present. With the exception of Andy, who had a natural dance ability, the rest of us had trouble learning even rudimentary choreography. Jeff would take a deep breath, and with eyelid virtuosity, turn to me and demand, "Pavlova, now please dance the Pony for eight counts."

As teenagers in theater camp, one of the incidents that cemented Andy's and my relationship had occurred while learning the choreography for the "Dainty June and Her Farmboys" number in *Gypsy*. The young choreographer, attempting to be as ruthless as Jerome Robbins or Jack Cole, singled me out in rehearsal for my ineptitude in mastering the tap routine. Andy vigorously sprang to my defense. "He can do it!" Genuinely touched by his faith in me, I was forced to whisper in his ear, "Pssst. I really don't think I can."

Andy stayed up with me until the middle of the night drilling that number over and over until I was able to keep up with the other Farmboys. Unlike that long-ago summer camp choreographer, Jeff Veazey never lost his patience with us. A task master but one who was never cruel, he devised dance numbers that got laughs—and not unintentional ones.

Babes on Avenue C

We opened the new Limbo Theater on November 9, 1984. Our gala opening night was not without incident. Kathie was set to arrive at my place around six o'clock to sew some straps on a gown before we headed to the Limbo Lounge. When I opened the door, she stumbled in, pale and moist as a plate of linguine minus the red sauce. She said she felt she was coming down with something, quite an understatement considering that she looked and acted as if she required embalming. I placed my hand on her forehead and it was burning hot. How was she going to handle her duties as stage manager? I laid her down on my bed. "Kathie, you should've stayed home. You can't call the show." Slurring her words, she refused to consider that possibility.

My immediate task, beyond playing Nurse Edith Cavell, was to get rid of the hair on my legs. I'd decided to try Nair, a depilatory cream. As I was standing in the bathroom in my underwear, slathering on the smelly sticky white stuff, Kath staggered toward me. "Charles, I think I need to . . ." She pushed past me in the tiny bathroom and reached the toilet just in time to throw up. I managed to hold her head and smooth back her hair as she sat on the floor with her face in the toilet bowl.

I thought to myself, *I must really love her*. Kath lay down in my bedroom and I phoned Aunt Lil. After I'd filled her in on Kath's condition, she counseled, "If her temperature goes past a hundred and three, you'll need to bring her to an emergency room." The emergency room? The audience would be arriving in an hour and I was covered in depilatory cream up to my crotch!

When it was time to rub off the Nair, strangely, not a single hair was removed. Had I not given it enough time? I'd have to get out a razor and begin shaving. This was not an activity with which I was all that familiar, and I immediately bloodied my ankle in three places.

Then the phone rang; it was Ken calling from the Limbo Lounge wondering when Kathie was going to arrive. I gave him the bad news that she wouldn't be coming at all. "Ken, I can't really talk right now. I'm in the middle of shaving my—" He asked me to look in his address book for the phone number of a veteran Broadway stage manager we knew. Carrying the phone with its long cord, I hobbled toward Ken's bedroom, which led directly into mine. As I was dictating the number, Kath rose to her feet like one of Dracula's brides and, without warning, projectile vomited all over me, the phone, and the bedroom wall.

We were both in a frozen state of horror. Kathie began to sob. Like something out of *The Exorcist*, my chest and my hair were splattered in vomit and my bare legs coated in white Nair and blood. Hanging up the phone, I couldn't believe I was hearing myself say in a gentle Spring Byington voice, "Don't worry, darling. I'll clean everything up." I turned to face an imaginary camera and screamed, "Aaaaaagh!" With that, I slipped on the watery floor, falling flat on my ass.

Things have a way of working out, though, don't they? Our lighting designer, Vivien, ran the show, the straps of the gown were attached with safety pins, Kath's fever and nausea subsided, and my legs, though scabbed in eight places, were smooth as silk. The show went on.

We began our season with three weekends of *Vampire Lesbians of Sodom*, followed by a new play, a spoof of sixties Mod London titled *Sleeping Beauty or Coma*. We brought back *Theodora, She Bitch of Byzantium* and planned to close in December with a Christmas show. Ken regularly attended Sunday services at the First Presbyterian Church on Fifth Avenue and 12th Street—one of the many ways in which he was the last person you'd expect to be producing shows in a bar on Avenue C. He felt that if we did a Christmas play we shouldn't spoof the sentimentality but embrace it. That fit perfectly in line with my love of Hollywood religiosity in film. I'm a sucker for any movie involving miracles, and if Jesus makes a cameo, the tears start flowing. But a story line just wasn't percolating.

One night after a performance at Limbo, Andy and I returned to the West Village and made our way into a small Italian restaurant. It was October; my numerous failed attempts at conjuring forth a suitably heartwarming yet hilariously camp story for our Christmas show were weighing on me. "Andy," I said, "we are not leaving this table until we come up with a plot."

By the time we'd finished our tiramisu, we had the entire scenario mapped out. In a melding of *It's a Wonderful Life* and the 1942 Lucille Ball–Henry Fonda movie *The Big Street*, I was to play a selfish tough-as-nails nightclub entertainer named Irish O'Flanagan who learns a very important lesson on

Christmas Eve. Andy would be Eddie, the busboy who loves her. We called the play *Times Square Angel*. I have a great fondness for the fantasy films of the 1940s, and it was easy for me to both have fun with the movie conventions and invest Irish O'Flanagan's redemption with genuine sentiment.

Toward the end of the play, when Irish receives her second chance, she hears Christmas carolers singing outside the nightclub. She exclaims to her faithful maid, "Throw open the window. I wanna hear that music. I need to hear that music. The most beautiful sound I ever heard!"

That play has been part of my life ever since. We did full productions in 1984, 1986, 1990, and 1991. Since 1998, *Times Square Angel* has been presented every year (except 2020, the first year of the pandemic) as a one-night event at Theater for the New City in the East Village, with Andy and me still in the cast.

Kathie and I found a great vintage forties gown of red silk crepe for me to wear in that first production of *Times Square Angel*. I'd seen it in the window of a secondhand shop and walked past that window lusting after it day after day. By the time I brought Kathie to the shop, the gown was off the display mannequin. When we went inside, we found an attractive woman trying it on, checking herself out before a full-length three-sided mirror. She caught me gazing at her and said, "It's so pretty, but I think it makes me look short-waisted."

I've rarely wanted anything as much as I wanted that red silk crepe gown.

"Well," I said, "I hope I'm not being too forward, but you have a classic movie star figure. You've got an Ava Gardner shape, and if the dress makes *you* look short-waisted, well, then there's a drastic flaw in the design." Flattered, she was inclined to agree. I waited until the second she left the shop: "Kath, help me into this dress!" The gown was everything I'd hoped it would be, and after I wore it in *Times Square Angel*, nearly everyone in the cast, male and female, maneuvered themselves into it at one time or another for some production or event.

A favorite Limbo play of mine from our early days was a romp we performed only nine times. The full title is *Pardon My Inquisition or Kiss the Blood Off My Castanets.* The play was a Spanish peasant stew mixing elements of *Carmen*, *Blood and Sand*, and *Marked Woman*, with more than a dollop of *A Tale of Two Cities.* I played dual roles: the tempestuous spitfire prostitute Maria Garbanzo and her look-alike, the tragic noblewoman the Marquesa del Drago.

We were rehearsing the first big tavern scene with the entire cast onstage. There was no end to the backslapping, foot stomping, macho exhortations to "Drink! Drink!" and heavy Castilian lisps. When we'd finished, Ken approached the stage to speak to the company. "That was like the worst hammy, clichéd, vulgar dinner theater production of *Man of La Mancha.*" He paused to let his words sink in. "*I love it!*" The scene concluded with a coup de théâtre in which I, as Maria Garbanzo, lure a handsome hombre played by Bobby Carey to the back of the stage, pull down his pants revealing Bobby's trademark perfect round naked butt, and, with my face hidden from view, proceed to perform fellatio on him to the cheering of the tavern crowd.

My two sisters attended the first performance. Afterwards, Betsy asked Margaret, "Do you think Charles really went down on Bobby?" "Of course not," Margaret replied sagely. "Charles would never mess up his lipstick."

The Bad Old Good Days or
the Good Old Bad Days

For the previous decade, I'd relentlessly pursued my path as a solo performer and along the way lost the joy in putting on a show. Before we became Theater-in-Limbo, that was true of all of us. We had been suffering from a near fatal lack of fun and were now deriving an exhilarating kick from this unexpected chapter in our lives. We weren't thinking about these plays as a shrewd career move. How could we? You'd have to be insane to imagine that what we were doing was a step toward anything except perhaps a case of bedbugs. We didn't have a backstage toilet. Hell, we didn't have a backstage, only a narrow space behind the stage wall where we'd gather single file during the show. The boys would pee in paper cups and line them up on the floor. Accidents happen when people must squeeze past to make their entrances. Yes, at times the hems of my gowns were stiff with urine but, *mes chères*, I was never happier.

As a writer, I enjoyed bestowing on my friends romantic visions of themselves. Julie and I bonded over our love for anything to do with sixties Mod London, so I wrote a play where she could play a Twiggyesque fashion model. For me, for the cast, and for many in our audience, devastated by the AIDS epidemic, our shows were a much-needed source of escape. For that one hour, we were in a collective dream.

Under Ken's sharp eye, Theater-in-Limbo evolved into a true ensemble. It's odd for me to come up with a sports analogy, but we derived pleasure from tossing the ball to each other. I'd set up Andy's laugh, and after he scored, he'd set up my laugh, and after I got my laugh, I'd set up Julie's laugh, and she would in turn set up Theresa's laugh. We may have shared the laughs, but we were incapable of improvising if one of us forgot a line. We'd just wait till the unfortunate victim recovered. Ken was the worst in a memorization disaster. No matter what the play, the role, or the situation was, if he lost concentration and blanked on a line, he'd resort to the same ad-lib, "I hate you! I hate you, you . . . you nut!"

A few years ago, I met the marvelous octogenarian character actress Beulah Garrick, who created the role of the loyal housekeeper Norah Muldoon in the play *Auntie Mame*. Late in the play's run, the original star, Rosalind Russell, left and was replaced by the British comedienne Beatrice Lillie. Beulah told me that during one performance, Bea Lillie forgot her lines and Beulah tried to save her by covering her mouth with a handkerchief and surreptitiously whispering the cue. Bea Lillie turned to her and, projecting to the last row of the balcony, requested, "Louder, Beulah!"

Though I wrote and appeared in these shows without any long-term goal or expectation, I also felt part of the grand tradition of the actor/manager. Bernhardt traveling around the world in a repertory of plays, Mrs. Fiske at the turn of the century introducing Ibsen to the hinterlands, and Katharine Cornell in the 1930s touring north, south, east, and west with a company of actors (among them the eighteen-year-old Orson Welles)—each of these actresses was a role model for me.

While I was reveling in this new life, the cloud of AIDS was always hovering overhead. If I were infected and became ill, how would I break it to Aunt Lil? Her brother Charlie's death in the Second World War had shattered her youth, and my mother's early death devastated Aunt Lil's middle age; my premature death would have destroyed her remaining years. And yet I knew that my family would rise to the occasion and I'd be loved and well cared for.

Aunt Belle, hobbled by arthritis, volunteered several days a week at Roosevelt Hospital's AIDS ward, pushing the magazine cart and providing grandmotherly affection to patients who were frequently abandoned by their own families.

Every week, we'd hear of another AIDS death: a friend's hairdresser, someone's brother, a popular singing waiter at a piano bar, a theatrical publicist, an up-and-coming painter. When would it reach my inner circle of friends? I'd grown up watching documentary footage of Auschwitz and Dachau and now my childhood terror of being transported to a concentration camp was rekindled by pundits like William F. Buckley espousing that those infected with HIV should be tattooed and quarantined in camps.

For gay men of my generation, this was our war, and many of us think of it much as our parents regarded World War II.

In 1995, that analogy hit home when I was appearing in an Off-Broadway musical called *Swingtime Canteen*, about an American all-girl band performing in London during the Blitz. Late in the run, Maxene Andrews of the Andrews Sisters joined the show. I received a letter from a man saying that he was bringing his lover, a devoted Andrews Sisters fan, and asking if they might meet Maxene.

Everything was arranged. After the performance, the two young men came backstage. The lover, in a wheelchair, emaciated and ravaged, was in the last stages of AIDS. He had a wonderful visit with Maxene, who was affectionate and darling with him. (Several months after she left *Swingtime Canteen*, Maxene would die suddenly of a heart attack.) When the couple was ready to leave, Maxene, with marvelous gallantry, gave a little salute and said to the desperately ill young man, "Good luck to ya, kid." At that instant, the two wars became one in my mind.

In 1984, with the plague circling ever closer, I was at last connected to a group of kindred spirits, feeling loved and appreciated, and enjoying a collaboration and camaraderie I had never known. For Theater-in-Limbo, it was the best of times and the worst of times. I feel guilty admitting that in a time of death and despair for so many, I was living through one of the most fulfilling periods of my life, but it's true. We were jesters during the plague.

I'm proud to have supplied some diversion, but I must bow to the brave, fierce commitment of the activists in ACT UP and TAG. These men and women, fighting for our lives, forced the pharmaceutical companies to change their protocols and shamed a homophobic government into admitting that the disastrous AIDS epidemic was real and pervasive.

Alphabet City Lights

There were other clubs in the East Village besides the Limbo Lounge, among them 8BC and the Pyramid Club, the most influential one. These venues hosted a roster of unique performance artists including Joey Arias, Ann Magnuson, Ethyl Eichelberger, John Kelly, Tabboo!, John Sex, Lypsinka, video artist Tom Rubnitz, and John Jesurun.

Some of these talented and profoundly original artists thought of Ken and me as interlopers, and not without reason. Ken was about as downtown as Flo Ziegfeld and determined to bring to our shows, no matter how miniscule the budget, a level of uptown polish. Apart from the work of the serious performance artists, many East Village productions were convulsively funny because of their improvised cheap theatrics. The length, pace, and comic invention of the shows were often dictated by the amount of alcohol or drugs the cast had ingested. Ken wasn't a deconstructionist or a theorist, but he possessed the gift of knowing how to produce a fast-paced, disciplined entertainment and direct a play with wit and brio. It was our degree of professionalism, exemplified by Ken, that our audiences found to be the biggest surprise of our shows.

During those first six months, there was a flurry of media interest in the outlandish performance art scene in Alphabet City, and Theater-in-Limbo was always mentioned. The zany and profane titles of our plays made good punch lines. That free publicity, along with word of mouth and a string of positive reviews in the gay paper the *New York Native*, helped ensure a long line outside the Limbo Lounge before every performance. And depending upon what was going on inside before our show, the wait could be interminable.

We almost never knew ahead of time how long the wait would be—once, the sudden appearance of the rock band the Butthole Surfers, performing an extremely long set, kept our audience outside on the street for well over an hour. Ken ran to the nearest deli, bought beers, and handed them out to the people in line.

Exiting the show could be an ordeal as well. It wasn't uncommon for Michael Limbo and his cohorts to begin splashing pink paint on the walls for a new art installation while our audience was still putting on their coats. Attempting to produce a play in a venue that had no desire to be disciplined created what Ken would dub "the eight o'clock surprise." We'd arrive to find an exhibit of vividly painted totem poles in the middle of the stage or all of the stage lights rearranged. We weren't the only ones who suffered when this happened: Poor Michael would find himself pushed in a corner and berated by two furious five-foot-tall Italian American women, Vivien and Kathie.

Celebrities as diverse as Jerome Robbins and Joan Rivers began making the trek down to the Limbo Lounge. One performance of *Vampire Lesbians of Sodom* was so overcrowded that it was in violation of just about every city code.

There were people perched on top of the ice machine. When the show was over, we scooted back to our regular West Village hangout, an Irish bar and restaurant called McBells. We had the proceeds from the night in cash, and Ken and I began counting it out in piles of hundred-dollar bills. It came to a total of over two thousand dollars. Ken turned to me wide-eyed and wondered aloud, "Is it possible that this thing we've been doing just for fun could be *commercial*?"

Given my nearly demented faith in myself, it's perplexing that I didn't have some fixed objective in mind, such as starring on Broadway or having my own television sitcom. During my solo years, I'd been climbing a jungle gym from one out-of-town booking to another, too focused on finding my next handhold to see them as steps toward an ultimate goal.

Ken swept me along with his determination to take *Vampire Lesbians of Sodom* to the next level. He used every contact he had to get producers down to the Limbo Lounge in hopes that they would move the play to a commercial Off-Broadway house. Several producers made the trip to Avenue C, and while they appeared to enjoy the show, they always passed. The lone exception was Arthur Cantor, a veteran Broadway producer who managed the historic Provincetown Playhouse on MacDougal Street in the Village. He was interested in having us at his theater, but disappointingly, didn't want to produce the show. Ken concluded that we'd just have to produce the show at the Provincetown Playhouse ourselves. The plan was to pair the forty-five-minute *Vampire Lesbians of Sodom* with another of our pieces, *Sleeping Beauty or Coma*, for a full-length evening. Ken devised a budget of $55,000, just enough to get us through opening night. A mere pittance for most Off-Broadway shows, but it seemed like an awful lot of scratch.

We spent the next five months on a scavenger hunt to raise that cash, selling shares in the show for $5,000 each. A quartet of young men who attended almost every one of our performances pooled their money and bought a share. Andy's mother, Rose; Julie's boss on Wall Street, Doug Lane;

Ken's employer, Michael Stewart; and Michael's sister, the novelist Francine Pascal, all bought shares. Ken's parents in Indiana came through and bought a share each. I'd assumed they had a vision of me as an evil siren who seduced Ken out of attending New York Law School. I was wrong. They were supportive of their son whatever path he chose.

I put the pinch on my sisters and Aunt Belle in my apartment over a nearly inedible spaghetti dinner; Margaret quipped that her five-thousand-dollar investment amounted to twenty-five dollars per strand of pasta. Aunt Belle gave what's called "front money," which means money that can be spent immediately. We were almost there, only five thousand dollars short. It was time to pay a call on Aunt Lil.

As we sat facing each other, we both knew we'd reached a pivotal moment. She'd spent the previous decade forever worrying that I'd never be able to earn a living. This play, with its lurid title, could very well put success, or at least solvency, within my reach. Had I stumbled onto the elusive lucky break that is the bedrock of show business lore? During my high school years, I'd taught Aunt Lil the value of employing the occasional well-placed profanity. At this key moment, she said, "Well, if I didn't give you the money, I'd really be a number one shithead."

Five Minutes to Places

B uilt in 1918, the Provincetown Playhouse was once the artistic home of a group of budding geniuses, among them the writers Eugene O'Neill and Edna St. Vincent Millay. By the time we got our lease, it had fallen on hard times and was considered something of a jinxed house. With rare exceptions, nothing ran more than a weekend, so we were able to negotiate an exceptionally low rent.

With our budget of fifty-five grand, Brian Whitehill was able to build a stylish, witty set, Vivien Leone could light us wonderfully, and John Glaser designed an array of gorgeous costumes ranging from metallic sixties mini-dresses to lace gowns with bat-wing drapery and hobble skirts out of Poiret. At last Kathie had a real wig budget—and she needed it since she had to design and create twenty-seven wigs!

While we prepared for the Off-Broadway production, Kath's elderly mother, Mrs. Caracciolo, came from Queens to stay with her for a few days. During her visit, it was necessary for me to stop by for a wig fitting. Kath was concerned that her mother might disapprove of a guy being fitted for a woman's wig.

Silver-haired and no more than four foot ten, Mrs. Caracciolo sat silently, hands folded, in a corner of the room. Wouldn't you know it, the wig we had to work on was the most excessive in the show, fire-engine red and teased with a wing on the right side of the hairdo. I put on the wig and sat on a stool while Kathie took her spiked hair pick and began lifting out the syn-thetic cotton candy–like hair, making it bigger and bigger. Mrs. Caracciolo sat motionless, observing us. Kathie and I were both self-conscious, Kathie nervously giggling and me trying to act like a "regular guy" who had no choice but to endure this woman's stuff.

Kathie stuck a hairpin above my ear to give the massive beehive a bit more definition. At last, her mother was compelled to speak up: "Kathie, she needs a little curl in front of the ear to give it softness."

Now that the stakes were so much higher, we wondered if the show itself needed to be "picked out" and expanded. Were we good enough? What do we do about Bobby? He was an amateur. Do we include everyone else in the Off-Broadway transfer but leave him out? Ken refused to consider it. "It would kill him. Besides, his wooden line readings and his ass are part of the charm of the show."

Julie was in a quandary. Unlike the rest of us, she had a real job as a Wall Street corporate librarian. She couldn't perform eight shows a week including matinees and keep her job. Should she give it up for a show that might close after a week? She agonized over that dilemma and came up with a compromise. In a novel career trajectory, she'd go from leading lady to understudy. As her replacement, Julie recommended a friend of hers, an actress named Meghan Robinson.

When Meghan (pronounced Meg-ANN) showed up at our apartment, it was infatuation at first sight for both Ken and me. I'd never seen anyone, male or female, wear that much makeup in midafternoon. Meghan, at twenty-eight, had the authority and rich contralto speaking voice of a stage actress from the 1930s. She had such vocal power that I once saw her disperse a gang of teenage hoodlums bent on attacking each other with a stentorian Lady Macbeth–like howl of "Stop this at once!"

Meghan lived on a miniscule struggling actress's budget. Her entire wardrobe consisted of four Betsey Johnson dresses, yet she was always the height of chic. The daughter of two bohemian artists, that dame could do more with a scarf than an origami master could do with a piece of paper.

But though Meghan joined the cast, she was never really part of the company. Ken and I instinctively treated her with the deference we would a visiting artist. That didn't always go over well with the rest of Theater-in-Limbo. And, with the mannered charm of an Ina Claire or Lynn Fontanne, Meghan could seem . . . well . . . patronizing. Bobby laughed it off when she patted him on the arm and cooed, "Bobby, darling, you're really holding your own with us." She tried pulling that on Andy, only he wasn't laughing. He never warmed up to her.

As the subjects of her condescension would invariably point out, she hardly possessed the resume to justify her grand manner. Meghan tended to embellish stories of her past, treating what had actually transpired as more of a starting point than anything else. A kind of film would dull her eyes as she made hay with the truth. Andy would whisper to me, "Did you hear what she said? She's making it all up." Her foolish self-inventions, instead of making her seem devious, gave her the vulnerable air of a sleepwalker.

As I came to discover, this somewhat imperious young woman was also capable of deep loyalty and tenderness for those she respected. She'd go to battle for you. Oh, I was mad about her.

Cast in place, we threw ourselves into preparing for our Off-Broadway debut. While we were in final rehearsals, I began to panic. This would be my first time facing the New York critics. I'd never imagined this was the vehicle that would grant me such an opportunity. A late-night bar entertainment, *Vampire Lesbians of Sodom* wasn't meant to be scrutinized. My solo material had more depth and substance. It seemed inevitable that I'd be unfavorably compared to Charles Ludlam. His plays were over two hours long and full of allusions to classic literature. His work had an intellectual heft and political relevance that elevated it beyond theatrical or film parody.

I sat down at the typewriter and began beefing up various scenes of the play. There had to be some way to make this burlesque sketch literary and deep. I presented the rewrites to Ken in the late afternoon. Surprisingly, he didn't reject them out of hand. I think he was concerned at the wispiness of the show as well. The next morning, he told me he'd woken up sweaty from a nightmare. In the dream he'd put in the rewrites, but after we performed them, the audience began booing. "This isn't the show we liked!" He leveled

with me: "This may not be what we hoped would be our big break, but this is
the show we have. We may not be the best judges. Let's leave it alone."

We began two weeks of previews. None of us had experience playing
eight shows a week, which included two shows each on Fridays and Saturdays.
Andy and I designed and applied our own drag makeup. When Bobby Carey
first saw Andy's attempt at blocking out his real eyebrows and penciling in a
stylized false brow, he quipped, "Andy, didja trace those brows around a Coke
bottle?" Accustomed to using cheap cosmetics from the drugstore instead of
professional theatrical makeup, Andy and I coated our faces with thick liquid
foundation and then powdered heavily. When it was time to freshen up our
makeup for the second show, we simply added more liquid foundation and a
dense new coat of powder. During the intermission, in the harsh light of the
dressing room, I noticed that Andy's makeup had cracked into a spider's web
of fine lines. "Andy, your face! Look at your face!" Then he pointed to me in
horror. "Look at *yours*!" A chip of hardened liquid foundation had fallen off
my chin like a jigsaw puzzle piece. We had learned an essential and irrefutable
truth—one must *never* put liquid foundation over dry powder.

The *New York Times* sent their critic D. J. R. Bruckner to the third-to-last
preview. His was the review that mattered. Without a positive *Times* review,
the show would quickly fold, and it wasn't likely we'd return to the Limbo
Lounge. It would be back to the temp pool for me.

In recent years, I don't want the distraction of knowing when the *Times*
critic is coming, but I didn't feel that way back in 1985. The entire cast knew
when Bruckner was in the audience. Our hearts may have been beating faster,
but the show went off smoothly; what he saw was representative of what we
were selling. An agonizing seventy-two hours loomed before opening night,
when the *Times* review would appear.

Opening night arrived with the seats largely filled with our friends and
investors. When it was over, half the audience wafted downstairs into the

greenroom. While we were all engaged in a champagne toast, a waiflike kid named Joey who worked as an assistant stage manager ran outside and found a newsstand. He returned waving the early edition of the *Times*. "The review! It's out!"

He tossed me the folded newspaper opened to the review. My hands began to shake as if the paper were on fire. I tossed it to Ken, who couldn't bring himself to read it either. My college roommate, Ed Taussig, grabbed the newspaper out of Ken's trembling hands. Ed read the review aloud, his voice catching with emotion. It was a rave. Everyone got mentioned: the actors, Ken's direction, the designers, Kathie's wigs. There was a paragraph devoted to my performance, thank you very much, and a prediction that the show would run for years. People were shouting and cheering, as if the *Titanic* had been raised with all the passengers and crew still alive.

In the cacophony I slipped away unnoticed, went into the dressing room, and shut the door. I sat down at the makeup table and was racked with sobs. It had been eight years of constant pushing toward a nebulous goal since I'd returned to New York, holding on to an increasingly frayed rope of belief in myself. Actually, it was more than eight years. It had been fourteen years since I'd arrived at Northwestern to discover that I had no desire to compete for roles that were alien to my nature and would have to create my own opportunities. I could hear the cheers of the cast and friends outside the dressing room.

Sitting in front of the dressing room mirror, I pondered what that *New York Times* review might mean for the show and for my future. Would the show run? Would I now at last be able to earn my living as an actor and writer? I calmed down and stepped outside myself. Staring at the heavily made-up and bewigged creature in the mirror, I asked, "What happens to you *now?*"

Many years later, I was walking in my neighborhood and ran into a journalist friend of mine who was accompanied by an older gentleman. My friend introduced his companion. "This is Don Bruckner." Don Bruckner was none other than the D. J. R. Bruckner who wrote our *Times* review. This was the first time I'd ever laid eyes on him. In a tremulous voice, I stammered, "You don't know . . . you don't know what you've done for me. I've had the most wonderful life. Your review is responsible for everything."

Don Bruckner was a reserved and taciturn gentleman. There was a nervous-making pause, after which he quietly muttered, "I . . . um liked the play."

Footlight Parade

1986. The first year of the run of *Vampire Lesbians* was like living full-time in a Coney Island amusement park complete with thrill rides, fun-house mirrors, and a haunted house. We had our photos taken with a dizzying assortment of backstage visitors, including Phyllis Diller, prima ballerina Cynthia Gregory, Lily Tomlin, and Yoko Ono. I enjoyed being wooed as a client by both ICM and the William Morris Agency, when a few months earlier neither would have hired me as an office temp. Six months into the run, we learned that our crotchety general manager, who forty years earlier had worked for producer Billy Rose, had misread the Actors' Equity Off-Broadway contract, and had vastly overpaid our cast. Before he resigned in disgrace, he strongly advised closing the show. Ken took over as general manager and kept the show going and going and going.

Working out of our West 12th Street apartment, Ken's new company manager, a dedicated young woman named Terry Byrne, did the weekly payroll at the kitchen table while I ate my Rice Krispies. A recurring aggravation for Terry was that the Provincetown Playhouse marquee for *Vampire Lesbians of Sodom* was repeatedly stolen in the middle of the night by thrill-seeking NYU students and others. Fiercely loyal, Miss Byrne, as we all came to call her, took the theft in a most personal manner. She'd sob and fume with the indignation of an O'Casey heroine as she dealt with an increasingly unsympathetic insurance company.

We'd been performing *Vampire Lesbians of Sodom* for over a year when the cast began to grow weary of making the same funny faces. None of us had experience appearing in a long run and it was a tough show to maintain as an actor. A drama or a comedy with some complexity gives an actor room to explore, with the potential to dig deeper into an emotional scene. The two one-acts that comprised our evening of entertainment at the Provincetown Playhouse did not offer many pockets of emotion to keep us fresh. The tendency was to invent new comic business and extend proven laughs with additional schtick.

Six months into the run, the show was a full twenty minutes longer. Ken put us through several brush-up rehearsals to "take out the improvements." The only member of the company not guilty of over-embroidery was Bobby, whom we'd lovingly dismissed as a sweet amateur. Over the course of several hundred performances, he'd become a disciplined professional. Exiting the stage with an air of pride, he'd shrug, "I don't know about youse, but I got my applauds."

Any time I'd see a show on my night off that excited me, my next performance would be visibly affected. Andy and I saw the great Martha Raye in her final cabaret appearance in New York. Her singing voice was in perfect condition and she performed her trademark songs in their original thirties swing arrangements. What inspired me was the uninhibited and frequently blue comedy bits she did between songs, at one point intentionally getting the microphone stuck in her mouth.

Around that same time, I also attended a mesmerizing performance by the ninety-year-old Japanese female impersonator Kazuo Ohno, the father of the starkly minimalist Hiroshima-inspired dance form known as Butoh. Resembling a skeletal ancient doll in a 1920s child's dress, he could take a hypnotic half hour to place his index finger to his hollowed cheek. My subsequent Butoh- and Martha Raye–influenced performances were fortunately not encouraged or repeated.

About six months into the run, Meghan started missing shows. She was a chain-smoker and was plagued by severe bronchial attacks. Several in the cast felt she was being a prima donna and creating illnesses because deep down she thought the show was beneath her. Julie was content with her role of understudy and was often backstage, regarding the sofa in the greenroom as the set for an ongoing talk show, with all of us her recurring guests.

There was great excitement among the cast the first time Julie had to go on for Meghan. She and Meghan were about the same size, so the costumes weren't a problem, but somehow, we'd neglected to have her try on Meghan's wigs. Meghan's first wig in the show, a shoulder-length blonde sixties Julie Christie bob, was so loose that even anchored with many pins, it threatened to slip off Julie's much smaller head. Naturally, this wasn't discovered until half an hour before curtain. Assessing Julie's fine, straight blonde hair, I said offhandedly, "Julie's own hair would look great in a short sixties asymmetrical Sassoon." With no time to lose, Julie said, "Cut my hair." Kathie, our stage manager and wig stylist, begged off, saying she had no experience cutting human hair.

I don't know why Julie turned to me. "Chawlz, you're gonna have to do it." With trepidation, I picked up Kathie's wig scissors and, taking a deep breath, began improvising my first asymmetrical Sassoon cut. It turned out rather well—parted on the right, tapered close around the ear, and with the left side longer and angled against the jawline. At least it was competent enough to get through the show, and Julie visited her own hairdresser the following day to clean up the rough edges.

At the end of each performance of *Vampire Lesbians of Sodom*, I'd make a curtain speech, still in character as a faux great lady of the theater imploring the audience to sign up for our mailing list. To make the pitch more entertaining, I'd improvise the titles of future plays they might see. One night, the title *Gidget Goes Psychotic* came to mind. It got a big laugh, and I used it as the final punch line of my curtain speech for the next year.

Eventually, Ken said, "You know, maybe we should do a show called *Gidget Goes Psychotic*. We've certainly been promoting it long enough." I saw his point; it would also get the company out of the rut of playing *Vampire Lesbians of Sodom* with no end in sight. We could do late shows of a new play on weekends at the Limbo Lounge after we finished our eight o'clock performances at the Provincetown Playhouse.

I wasn't that keen on the subject matter, however. I found no glamour or grandeur in the Frankie and Annette beach party movies or in the film and television series *Gidget*. The shows I wrote for Theater-in-Limbo were built on fantasies of who I'd like to play—an ageless vampire actress, a Byzantine empress, a mod fashion designer. Then it occurred to me that perhaps Gidget's emotional problems could manifest in multiple personalities: a supermarket checkout girl, a vain male model, an elderly female public radio talk show host, and, best of all, a Cruella de Vil–like dominatrix named Ann Bowman.

By this time, I'd written so many roles for our ensemble that the new play nearly wrote itself. Everyone was cast in variations of roles they'd played before but in a different movie genre. For Meghan, who'd recently left her *Vampire Lesbians* roles, I wrote the character of Gidget's sexually repressed mother, and we costumed her to resemble the early 1960s Joan Crawford. When the play is produced around the country, Mrs. Forrest is usually cast with a man in drag. It seems an obvious choice, but they lose a potentially poignant moment. Toward the end of the play, there's a brief flashback that refers to the 1964 Hitchcock film *Marnie*, where we have a glimpse of Gidget's mother in her early days as a prostitute. For that scene, Meghan wore a soft flowing wig and a tight gown that exposed her slender young woman's figure. The dragon lady was suddenly seen as a vulnerable victim.

As this story demanded a larger cast of characters, I wrote roles for our two excellent understudies, Michael Belanger and Judith Hansen. Julie Halston sat this one out. By this time, she'd left *Vampire Lesbians of Sodom* to focus on her Wall Street business career. Her company even sent her on a quick trip to Alaska to train her as a gold analyst.

To replace Meghan in *Vampire Lesbians*, we held auditions and found a marvelous actress with startling Bette Davis eyes named Becky London. A recent graduate of the Yale School of Drama, her versatility and willingness to throw herself into any wacky situation onstage and off fit in with us so perfectly that I wrote a role for her in our new play as well—as Gidget's best friend, Berdine.

Within a few months we were ready to go. As soon as the curtain came down at the Provincetown Playhouse, we'd jump into cabs, wig caps still pinned on, and speed across town to the Limbo Lounge. Our audience would be already seated in the house as we raced down the aisle to boisterous welcoming applause and dashed backstage to throw on our new costumes and wigs. It was exhausting, but we were young and buoyed by the energy of the crowd.

Our audiences at the Provincetown Playhouse a year into the run weren't nearly as demonstrative. They were largely tourists and, in many cases, non-English speaking. On a scale of one to ten, ten being uproarious, the laugh-o-meter was down to four, three for a Sunday matinee. There was one show where we didn't receive a single laugh. It was like performing underwater. Ralph Buckley, who'd replaced Ken in the show so Ken could devote his energies to being general manager, felt self-conscious maniacally mugging to no effect, and he started to laugh. Normally, I'm a strict school-marm about stage crack-ups, but the situation was so absurd that I began to laugh as well, and then Andy, Theresa, Becky, and Bobby all started giggling. Picture the audience expressionless and the actors busting a gut.

Another night, a straight couple sitting in the front row held their opened playbills over their faces with their eyes barely visible throughout the entire performance. In the wings, we all wondered what the hell was wrong with them. It was Bobby who clued us in that they were probably worried they'd get AIDS from our accidental expectorations spraying over the foot-lights. We really needed the fix of connecting once again with our original East Village audience.

The response to *Gidget Goes Psychotic* was so strong that we decided to transfer it Off-Broadway as well. There was some concern that there'd be copyright problems with the title *Gidget Goes Psychotic* and I was more than happy to retitle it *Psycho Beach Party*. What had begun as a spoof of a specific movie and TV series had become a more complex piece of writing. The newly renamed Chicklet, the mixed-up heroine of my play, ultimately accepts that the personae emerging from her are all facets of her truest self. Chicklet, *c'est moi!*

I discovered early on that my audience easily accepted me as a female character and didn't enjoy being shaken out of that illusion. My attempts at humor pointing out my masculine gender usually fell flat. The one time this worked was in the first scene of *Psycho Beach Party*. Chicklet and her friends Berdine and Marvel Ann go to the beach and Chicklet remembers she for-got to put on the top of her bathing suit underneath her sundress.

CHICKLET
Darn it. It's in my bag and there's no ladies room to change in.

MARVEL ANN
There's no one around. You better hurry.

BERDINE
You can't take off your top here.

CHICKLET
Hold the blanket up and no one will see me. (They hold up the blanket,
Chicklet takes off her smock, revealing her nude flat chest.) I'm hopeless.
I'm built just like a boy. I wonder if I'll ever fill out.

Exposing my smooth skinny male chest gave us one of the most extended laughs we had received to date.

Meghan's physicality also contributed to the gender fluidity of our shows. The two of us were the same height, and with her grand manner, vividly painted face, and nearly baritone voice, some people assumed she was also a guy in drag.

This happened offstage as well. Once we were walking along the beach in Cherry Grove on Fire Island. Meghan was wearing a 1940s flower-printed sundress edged with ruffles and had applied a heavier maquillage than is usually worn for a day at the beach. A man approaching us seemed to recognize her. Ignoring me, he took a deep bow and exclaimed, "Oh, Mr. Busch. I'm such a fan. I've seen *Vampire Lesbians* over ten times!" Meghan was not amused.

As our company prepared for the Off-Broadway transfer of *Psycho Beach Party*, we gradually replaced the remaining members of the original cast of *Vampire Lesbians of Sodom*. We auditioned many actors for my role and yet no one seemed quite right. We weren't sure what we were looking for, a comic drag performer or an experienced actor. We needed both in one person.

The audition process dragged on for months, and the strain of preparing the new show while playing my *Vampire Lesbians* roles with seemingly no end in sight stretched my nerves to the snapping point. There was one performance where, blinded by the footlights and peering out into the dark void, I thought I detected a figure slowly creeping up and down the aisle. By the time we reached the climax of the play with the entire cast onstage, I'd worked myself into a fevered pitch of hysteria, convinced that I was to be the target of an assassin's bullet. My cast mates were mystified as I roamed the stage in constant frenetic motion and then employed my perplexed leading man, Arnie, as a human shield. It turned out that my shadowy assassin was merely an elderly man with bad circulation and a need to stretch his legs.

At the end of yet another day of disappointing auditions, in walked beautiful twenty-three-year-old boy named David Drake. He was a friend of our publicist and had seen the show dozens of times. He had memorized my performance down to the tiniest detail. David was cast, and Ken had no explain the thought process behind my florid comic choices to our new star

While David started out as an expert carbon copy, after playing the role for a few months, he found an original way into the character of Madeleine Astarté. He stayed in the role for about two years, racking up more performances than I had. He left *Vampire Lesbians* for another show, and other Madeleine Astartés passed in and out of the production. I returned for brief engagement when we were between leading ladies, and then David came back to close the show at the end of its five-year run.

I'm subject to a recurring dream in which someone informs me that *Vampire Lesbians* is still open after more than thirty-seven years. In true Actor's Nightmare fashion, I'm obligated to take over my old role without any rehearsal, with a supporting cast of strangers and wearing the original costumes, which are hanging on a rack, faded, torn, and sticky with mildew. As usual in this sort of dream, I can't find my shoes.

There's Always Tomorrow

A unt Lil was greatly relieved that my career had finally taken off. The night the *New York Times* review of *Vampire Lesbians* came out, the doorman of her building rushed it upstairs for her to see. She told me she found herself speaking to my late mother: "Gertie, our boy's going to be all right." One would think that after all her effort and devotion, not to mention her participation as an investor in my shows, she'd be sitting front row center at each opening night.

In fact, the one and only time she saw me onstage was when I was a seventeen-year-old apprentice at the Lake Placid Playhouse and played the elderly Merlin in the musical *Camelot*. Aunt Lil took an eight-hour bus ride to see me in the role. For the next three decades she would reflect upon my "extraordinary" performance. "You *were* Merlin." I was indeed good as Merlin. My turn as the wizard and mentor to the young King Arthur was the first time I played an idealized version of Aunt Lil. It would be far from the last.

After a year in *Vampire Lesbians of Sodom* and ten months in *Psycho Beach Party*, it was becoming clear that Aunt Lil had no intention of seeing me in one of my drag roles. We finally sat down and thrashed it out. She explained, "We're so connected. There is no way I could sit back and objectively enjoy myself. The whole time I'd be worried that the audience might not like you or would be unkind."

I tried to reassure her that it wasn't likely I'd be pelted with tomatoes. But there was more to it. "You know that sort of show isn't for me. I wouldn't get it, and ultimately, my opinion is of no importance. I could lie and smile,

but you'd know how I felt. It would put a shadow between us. It's best that I support you in every way and love you, but just stay home."

About a year later I was appearing in my play *The Lady in Question* at the Orpheum Theatre on Second Avenue. Aunt Lil and Margaret and I had lunch in that neighborhood before my Saturday matinee. Afterwards, I walked them over to the theater to see the magnificent old-fashioned marquee and the photos out front. Aunt Lil was moved to see my name in such big letters. They planned to walk the mile up Second Avenue back to Aunt Lil's apartment in Murray Hill, and I left them to go backstage.

When the play started, I began to obsess that Margaret had persuaded Aunt Lil to slip in and see the matinee. There wasn't a moment of the performance that I didn't wonder if Aunt Lil was approving or disturbed. I'm sure the audience didn't notice, but I felt I'd given a terrible performance. It turned out she wasn't there, but that was enough for me to see that her attending one of my shows would be every bit as impossible for me as it would be for her.

On the other hand, my father had no problem seeing me onstage. He was living in Florida with his third wife, Irene, doing phone sales for a large sheet music publishing company. About once a year, he'd come to New York to meet with his major customers and Margaret and Betsy would take him to whatever play I was currently appearing in.

I still found it awkward giving myself fully to him without feeling I was betraying Aunt Lil. It was difficult because Daddy demanded nothing of me and was grateful for any sign of affection. Hopelessly stagestruck, he loved being given a private tour backstage. I could see him breathing in the ambience of the empty theater as he moved about the stage set. He was always demonstrative in his praise of my performance, though he inevitably went too far by saying something vaguely creepy such as, "I find myself oddly attracted to the women you play."

My father was active in community theater in the Miami area, and during one visit, he made a point of telling me about a performance the theater company had given to raise funds for a local AIDS charity. I'd never discussed my sexuality with him and sensed that he'd brought up the AIDS fundraiser as an opening for me to casually address being gay. I was hardly in the closet, but I chose not to let the conversation move in that direction. I suppose I made that choice knowing that the discussion would bring us to a degree of openness that I didn't have with Aunt Lil and would somehow give him the upper hand in the unspoken competition between the two of them.

Dark Victory

Even with the darkness of AIDS creeping ever closer, I put off being tested, sure the law of averages would dictate that I was HIV positive. I dreaded the finality of that grim diagnosis. At last, summoning up my courage, I went to a dismal free clinic in Chelsea, had the blood test, and waited an agonizing week for the result. It came back negative. How the hell had I escaped that virus? It made no sense. Others in my circle were not as fortunate.

Charles Ludlam died from complications of AIDS in 1987. At the height of his powers, he'd had his biggest hit with *The Mystery of Irma Vep* in 1984 and followed it up with several other successes. He was on the verge of a major career move with Joseph Papp's New York Shakespeare Festival and had made a splash in the hit film *The Big Easy*.

Ludlam was one of the first great cultural figures to die of AIDS and his obituary was deservedly on the front page of the *New York Times*. We opened *Psycho Beach Party* shortly after he died and most of the critics seemed to feel an obligation to portray me as Ludlam lite and mourn the loss of a superior artist. I like to think that over the course of the decades that followed I've moved farther from his influence, but I will *always* be proud to be in his direct theatrical line.

The epidemic finally reached the doorstep of Theater-in-Limbo. First, our choreographer Jeff Veazey became ill and died quickly. Jeff's closest friend was the choreographer and director Susan Stroman. They'd met as chorus dancers, and even as a young woman, Susan was sensitive about her age and shared it with no one, Jeff included. When Jeff was on his deathbed, in the barest whisper he asked her to finally divulge her age. Susan told him, and then immediately followed with, "I'm leaving right now for the deli, and when I get back, you'd better be history."

One day Bobby Carey, our beautiful boy, told us that he was HIV positive. He appeared perfectly healthy, however, and announced that his 1989 New Year's resolution would be the unveiling of an even more spectacularly muscular physique.

As had been the case with *Vampire Lesbians of Sodom*, Meghan began regularly missing performances of *Psycho Beach Party*. She developed severe bronchial problems that we blamed on her chain-smoking. One time backstage, she coughed so forcibly she cracked a rib. She came down with pneumonia and was hospitalized. After that, she returned briefly to *Psycho Beach Party*, but finally gave her notice for the role, and Becky London's good friend Dea Lawrence took over as Chicklet's mother.

Though she'd left the cast of *Psycho Beach Party*, Meghan was still a part of Theater-in-Limbo and would appear in the new play I was working on.

This play came about when Kyle Renick, the artistic director of the WPA Theatre on West 23rd Street, expressed a desire to work with Ken and me. The three of us got together to discuss what sort of play I might write for his theater. What would be a fun classic movie genre for me to explore? While Ken and Kyle tossed around ideas, I suddenly thought of a gown that was hanging neglected in the back of my closet.

A year earlier, our wardrobe master at *Psycho Beach Party*, Bobby Locke, had created a gown for me to wear at an AIDS fundraiser, a drag ball held at the Waldorf called "Night of a Thousand Gowns." In many of my favorite movies, when the leading lady appears at a nightclub or ball, she wears a relatively simple white gown in contrast to the glittery costumes of the supporting cast and background players. Together, Bobby and I created a look inspired by the white crepe gown designed by Adrian for Katharine Hepburn in *The Philadelphia Story*. Long-sleeved with a gold waistband, military collar, and epaulettes, it made a striking impression at the ball.

I mentioned the gown to Kyle and Ken because it could be something Joan Crawford or Norma Shearer might've worn in an anti-Nazi melodrama such as *Escape* or *Above Suspicion*, a film genre I've always had a fondness for. Kyle also expressed his enthusiasm for those patriotic espionage thrillers, and by the time our chat concluded, we'd all agreed that I'd write a 1940s wartime suspense comedy/drama for Theater-in-Limbo to perform at the WPA Theatre. And one of the costumes was already made!

By our standards, *The Lady in Question* was a lavish production, with a grand staircase leading to a second level. This was the first of my plays intended to be performed in an actual theater, not on a shoestring budget in a club, and that was based on a film genre I sincerely loved. These melodramas often linked Nazism with a penchant for highbrow culture, particularly classical music and in this new production I played Gertrude Garnet, an egocentric internationally acclaimed concert pianist on tour in Bavaria in

1940 who comes to her senses and courageously involves herself in a plot to rescue an imprisoned actress, played by Meghan.

Gertrude Garnet became my favorite role to date. Toward the climax of the second act, Gertrude is being interrogated by the Nazi Baron. She drops her high-tone pretentions, returning to her earlier self as Barrel House Gertie, the kissing kitten of the keys, and gives as good as she gets.

BARON

Why should you be so loyal to your country? I thought you considered yourself a citizen of the world, Madame Gertrude Garnet (Gar-nay).

GERTRUDE

The name's Gertie Garnet (in the American pronunciation). And I'm a citizen of Brooklyn, New York.

BARON

This Brooklyn, it will soon be part of the Third Reich.

GERTRUDE

(With defiant pride) Brother, you may take the Maginot Line, but you'll never take the Canarsie Line.

The play was a hit at the WPA. Andy made a splash as Lotte, a maniacal young girl—the *New York Times* named him the scene stealer of the week, and he received a caricature by the legendary Al Hirschfeld. We finished our initial seven-week nonprofit engagement and then shut down to make plans for a commercial Off-Broadway transfer.

Meghan asked to meet with Ken and me at our apartment to discuss something of importance. I hadn't seen Meghan outside of the theater in quite a while. With the strong sunlight streaming through my living room window, I noticed for the first time that her dark brown curly hair—now tinted auburn—was noticeably thinner. An expert at hair and makeup, she had it pinned up in a way that disguised her hair loss. I also noticed a few tiny skin tags by her cheekbone. In a calm and measured tone, Meghan told us that she was determined to continue in her role for the Off-Broadway transfer of *The Lady in Question*, but she wanted to fill us in on the truth behind her health issues.

She had AIDS. Because she was a woman, the possibility hadn't occurred to us. It was clear that she wasn't prepared to reveal any details about how she was exposed to the virus. It was none of our business. She made us promise that we would keep her diagnosis a secret. She knew that any word of it would brand her unemployable and, in many circles, a pariah. We assured her that we'd tell no one.

A few months later, we began performances of *The Lady in Question* at the Orpheum Theatre. The show looked fantastic on the large stage, and it was exciting to be able to play to a balcony for the first time. I'd been performing to an imaginary balcony for years, so I was prepared. The reviews came out on opening night while we were celebrating with a party at the neighborhood restaurant Spaghetteria. The *New York Times* review by Frank Rich was read aloud, and it was the best review any show of mine has ever received. It cited Meghan as a standout and said a comic high point was her slapstick ascent up the staircase. I remember feeling so happy for her and yet also painfully aware that this would most likely be her last play.

The next performance after a lauded and successful opening night is always special. The audience is excited because the hunch they had when they bought tickets in advance was proven to be correct. The actors are relieved that the pressure of critics' previews and opening night is behind them and are ready to give their best.

Meghan arrived at the theater out of breath, her face coated in perspiration. Panting, she told Ken and me that she had a temperature of 104. Her understudy, Judith Hansen, had just been put on contract and hadn't had an opportunity to rehearse the role. We felt our only recourse was to cancel the performance. Meghan would have none of it and grew angry when Ken insisted that he couldn't allow her to perform. While all this was happening, the rest of the cast were gathered in the greenroom.

Later, Julie told me that was the moment everyone in the company at last realized the truth of Meghan's illness. Bobby already knew. During Meghan's most recent hospitalization with pneumonia, he had stopped by for a visit and found her asleep. He saw the medication bottles on the tray beside her bed and recognized them as AIDS medications. It speaks well of Bobby that he never divulged that knowledge.

Meghan refused to capitulate to common sense and the show went on. It was excruciating watching her perspire under heavy gowns and furs but still give a highly energized performance. The big slapstick scene that Frank Rich mentioned in his review came in the second act. Meghan's character, Raina, a desperately ill actress, has been rescued from a Nazi prison and is hidden in a catacomb beneath the Nazi Baron's schloss. My character must divert the Nazis while Raina climbs out of her wheelchair and drags herself up the steep staircase so she can hide in one of the upper rooms. The audience, unaware of the real actress's suffering, was laughing uproariously as Meghan-as-Raina repeatedly fell down the stairs and pulled herself up again on to the banister.

During her long ascent, I had a constant stream of dialogue as my character, Gertrude, madly invented a story to divert the Nazis' attention. Distracted by concern for Meghan, I began rushing my lines. I looked upstage and she shot me a fierce glare that made it clear she thought I was wrecking the timing of her bit. I managed to slow down, thinking that surely she would at least cut her final somersault. She didn't, and her surprise athletic exit resulted in a huge round of applause. When the play was over, Ken had a cab waiting outside the theater. He bundled up Meghan, still in her stage makeup, and whisked her uptown to the hospital.

Judith took over her role until Meghan recovered from her bout of pneumonia and was able to return to the show. The production did well for the first few months, but then the box office began to dwindle. The play lacked a bold title like *Vampire Lesbians of Sodom* to help in drawing an audience. The weekly expenses were high, and *The Lady in Question* closed after six frustrating months.

After Meghan left the show, her health dramatically worsened as she was subjected to every opportunistic disease. She grew emaciated and disfigured by large purple Kaposi's sarcoma lesions. Still, she had the quixotic vision of working again.

Ken and I were making plans for a Los Angeles production of *Vampire Lesbians of Sodom* with Julie returning to play the roles she'd originated at the Limbo Lounge and that Meghan had played Off-Broadway. Meghan insisted we have lunch near her apartment in the West Village. She sat before me, bones protruding from her shoulders and a large KS lesion under her eye. What did she see in the mirror that allowed her to insist that Ken and I take her to Los Angeles with the production? She asked passionately, "If you and Ken won't hire me, who will?" I said something to the effect that her immediate goal should be to get stronger. We didn't have to make any decision at this time. One had to salute this woman of great character with her actor's ego intact and her noble, mad refusal to face reality.

During her final lengthy hospitalization, she was systematically robbed of every vestige of vanity. She lost the power of speech. I held her hand and attempted to say something comforting, but who was I fooling? "How fortunate that you're a great actress who can express so much with just her face." Her younger sister, Maura, was almost always at her bedside.

I arrived one afternoon, and Meghan was alone in the room, asleep. She was totally bald. The nurse told me that Meghan was suffering from a swelling of her brain that triggered a torturously painful headache. They'd given her a drug to ease the pain, but the drug also caused all her hair to fall out. Was she to be spared nothing? Couldn't she greet Death with a full head of hair?

I left Meghan's hospital room and went directly to the midtown studio of my friend John Schneeman, a Broadway costume tailor. I filled him in on Meghan's latest catastrophe. I told him that I knew she had little time left but that I wanted to get an old-fashioned hatbox like the one my aunt used to have and to fill it with fun, stylish turbans and eighteenth-century mop caps. John put aside his work and we sprang into action.

I drew a sketch, and on the spot, he cut and constructed the hat. We spent a few hours creating five different varieties of head coverings. I found a round cardboard hatbox at an art supply store and filled it with pink tissue paper and artificial roses. I placed the hats among the flowers and sprinkled the entire thing with Chanel No. 5.

I headed back to the hospital the following day with my hatbox. Placing it on the bed, I put on a big show for Meghan and her sister, Maura, assuming the voice and mannerisms of a flighty 1930s gay milliner. The hospital room took on an entirely different character as the intoxicating scent of Chanel No. 5 wafted in the air. I sat back and watched the two sisters pick the hats out of the box. I loved hearing them laugh as they discovered each item.

Meghan, mute and skeletal, managed with her innate sense of fashion to adjust the hats in a piquant way. I never saw her again. She refused to have any more visitors. Later I was told that, consumed with anger, she turned her back to the wall and waited for death to come until, at last, it did.

Bobby's health rapidly declined over the next year as well. In the final weeks of his life, he moved back to his parents' home in New Jersey, where he died. Ken rented a car for a group of us to attend Bobby's funeral over an hour and a half from Manhattan.

Bobby was our rambunctious little brother. How could he be gone? Ken particularly felt the loss, as he and Bobby had been in an intense romantic relationship before we started our company. We all sat together in one row of the church. The minister began his sermon, and as he droned on with a variety of generic platitudes, it became obvious he knew nothing about Bobby. Toward the end of his sermon, he added, "But, and this is a big but . . ." Considering that Bobby was famous for his derriere, the minister talking about a "big but" released our tension and one could feel the pew shake with our suppressed cathartic laughter.

A Gift from a Star

The first Limbo play without either Meghan or Bobby was *Red Scare on Sunset* in 1991. Shortly after we opened, I received a letter from an audience member praising the production. He added at the end, "I was glad to see that the young man who usually removed his clothes in your shows was not in this production. His lack of acting talent was at odds with the rest of the cast." The writer of that letter couldn't have realized that in an ensemble, there are qualities besides talent that can make one indispensable. Bobby's irrepressible silliness kept us entertained backstage at times when we'd otherwise have been overwhelmed by tension or sadness. He was also the one to deflate any pomposity I may have been subject to. At times when I'd get rather grand, Bobby was always able to take me down a peg: "Oh, you're very important, aren't you?"

Red Scare on Sunset is set in Hollywood during the fifties, the era of the blacklist. Instead of writing about a leftist artist hounded out of her career, I chose to make the play a satirical right-wing nightmare. My character, a guileless Indiana-born and -raised movie star named Mary Dale, discovers to her horror that the director of her current film, her best girlfriend, her houseboy, and her husband are all part of a malevolent Communist takeover of Hollywood. Julie played Pat Pilford, a popular red-baiting radio star, who early in the play warns me that my husband, an artistically frustrated film actor, may be cheating on me with a left-wing Method actress. Pat lays it on the line: "Face it, girl. Your enemy isn't pussy. It's Stanislavsky."

One of the greatest of stage actresses, four-time Tony Award winner Zoe Caldwell, attended a performance of *Red Scare*. We shared a bit of a history. In 1968, when I was fourteen, I was taken to see her in *The Prime of Jean Brodie*. Aunt Lil and I were both overwhelmed by the play and her performance. A small woman, Zoe had the bigger-than-life nineteenth-century aura of a Bernhardt. Her physical presence and emotional intensity were spellbinding, and as with Sarah Bernhardt, her stylized movements evoked classical sculpture yet still seemed honest and human.

After the matinee, I went backstage. I'm quite sure that Aunt Lil wasn't with me. It's likely that she asked the stage doorman if I could meet Miss Caldwell and then remained outside. Miss Caldwell's dressing room door was open, and I found her alone at her dressing table. I looked young for my age, so her curiosity may have been piqued by this thin adolescent boy visiting her after her performance in a very adult play. She offered me a seat and took the time to ask me about myself. I told her that I wanted to be an actor. She tilted my chin to the light and said in her crepuscular theatrical voice, "Well, you have the face of an actor . . . but, of course, that means nothing."

At the end of my audience with her, she grasped my hands. "Whenever I'm in a play, you must promise to come back and see me."

I vowed I would but never did. Mounting adolescent insecurity prevented me from solidifying that relationship. Yet I dreamed that one day she'd see me onstage and think that I was worthy of her early interest.

In 1991, I was performing in *Red Scare on Sunset* at the WPA Theatre. I was corresponding with a college directing student named Matt and had shared with him my Zoe Caldwell story. That semester, Zoe taught a master class at his university and attended his student production of one of my plays. "Matt," I said, "you've gotta give me her address." I wrote to her how kind she'd been when I visited her backstage after *Jean Brodie* and what it would mean to me to have her see *Red Scare on Sunset*.

A few weeks later, I was sitting in my kitchen when the phone rang. I picked it up and heard that unmistakable voice. "Charles Busch? This is Zoe Caldwell." I nearly dropped the receiver. She cut to the chase. "I received your letter. I'm coming to see your play, but I won't tell you when."

It was a Friday night performance. We'd been having extremely receptive audiences but this one was deadly, with few laughs and little energy coming from the audience. At thirty-seven, I believed that the answer to a quiet house was to do everything in your power to seduce them—to be more energized and more inventive. At times, this desperate tomfoolery would pay off. That night I did everything but stick a cucumber up my rectum.

I was trooping dispiritedly back to the dressing room when our house manager caught up with me. "There's a Zoe Caldwell here to see you." Oh my God, why, why, why did she have to come on this of all nights? Suddenly, she appeared: more petite than I remembered and dressed all in black; black slacks, black turtleneck sweater. There was that vulpine face with its piercing eyes heavily circled with black kohl.

She spoke no pleasantries but cupped my face in her hands. "You are so beautiful. So beautiful . . . but you were pushing tonight." Her eyes blazing, her rich tomb-like whisper tore into me. "You were mugging, and overacting, pandering to the audience and underlining every laugh. I don't want to *ever* see you do that again. You're better than that. Do you hear me? You're better than that."

She mocked me with a campy buck and wing dance step to illustrate my hammy excessive performance. I didn't defend myself. I made no excuses and absorbed every word. When she'd finished speaking, I awkwardly thanked her for coming and asked if we'd ever see *her* onstage again. Her face flushed and her eyes widened and darkened. In something between a hiss and a hushed cry she whispered, "I shall never act again!"—and in a flash she was down the stairs and gone. Little did either of us know that only a few years later she would return to the stage and have one of her greatest triumphs, winning yet another Tony Award as Maria Callas in Terrence McNally's play *Master Class*.

I wasn't the least bit critical of her behavior backstage that night. Disappointed, yes—of course I was hoping she'd think I was perfection—but I appreciated that she took the time to straighten me out. She didn't have to come backstage at all. And once she did, it would've been far easier just to say, "I enjoyed the show. Have a good rest of the run."

I can't say that there was an overnight shift in my acting style, but Zoe Caldwell's fierce critique began a thirty-year journey toward simplifying and playing truthfully, a journey I'm still on today. Many years later, attending a tribute to her friend Audra McDonald at the New Dramatist's luncheon, I found Miss Caldwell sitting at her table, rigid and diminished from Parkinson's disease. I knelt and kissed her hands and was able to thank her for the gift she had given me.

It's Love I'm After

1989. During the four years after my breakthrough with *Vampire Lesbians*, I was so busy working and enjoying the high of earning my living in the theater that I never thought for a moment about wanting a boyfriend. None of us in Theater-in-Limbo were in any relationship beside the ones that we had with each other. Now that the novelty of having an actual career was wearing off, when I wasn't at the theater I'd sink into a dank feeling of loneliness.

I was friends with the gay film historian Vito Russo, author of the seminal book on LGBT imagery in the movies, *The Celluloid Closet*. He'd acquired a print of the 1950 women's prison film *Caged* and was planning to screen it in his apartment. Vito had the best parties, full of writers, actors, directors, artists, and activists, many of them highly attractive.

I went to Vito's screening with the single-minded intention of finding a boyfriend. My previous two dates had been fiascos. I was still too new to the celebrity game to distinguish between a fella wanting to be friends with a celebrity and one actually having the urge to jump into the feathers with me. Truth be told, I still can't always tell the difference, and it can prove embarrassing.

Well, I left Vito's party with two business cards, went on dates with both gentlemen, and chose Eric Myers. Eric was an established film unit publicist the same age as me. He was easy to talk to, highly intelligent, and handsome in a classic 1930s Franchot Tone/Douglass Montgomery/Richard Cromwell/Phillips Holmes sort of way. In fact, Eric almost always dresses in vintage clothes. The night we met, before the feature, Vito played a clip from a Universal B-movie musical and Eric immediately identified the energetic blonde star as actress/dancer/recording artist Jane Frazee. I was duly impressed and strangely turned on.

Eric was passionately interested in film, theater, opera, and architecture. An expert on art deco design, he'd co-written two coffee-table books on the history of art direction in the movies. His memory for film history facts is phenomenal . . . well, pre-1946.

Shortly after we met, Eric and I attended a party where we encountered Stephen Sondheim—a first for both of us. Mister S., seeking a worthy trivia opponent, looked me in the eye. "You must know everything there is about the movies," he said. He began firing questions at me, rat-a-tat-tat. I believe the first was, "Give me two films starring Paulette Goddard and directed by Mitchell Leisen." I was so intimidated that if he'd asked, "Who played Dorothy in *The Wizard of Oz*?" I would've stuttered, "Um . . . uh . . . Deanna Durbin?" Eric had no such problem. Sharp as a fresh Gillette blade, he blurted without a moment's hesitation, "*Hold Back the Dawn* and *Kitty*." Sondheim fired back at me, "Not fair! You're cheating!" He was determined to stump me with two more arcane questions, and each time I blanked, Eric came in for the save. How can you not fall for a guy like that?

Eric fit in well with the members of my troupe, and he was the first boyfriend that I integrated into my family. Aunt Lil, Aunt Belle, and my two sisters all took to him immediately. Eric even joined me on a rare trip to West Palm Beach to visit my father, where they bonded over their mutual love of opera. Eric was a gold mine with his knowledge of the complete discography of Croatian soprano Zinka Milanov. I'm grateful that Eric encouraged me to maintain a relationship with Daddy up until my father's death in 2002.

When I met Eric's family in California, they embraced me wholeheartedly as well. His father, Julian Myers, regarded as the dean of Hollywood publicists, was an endless font of anecdotes from a long career in the film business. While working at 20th Century Fox, he'd been responsible for a celebrated publicity stunt. For the 1950 premiere of *All About Eve* at Grauman's Chinese Theatre, Julian convinced the Hollywood Roosevelt Hotel across the street to block out all the neon letters on their rooftop sign except for the EVE in Roosevelt.

Eric and I made the decision early on never to live together. Each of us had recently acquired co-op apartments that we loved and weren't inclined to share. His apartment was austere in its streamlined art deco beauty. After Aunt Belle had dinner there, she muttered, "That's the most goddam depressing apartment I've ever seen." What she deemed depressing I found minimalist and sleek. Eric's fascination with art deco architecture led him to visit cities such as Tulsa and Kansas City that hadn't been transformed by urban renewal projects in the sixties, leaving their 1920s buildings still intact. I'd balk at joining him on those trips, and yet every time he returned, I'd regret it after hearing about the old vaudeville theaters he'd toured and his visits to the childhood homes of Louise Brooks and Vivian Vance.

He had so many interests that I genuinely wanted to know what he was up to every day. For a long time, he tried to get me to travel with him on an extended tour of Eastern Europe to explore our Jewish roots. "Charles, we could visit Poland. We could visit Auschwitz." I looked at him askance. "Auschwitz? I couldn't emotionally handle the last revival of *Follies*."

In time, Eric became fed up with his publicity career. Although the films he worked on allowed him to spend months in locations such as Tokyo, Paris, and Prague, the role of a unit publicist is a thankless one. As liaison between the film stars and the press, he was the whipping boy when the A-list talent, feeling out of sorts, capriciously refused to speak to the film crew from *Entertainment Tonight*. Eric transformed his life when he began a new and successful career as a literary agent.

We lasted twenty-three years as romantic partners. Gradually, we grew apart, and the eccentricities that we'd once found endearing in each other began fraying our nerves. Instead of seeing each other five nights a week, it became three, and then just weekends. It seemed as if we were nicer to our friends than we were with each other and so we chose to continue as friends. It was a simple breakup as breakups go, with me returning to Eric the few items he kept in my apartment—his sleep mask, his mouth guard, his earplugs, and a small cache of Ambien.

A few years before, my friend Barry Kohn invited us to a Passover Seder at his apartment on Central Park South. I'd been to enough Seders. While Aunt Lil rejected all traces of organized religion, Aunt Belle clung to the barest minimum of observance. At one of her last Seders, everything had gone wrong, from a soapy sponge falling onto the sweet potatoes to Eric sitting on a rickety antique dining chair and having it collapse beneath him. The only scripture read at Aunt Belle's Seders was the Four Questions, among them, "Why is this night different from all other nights?" That night, Aunt Belle took a final swig directly from the bottle of Manischewitz Concord Grape before barking, "I'll give you a fifth question—when will this fucking night ever end?" I had no desire to attend another Seder, particularly one that would be a real Seder and not a travesty like those of Aunt Belle's, which at least had the virtue of being shorter.

At a traditional Seder, everyone at the dining table reads a passage from the Haggadah, which tells the story of the first Passover. You go round and round until the whole thing is read. In an Orthodox household, it can go on for hours. Barry and his wife, Brina, use an abbreviated version, but it still seemed a chore.

Barry is a retired allergist and the inspiration for my play *The Tale of the Allergist's Wife*. He'd recently become friends with Angela Lansbury, who'd just returned to the stage after an over twenty-year absence. She was doing a Terrence McNally play called *Deuce* co-starring another great lady of the American theater, Marian Seldes. I suggested to Barry on the phone, "You should invite Angela and Marian." I was half-joking, but Barry replied, "That's a great idea. I will."

It was a small group: Barry; Brina; Angela; Marian; Eric; the actress Cherry Jones and her partner at the time, future Emmy Award winner Sarah Paulson; and me. Angela confessed that this was the first Seder she'd ever attended. We all sat at the table and began reading from the ancient text that told of the Israelites' escape from slavery in Egypt.

Suddenly, it hit me that I was *acting* with Angela Lansbury, Marian Seldes, Cherry Jones, and Sarah Paulson. I felt pressure to give a performance up to the standards of this estimable company. It was spellbinding hearing them read with their distinctive voices, particularly Angela with her bright Anglo-American accent and Marian in her low cathedral-like whisper. You would've thought they were co-narrating a program on the History Channel. When it came around to me, I made every effort to enunciate perfectly and read with emotional expressivity. I thought I was doing very well.

When I finished, Eric hissed in my ear, "I can't believe you're reading the Haggadah as Joan Crawford." I whispered back defensively, "I'm giving it vocal color." As each guest took their turn after me, I was competitively flipping through the small book searching for my next passage and thinking, *My part stinks. I can't do anything with this*. When at last it was my turn again, I employed every bit of vocal virtuosity to make something of my dreary lines. This time Eric whispered, "I never knew the word 'Jew' had so many syllables."

Except for when I pursued a relationship with Eric, I've never made the search for a romantic partner a priority. My great love has been my creative life. Not my professional life—my creative life. Acting, performing, but mostly writing. At times it's been a cruel love, when the exposure of the limitations of my talent has left me feeling frustrated and even, at the risk of sounding melodramatic, betrayed. Fortunately, my great love has always managed to return in some fashion and hopefully will be with me until the end.

Leaving Oz

1998. Once every ten years, with little effort on my part, I get an offer to appear on a TV show. I played a role on the HBO prison series *Oz* due to an idle remark I made to my late, deeply missed manager Jeff Melnick. "Do you ever watch *Oz*? It must be cool to be on an edgy series like that." I've never pursued an acting career outside of my own plays, but Jeff wouldn't accept that. He once phoned the Royal Shakespeare Company in London to suggest they bring me over to play Juliet. (PS: They didn't jump.)

After my comment about *Oz*, Jeff phoned Georgianne Walken, the show's casting director, who, unlike the Royal Shakespeare Company, thought having me on was a dynamite idea. She contacted *Oz*'s creator and producer, Tom Fontana, who, in the small-world department, had known Meghan and had seen us in *Vampire Lesbians of Sodom*.

When we got together at his office, only a few blocks from my apartment, Tom asked what sort of character I'd like to play. I told him that while

I adored the sordid realism of the show, I was just about the least *street* person who ever lived. Perhaps I could be someone deceptively vulnerable and refined but with the cold heart of a merciless killer. I submitted as examples Gene Tierney in *Leave Her to Heaven*, Joan Fontaine in *Born to be Bad*, and Olivia de Havilland as her own evil twin in *The Dark Mirror*. Worried that his frame of reference might lean more toward the films of Scorsese and Tarantino, I was relieved when he knew exactly what I meant.

A few months later I received a call inquiring about my availability to play the role of Nat Ginzburg. The character was as I'd described. Nat was a well-educated, articulate drag performer who in a fit of pique threw acid in another queen's face. Once in prison, he was enlisted to seduce an elderly retired mob boss and smother him with a pillow. That bit of mischief landed him on death row.

My first few episodes went so well that I was brought back for another season. As my second season progressed, the other prisoners on death row were executed, one by one. I've neglected to tell you that Nat Ginzburg also had full-blown AIDS. Between his advancing illness and being condemned to death by a judge and jury, my prospects of returning for a third season didn't look promising. In each successive episode, it was evident from the way the makeup man was applying more and more dark shading under my eyes that my days on *Oz* were numbered. If I was to be written out, I was hoping to leave in an exciting, memorable way, by lethal injection or, better yet, the gas chamber. I wrote a note to Tom Fontana.

Dear Tom,

I'm sure you have it all worked out, and I'm sure it's marvelous, but if you haven't, wouldn't it be interesting if I demand to go to my execution dressed as Susan Hayward in I Want to Live!*? Rita [Oscar winner Rita*

Moreno, an Oz series regular who played the nun Sister Pete] could come
to my cell and help me paint my nails and then, with great defiance, I
walk the last mile to my execution in the gas chamber. What do you think?

Charles

A few days later, I ran into Tom on the set. He said, "I got your letter.
Some interesting things there. Let me think about it."

The script for my final episode arrived. Yes, I got dressed up as Susan
Hayward and yes, Rita Moreno as Sister Pete helped me paint my nails, but
then it veered away from my suggested scenario. As Sister Pete is applying
his nail polish, Nat grows faint. Sister Pete gently advises him to lie down on
his cot; she'll finish his nails in the morning. The morning comes—but when
the warden, the priest, the guards, and Sister Pete arrive at the cell to escort
Nat to the gas chamber, they discover that he has eluded execution by dying
in his sleep. Died in his *sleep*? That wasn't the way it was supposed to be. No
defiance? No final middle finger to the world that spurned him?

The day arrived for what I'd hoped would be my epic farewell to *Oz*. Rita
and I played our nail polishing scene. It was filled with great dramatic opportunities for Sister Pete, and EGOT winner Rita Moreno certainly made the
most of them. We broke for lunch. When we returned to the set, I lay down
and played dead. The camera slowly panned over my serenely composed visage and then moved to the group of prison personnel.

We did the first take and the assistant director yelled, "His eyes were
twitching." I had no idea. I apologized to everyone assembled. Before we did
a second take, Rita came over to the bed and whispered, "Honey, here's a trick
I learned during my early days at Fox. Before they call 'action,' close your eyes
tight for five seconds, then relax them. Your eyelids won't twitch." I gratefully
took her advice. Take Two and, again, the assistant director shouted, "What

are we gonna do? His eyes were twitching." I was getting anxious. Things had to move quickly on *Oz.*

This time my friend BD Wong, who played the priest Father Ray Mukada, came over to my cot and whispered, "Here's a trick I once learned. Open your eyes wide for five seconds before they call 'action,' then close them. Good luck." We did a third and an unheard-of fourth take and my eyelids were now blinking out of control like oranges and lemons in a slot machine jackpot. The director of photography looked ready to put me out of my misery for real. The last shot of Nat Ginzburg ended up being a quick pan over his dead face, the focus swiftly switching to linger on the mournful mugs of Sister Pete, Father Ray, the warden, and the guards.

After my role had wrapped, I came up with yet another suggestion for the show. I mailed a quick missive to Mr. Fontana: What if Nat Ginzburg had a twin sister named Natasha, played by me of course, who under another name seeks revenge by infiltrating the walls of Oz by becoming a prison guard? Tom's a lovely but terribly busy man, so there could be any number of reasons why he never had a chance to get back to me.

Winter Meeting

1995. The nineties brought an important new person into my life: a young man named Carl Andruskevich. I'd written the book to a 1940s musical revue, *Swingtime Canteen*, which Ken directed. It was playing Off-Broadway and starred two-time Tony nominee Alison Fraser (for *Romance/Romance* and *The Secret Garden*). The production needed a new wardrobe person, and two candidates were up for the position: one, an experienced but rather dour older woman, and the other Carl, a twenty-four-year-old aspiring actor with no wardrobe experience but who was a major Alison Fraser fan. The choice was Alison's, and with the imperious authority of a Messalina, she came to a decision. "I'll take the boy."

Six months into the run, Alison left to do another show, and I assumed her role of Marian Ames. Carl was surprised that I showed up for the photo call alone, with a ten-year-old brassiere and no self-important airs. I was taken with how expertly he took care of me. He told me that he'd been living in Chicago, where he'd played his first drag role, to which I remarked, "With that face, honey, you must've been gorgeous."

We hit it off. Not much later, I offered to pay him to wallpaper the small entrance foyer in my apartment. The paper I chose was a complex Chinese toile, and the space had a tricky archway. I gave him the rolls of paper, and then left for the day with a jaunty "Bye, kid!" When I returned, he had done a perfect, meticulous job. Unlike me, Carl is incapable of giving less than 100 percent of himself to any assignment.

I did have to straighten the child out on a couple things. One time he showed up at my place bemoaning the humiliation of being a wardrobe person and having to wash out all the actresses' sweaty panties. "I've really paid my dues," the twenty-four-year-old groaned. This statement brought out the wise Yoda-like mentor in me. "Listen, you haven't paid your dues until you've worked as a stripper and a whore. When you've earned your rent lying on your back, then come and tell me you've paid your dues, kid." There are times when one must provide the young with a sense of perspective.

Carl began as my dresser but he evolved into my close friend, confidant, and surrogate son. A turning point in our relationship came when I was asked to perform at Manhattan Theatre Club's annual gala. I was invited because a musical I was writing, *The Green Heart*, was in development with them. The gala was a major event, held in the largest ballroom at the New York Hilton on Sixth Avenue, and on the bill were performers from almost all the hit Broadway shows of the season. I was to perform a solo comic monologue with musical underscoring in which I played an emotionally ravaged Manhattan housewife. It was a character who later became the starting point for my play *The Tale of the Allergist's Wife*.

I'd performed the piece dozens of times and was confident that it would make a fine impression. I brought Carl with me to the tech rehearsal as moral support. After seeing me run through the piece, the Manhattan Theatre Club's artistic director, Lynne Meadow, suggested that I shorten the piece by editing out a few lines from the middle. I thought it unnecessary to cut what amounted to at most forty-five seconds, but wanting to please this important lady, against my better judgment, I agreed.

As soon as we were alone, Carl was adamant that I not cut the lines. "You've done this piece so many times. You know it by heart. If you cut those lines, under the pressure of the moment, you'll get mixed up and blank. You must tell Lynne that you cannot make that edit." He was so right. I did exactly what he said. Lynne came around, since it had only been a suggestion on her part, and I was a big hit at the gala, contributing to my ongoing relationship with the Manhattan Theatre Club. It also cemented my faith in Carl as a coolheaded voice of reason.

Oh, I should add that Carl also spoke to the tech director of the event and explained that since I'd be wearing a red sequined gown, it might be best to light me with a more flattering amber gel. After several years of relying on his opinion and judgment, I made him the director of my plays. I needed someone to fill the role because Ken was growing increasingly frustrated with the life of an itinerant theater director.

Ken had a full directing career away from Theater-in-Limbo, which included two more plays at the WPA, two shows at Joseph Papp's Public Theater, and the first revival of Mart Crowley's *The Boys in the Band* in London and New York. Weary of the peripatetic life of a freelance director, he received his PhD and is now enjoying a fulfilling career as the chairman of the theater department at a major East Coast university.

Carl has developed into a fine director, with a visual and dramatic flair and great sensitivity to actors. He also knows me so well that he is an excellent dramaturg for my work. He'll ask exactly the right questions to fuel my imagination. Together we've worked on eleven new plays, numerous revivals of my old work, and several film projects.

Not long after we met, Carl began accompanying me to various theatrical social events. At one Broadway opening, I introduced him to Valerie Harper. "Valerie, this is my friend Carl Andruskevich." Valerie replied, "Wonderful meeting you, Carl Andrew." The name was a mouthful. We began compiling a list of possible new last names, including variations of his first and middle names. Carl Gregory, Gregory Carl. We jotted down a shortened version of his mother's maiden name, Zanichkowsy: "Zanuck." It didn't seem quite right.

I was asked to emcee a fundraiser for Juilliard's troupe, The Acting Company. Carl accompanied me, and we were to be seated at a table along with Carol Burnett and the costume designers Bob Mackie, Ray Aghayan, and Florence Klotz. When we arrived at the table, we saw that place cards had been set. Carl looked around for his and was confused when he found one with the name "Carl Andress." It had been a whim of mine when I sent in our names to the benefit committee. I asked him, "So, whaddya think? Does it do anything for you?" He took about three seconds to nod. "Carl Andruskevich is dead. Carl Andress lives."

The Lyp and I

How do I respond to being referred to as a "drag queen"? I'm of an older generation of performer who bristled at those words. Actually, "bristle" is too mild a description. We became downright unhinged. When that term was applied to us, we felt we weren't being taken seriously as writers and actors. In days of yore, "drag queen" implied someone dressing up for the outrageous fun of it, possibly having a drug and alcohol problem and a distinct lack of professional behavior. We came up with all sorts of alternative terms to assist the press in defining us. It may have been Jim Bailey who coined the phrase "gender illusionist."

Perhaps it was disingenuous of me and my colleagues to refuse to acknowledge the profundity of what creating art through a female persona truly meant to us. We demanded instead that it be stated without any ambiguity that dressing up in women's clothes was strictly a professional choice. I read old interviews I gave where the subject came up and I'm mortified by my glib, evasive responses. "I've got great legs and I know what to do with them." I wanted to be regarded as an actor who just happened to specialize in playing female roles, not as a psychological case of alter ego possession à la Dr. Jekyll and Sister Hyde.

In the early nineties, I had a truly humiliating experience on the daytime talk show *Donahue*. I was asked to be part of an episode exploring "drag as an art form." It was during the Off-Broadway run of *The Lady in Question*, and we hoped this national TV exposure would boost the box office. *Donahue* was considered the classiest show of its ilk. The producers had assembled an impressive panel of performers including John "Lypsinka" Epperson, Ira Siff of the all-male Gran Scena Opera, and members of the drag ballet troupe Les Ballets Trockadero de Monte Carlo in addition to Arnie Kolodner and me.

Arnie and I performed a short scene from the play. Our affectionate 1940s movie parody dialogue didn't have the slightest edge of biting satire or sexual innuendo and we received steady laughs and strong applause from the ladies in the studio audience. The congenial host, Phil Donahue, asked a few of the women if they enjoyed us and each of their comments was highly flattering.

Then he felt compelled to turn the discussion around. "Who here is troubled by this?" When the microphone was shoved into the faces of several affronted females, we got tight-lipped variations of "I don't understand why they feel the need to express themselves this way." The worst was a shrugged "Well, as long as they're not hurting anyone." Any illusions I may have harbored that I was a respected figure in the theater were dashed.

Today, the performers who compete on *RuPaul's Drag Race* refer to themselves as drag queens with pride. They've extended the entire concept of drag, which can now embrace trans men competing as drag queens and performers sharing their journey toward self-acceptance as trans women. National exposure from RuPaul's hit TV series has given many of these talented performers great opportunities and they've run with them, appearing in Las Vegas, in stadiums around the world, and on Broadway.

I belong to two worlds: the theater and the drag community, and I'm proud that both claim me as their own. Embodying a female character has been a major part of my creative life. I will not dismiss or belittle it. And I can't easily separate the lady from the gentleman. The lady is not simply an adopted theatrical persona. Although I've taken great pains to create a feminine illusion on stage and film and I enjoy all that this entails, the paraphernalia of drag is not necessary for my own belief in the women I play. I've performed feminine roles on radio and in staged readings without costumes. It's not about visual transformation. To go from male to female is as effortless for me as walking from one room to another.

In 1997, John Epperson and I were asked to participate in the HBO documentary *Dragtime*. We would be profiled along with several other notable drag performers. The schedule called for John and me to be interviewed on camera together in our male attire, then return in the evening in full drag to perform a duet in a club setting.

John and I showed up for our joint interview. No wigs, no makeup. We waited patiently while they set up the lights and camera. Our innate shyness took over. Although we were the center of the activity, we were mostly ignored. The shoot was over in less than an hour. As we were leaving, I turned to John. "They may think we're pushovers now, but it's gonna be very different when we return tonight."

It certainly was. Those recessive mild-mannered guys were replaced by a pair of glamorous "stars" exuding confidence and steely professionalism. Between the wigs and heels, we were each at least two feet taller. We had strong opinions on which light was more flattering. We restaged our musical number. We knew best how to present ourselves. The producers, director, and crew found all our notes and changes to be 100 percent on target and treated us with deference and respect. It took me a few more years to learn how to be that kind of woman while dressed as a man.

Everything Leads Me to Thee

1999. Aunt Lil, beset with myriad physical problems, was at New York University Hospital. She'd fallen in her apartment attempting to walk across the room unaided. Her prognosis rapidly descended from bad to gravely serious. I arrived at the hospital and found Aunt Lil surprisingly energized. Lying propped up in her hospital bed, she was downright loquacious. Then I realized that she was in the 1930s and believed that I was her dead brother, my namesake. I decided it would be foolish to try to steer her back to the present as she seemed perfectly comfortable being with Charlie in the thirties.

Pointing, she asked me to get a shawl out of the dresser drawer. A slight problem was that there was no dresser. The only thing I could think of was to mime opening a drawer. I placed the imaginary knobs far apart and even gave a realistic yank. Evidently, only in the movies can you join someone in her hallucination. Aunt Lil snapped, "What are you doing?"

Aunt Lil was the sanest and steadiest person in the world. I couldn't bear seeing her in this overmedicated delusional state. I kissed the top of her head and rushed out of the room, leaving her with her ghosts and the private nurse.

That night around 9:00 PM the hospital called me at home. A woman said, "Mr. Busch, your mother is on life support. I'd suggest you get here quickly." Aunt Lil legally adopted me during my adolescence, mainly for tax purposes. Still, it felt odd hearing her referred to as my parent. It shouldn't have. In almost every way, she was both my mother and father.

I phoned my sisters and raced to the hospital. I was the first to arrive. One of my favorites in Aunt Lil's repertoire of anecdotes was the story of being with her father for the moment of his death. She held him and watched him leave. It was a cherished memory. For the past eight years of Aunt Lil's decline, I'd counted on this conclusion for the two of us.

Entering the hospital room, I was confronted with the sight of a respirator tube in her mouth, which caused her nose to be pushed to one side. A machine to her right displayed the regular peaks of her heartbeat. I climbed onto the bed, snuggling next to her, and buried my face in her long beautiful grey hair. I murmured in her ear over and over, "Thank you. Thank you. Thank you. Thank you." Was she far away? Could she hear me? I had so much to thank her for. She had saved my life. She made everything possible. As a teenager, I'd read that Marie Antoinette and her intimate friend Count Axel Fersen exchanged rings with the inscription "Everything leads me to thee." Everything leads me to Aunt Lil.

It wasn't completely one-sided. From my earliest childhood, she was captivated by my creativity. She derived great joy helping me bring my ideas to fruition. As a child, I carried her with me into a fantastic world she would otherwise never have known. She had been a nurse, a teacher, a wife. I allowed her to be an artist. It was a forty-five-year collaboration that benefited us both.

I once told her, "You make a secret out of what you eat for breakfast." How often had she told me, "There are things I don't discuss, even with myself." I'd always wondered why Aunt Lil left the nursing profession while still in her twenties. To the end of her long life, she identified as a nurse. In fact, her nursing skills were the only thing Aunt Lil would allow herself to take pure pride in.

A few weeks earlier, Aunt Belle, in a resentful mood and fed up with her sister's elderly crankiness, had revealed Aunt Lil's deepest-kept secret. In the

1930s, nurses often took multiple shifts back to back, sometimes working a forty-eight-hour stretch. Desperate to earn more money at the height of the Depression, Aunt Lil had overextended herself. She placed a heating pad on a patient, left the room, and fell asleep from exhaustion. The patient was severely burned and Aunt Lillian's career as a nurse was over. How many times had she lectured me on the importance of anticipating someone else's needs? The guilt and shame must have haunted her. "There are things I don't discuss, even with myself."

I lay quietly by her side. A tap on my shoulder. It was the nurse. "Your mother is gone." "What?" "She passed." It couldn't be. Her chest was still moving. I looked at the machine and saw that the line was flat. It was only the respirator making her chest rise and fall. I had missed the instant when life left her. Goddam modern medicine. Goddam modern world.

I knew my sisters would be there shortly. I instructed the nurse to remove that obscene respirator tube. She told me to step outside until it was done.

Although Aunt Lil had abdicated her position as family matriarch several years earlier as she retreated into her final role of ancient invalid, I'd felt that as long as Aunt Lil was on this earth, nothing could harm us. She'd often warn Margaret and Betsy and me, "Don't think of me as Mrs. God." How could we not when she had orchestrated our lives with such unerring perception?

When I returned to the room, Aunt Lil looked infinitely more attractive without the tubes and paraphernalia. Her nose was still somewhat pushed to the side. As if I were molding clay, I gently manipulated her nose back to normal. Her long hair was matted and caught under her back. I couldn't find a hairbrush, but I pulled her hair forward and draped it romantically about her shoulders. She would have appreciated the care I took.

My two sisters arrived. I stepped aside and remained in the back of the hospital room, offstage, allowing them their time with her. Each of us had our own unique relationship with this complex woman.

Betsy commented, "It's not really her, is it?" I don't know why her remark bothered me. Perhaps it had something to do with my own vanity in having attempted to make Aunt Lil presentable before their arrival. I didn't want to intrude on my sister's emotions but I was compelled to disagree. I wasn't ready to let go. "It's her skin. It's her hair. It's still her."

Tales of the Allergist's Wife

2000. Unlike most playwrights, I never went around saying to myself, "I've got to get a play on Broadway." Off-Broadway was my province, and I was content there. For one thing, nearly every play I'd written was intended as a vehicle for me to play a female character. Perhaps it was shortsighted, but I accepted that my brand of drag theatrical parody wasn't Broadway material.

One of my rare "not starring Charles Busch" assignments was writing the book to a musical called *The Green Heart* that was produced by Manhattan Theatre Club. Ken was directing, but we found ourselves in an unfamiliar environment where we didn't call all the shots. Rehearsals and previews were highly charged and full of big personalities with conflicting visions of what was needed to put the show over.

Perhaps due to my early training with Aunt Lil in the art of observing the greater picture, I've become something of a strategist in creating professional alliances. In this case, I established a relationship with Lynne Meadow, the artistic director of MTC. What clinched that friendship was an early meeting of the creative team, where Lynne, an imposing six-foot woman, expressed a characteristically strong opinion. I'd only been around her a few weeks but felt so comfortable and easy in her presence, I laughed and, forgetting to self-edit, said, "Lynne, that's the dumbest idea I've ever heard." Dead silence in the room. I'll bet no one had said such a thing to Lynne Meadow in at least thirty-five years. At first poker-faced, Lynne began to giggle and then guffaw. Everyone took that as a cue to join in. Still laughing, she was forced to admit, "I guess it *was* a pretty stupid idea." On opening night when the mixed reviews came out, Lynne took me aside. "Charles, I'd like MTC to be your artistic home and I want to produce and direct your next play."

It didn't take a genius to figure out that the MTC audience leaned toward the conservative. Older and able to afford the much-in-demand subscription series, they preferred plays set in well-appointed Manhattan living rooms. Perhaps *Vampire Lesbians of Sodom: Part Two* would not be the wisest direction to go for this new venue. Several years before, I'd created a character named Miriam Passman, a culturally striving Manhattan housewife, in a ten-minute sketch for a solo show. I had performed that piece at a recent MTC gala. I'd long considered writing a full-length play about Miriam—here was my opportunity.

I worked on the play for about a year. For the first time, I explored the specific world in which I'd grown up—the urban Jewish upper middle class. Miriam Passman evolved into Marjorie Taub.

During this time, I attended an evening of one-act plays called *Death Defying Acts* starring Linda Lavin, which demonstrated to me that she was the perfect actress to play Marjorie. When Lynne Meadow read the script for *The Tale of the Allergist's Wife*, she loved it, had no cavils or quibbles, and wanted to schedule a reading as soon as possible. She asked who my ideal leading lady would be and Linda Lavin's name sprang from my lips. Fade out, fade in, Linda did the reading and, well, never have I seen an actor do a cold reading the way she did that day, with every color and nuance present. It was a fully realized serio-comic performance and a great one.

After the reading was over, Lynne and I bounded over to shower Linda with well-deserved hosannas. Like puppies we begged, "So, will you do the play?" Linda pursed her lips. "Hmmmm. I dunno. This is something I really have to ponder." She pondered for nine months, vacillating in her decision. Marjorie Taub was a demanding role with one raging aria after another. Linda, having just begun her romance with Steve Bakunus, who would shortly become her third husband, wasn't sure she wanted to work that hard.

I followed Linda to Los Angeles, where she was appearing in another play, to have lunch with her at Orso, and pursued her in New York to the bar at Joe Allen, trying to squeeze a commitment out of her. I wrote her shamelessly excessive love letters comparing her to Dante's Beatrice. I finally wore her down, and we went into production in 1999.

How lucky was I with this cast? If you've written a New York comedy about Upper West Side Jews, you can't do better than Tony Roberts. He has a relaxed comic style honed by his collaborations with Neil Simon and Woody Allen. We found a charismatic young actor, Anil Kumar, to play the otherworldly doorman. The role of Linda's dyspeptic elderly mother, Frieda, was difficult to cast. We saw a gallery of well-known character actresses. Accomplished as they were, they all came off a bit synthetic and too much like a musical comedy New York Jewish mother. Then in walked a fragile old woman none of us had heard of: Shirl Bernheim. She entered the rehearsal room slowly with the aid of a walker. She read the role perfectly, with an authenticity that took any bit of artificial sitcom out of the play.

Shirl was definitely not a cute little old lady. There was something dark and brooding underneath the pained wince of a smile, and you never quite knew how she'd respond to a simple "How are you today, Shirl?" You just might get "Why the hell are ya askin' me that for?" She was over eighty years old, still recovering from a broken hip, and there was concern that she might not have the stamina for an eight-show-a-week schedule in an emotionally taxing role.

MTC contacted Shirl's doctors who warily gave their consent. The next step was to have Shirl read with Linda, as their mother/daughter scenes were an essential element of the play. We brought them in. With a callback audition, there's always the worry that yesterday's miraculous discovery will be, on second viewing, a crushing disappointment. Shirl hobbled in on her walker, took one look at Linda seated in a folding chair at the worktable, and rolled her eyes. "Jesus Christ, this lady scares the crap out of me." They read the scenes and we were relieved to find that Shirl was every bit as marvelous the second time around. Linda was pleased that we'd found her a worthy stage opponent.

The final role to be cast was that of the mystery woman, Lee Green, who enters the Taubs' lives and seduces Marjorie and Ira into a ménage à trois. I envisioned the character as a somewhat dowdy older woman who's innately seductive not due to her beauty but because of her sexual confidence. (I saw the essential joke of the play as it being a sexual romp with three of the most unlikely middle-aged participants.)

A list of potential actresses was drawn up, none of whom seemed terribly exciting. My manager, Jeff Melnick, suggested Michele Lee. Michele was anything but dowdy, but her participation could be newsworthy. Among her other Broadway credits, Michele had received a Tony nomination for her starring role in the musical *Seesaw*, then settled into a fourteen-year run on the hit television series *Knots Landing*. She had recently starred in highly rated TV biopics of country singer Dottie West and *Valley of the Dolls* author Jacqueline Susann.

Michele was excited about doing the play and flew in from LA to meet with us. From that first meeting at MTC, Michele and I became buddies, and any earlier concept of mine for the role seemed shortsighted and unnecessary.

We were all delighted to have her join the production. Michele is the kind of dazzling bigger-than-life personality that is exceedingly rare in these careful, bland times. But there's also something soft and lovable about her. The combination is quite irresistible. Count me among those under her spell.

When It's Best for a Playwright
to Keep His Trap Shut

Linda and Michele were longtime friends, having both started out on Broadway in the early sixties and then enjoyed major television success in the seventies and eighties. It was delicious fun for me to watch them catch up on the first day of rehearsal.

> *Michele:*   *Linda, I was at both of your weddings.*
>
> *Linda:*   *You were at my wedding to Ron? I don't think so.*
>
> *Michele:*   *I was there, and at your next wedding.*
>
> *Linda:*   *Hmmm. Maybe you were. I've blocked it out. I was present at your wedding to Jimmy Farentino.*
>
> *Michele:*   *No, sweetie, you were at my second wedding, to Fred.*

Linda is a great actress. She has both a comedy technique as precise as a surgeon and an emotional depth that can be devastating, making it possible for her to play everything from *The Last of the Red Hot Lovers* to Mrs. Van

Daan in *The Diary of Anne Frank*. One doesn't have that ability to dive into chasms of emotion without being something of a complex personality offstage. One day Linda is a naughty, amiable companion with a gallant generosity of spirit and the next she's closed out the cash register, locked the door, and pulled down the front gate.

During a tech rehearsal one day, I was seated in the theater next to our set designer, Santo Loquasto. The actors were on a break and Santo and I observed Linda perched on the edge of the stage, lost in thought. She had no idea we were watching and in the course of sixty seconds her finely boned face registered various shifts of subtle emotion. Santo whispered, "Look at her. She's absolutely fascinating."

I learned so much from studying Linda in the rehearsal room. Stone by stone she laid down a foundation of honest emotion for each scene. Once I asked her if it had been horribly depressing appearing eight times a week in *The Diary of Anne Frank*. She said it wasn't difficult in performance. It was the rehearsals that were harrowing because that's where she was exploring her feelings of terror. A visitor to our rehearsal room would've assumed Linda was working on scenes from Ibsen or Strindberg.

By the beginning of the third week of rehearsals I was getting anxious at my comedy being performed as a reflective drama and I whispered to Lynne, "Um, when do you think she'll start being funny?" During that final week and a half, Linda began flirting with the comic elements in the play and then brought them to magnificent full bloom. An actor must possess great self-assurance to use the rehearsal period working in such an exploratory manner rather than cementing easy comic line readings for the approval of the few spectators in the rehearsal room.

Our other leading lady, Miss Lee, maintained the swagger of a Broadway diva, but inwardly she was fearful about being back onstage after so long an absence. I could see Linda becoming impatient with Michele's insecurities in the rehearsal room—Michele seemed to prefer talking about her character rather than playing the scene.

It was difficult adjusting to my role as playwright and not playwright/star. In my collaborations with Ken for Theater-in-Limbo, I was always respectful of his role as director but I also felt free to discuss the play with the actors, perhaps because the entire cast was composed of our closest friends. In this new situation it was prudent to conform to the traditionally strict protocol that the playwright remains silent unless called upon to clarify a point or make a change in the text.

When she's directing, Lynne Meadow is very much the leader; she has sonic radar in her head that lets her know instantly if someone's having a conversation about the play without her. Actors in rehearsal are extremely vulnerable and a writer who chooses to make an interpretive suggestion must tread with utmost diplomacy or risk triggering a scary thespian meltdown.

Lynne enjoyed having me sit beside her; I was like a funny younger gay brother for her. I was grateful. Many directors prefer to have the playwright banned from the room until the final week of rehearsal. I wanted to please her and she was protective of both me and the play. Dialogue comes easily to me, and I can deliver new lines within minutes. During *The Allergist's Wife* rehearsals, if an actor questioned a line, Lynne held me back from agreeing on the spot to rewrite it. She would say, "Before Charles makes any change, I'd like to do more work on the moment."

Our costume designer, Ann Roth, was another dynamic personality. Ann's career stretches back to the early sixties and she won an Oscar in 2020 for her work on *Ma Rainey's Black Bottom*. In so many classic movies, she's provided the image that remains with us, such as Jon Voight's fringed suede jacket in *Midnight Cowboy* and Jane Fonda's plunging backless gown in *Klute*. Ann attacks the character's costume not visually but behaviorally.

When we discussed the wardrobe for the elderly mother, Ann did a sort of free association exercise. "She's on a walker. She can't carry a bag. Her glasses are on a chain. She needs pants that she can slip down easily. Elastic waistband. She's frugal and housebound so she sends nothing to the dry cleaners. Machine washable." Ann is a tough, salty presence, rather like Elaine Stritch playing the role of a veteran costume designer—minus the arsenic.

By the end of the rehearsal period, the production was in excellent shape. Lynne had worked privately with Michele. The mysterious alchemy between a sensitive director and an excellent actress resulted in Michele giving a true star performance in the first preview. Having an audience was a big help, as well as the flash of the new purple lace bra Ann Roth gave her to wear in Act Two, Scene One.

Around this time, the actor Ron Rifkin, who was appearing in another play at the time, received a harsh review from the Times critic Ben Brantley, who lambasted him for being "over the top." Linda became convinced she'd be next on the frying pan for giving an excessive performance. For the last preview show of the week, without informing anyone, she chose to take her performance way down—from, let's say, a ten to a four and a half. Lynne and I were aghast. It was an entirely different play and a grim one.

Linda's character of Marjorie begins the play in a deep depression; it's only entertaining if her depression is in 3D and Cinerama. She's Medea in a chenille bathrobe. If she's histrionically pleading with the gods for a sense of meaning to her existence, her plight is not only comic but oddly universal. When the performance was over, Lynne turned to me. "What do we say to her?" "Say nothing," I replied. "Linda is so smart, I'm sure she realized that she jettisoned most of the laughs." We went backstage and were greeted by an ebullient Linda. "So, what did you think? It really worked, didn't it?"

Lynne was unable to remain silent. "Linda . . . You . . . you can't do it this way. You can't." Linda's face hardened into an impassive mask redolent of Gale Sondergaard in *The Letter*. "I don't want to talk about it." Lynne softened her approach. "I do have some blocking notes I'd like to give you." Linda cut her off tersely. "You can call me." With that she turned and shut the dressing room door. Lynne tried phoning her several times but Linda never picked up. When we returned after the day off for the next preview performance, Linda brought back her original theatrically mercurial characterization and the show went well.

The following night's performance was a strain on my sanity because the producer/director Hal Prince was coming to the show. Hal was Linda's longtime mentor and dear friend and his opinion meant everything to her. We worried that if he told her she was pushing or too broad we'd be finished. Well, Linda gave a glorious, bold performance the next night and Hal loved it and the play, allowing us all to heave a huge sigh of relief. From that point on, Linda never strayed from her commitment to her brave conception of the role.

The play was well received when it opened at MTC, and it was amusing seeing the subscriber audience get a kick out of a play that took satiric aim at them.

IRA
Marjorie, if I were half as intellectually curious as you.

MARJORIE
Curious, yes. Profound, no.

IRA
What do you call profound?

MARJORIE

The ability to think in the abstract. Oh, Ira, can't we just face it? We're Russian peasants from the shtetl. We have no right attending art installations at the Whitney. We should be tilling the soil, pulling a plow!

IRA

You're so tough on us. You know, that last production of Waiting for Godot *affected me deeply. I had the sense that I finally understood what that play was about.*

MARJORIE

You understood the story. You think it's about two guys who get stranded by the Tappan Zee Bridge. They're not waiting for Triple A. It's about—I can't even explain what it's about. That is my conundrum. I'm a fraud. A cultural poseur. To quote Kafka, "I'm a cage in search of a bird!"

I received a congratulatory note from a couple I'd never met, Paul Newman and Joanne Woodward, thanking me for writing a play that had them laughing "like two old whores."

Shortly after we opened, plans began to move the play for an open-ended commercial Broadway run. Manhattan Theatre Club partnered with a great team of producers: Douglas S. Cramer, Carole Shorenstein Hays, Stuart Thompson, and Daryl Roth. This marked the beginning of a professional and personal relationship with Daryl that has seen us through many stage productions and films; we have a friendship that continues to this day. Although we're close in age, Daryl—blonde, beautiful, soft-spoken but with a core of steel, the producer of seven Pulitzer Prize–winning plays and unwavering in her commitment to LGBT artists—embodies the kind of elegant surrogate mother figure that I get all moony about.

I had fantasies of the show's Broadway poster being something on the order of the haunting James McMullan design for *Six Degrees of Separation*. The ad agency SpotCo showed me a prototype. Designed by the *New Yorker* cartoonist Roz Chast, it was a cartoon of a frazzled lady poking her head out of a shopping bag. I'm embarrassed to admit that I wasn't familiar with the oeuvre of Ms. Chast. That night I had dinner with my two sisters and bitched about the poster and how I was being marginalized and not taken seriously as a playwright. When I mentioned that it was designed by a person named Roz Chast, their eyes bugged out.

They excoriated me for being such an ignoramus as not to realize that this was an incredible coup. Evidently Chast, the cartoonist laureate of the Upper West Side, never did commercial work. This was the greatest thing that had happened to the *three* of us in our entire lives! Okay. Okay. When I got home, I looked at the drawing again and grudgingly admitted to myself that it was witty and certainly unlike any theatrical poster I'd ever seen. I was reconciled that the play was indeed a comedy, had to be sold as such, and the team at SpotCo weren't dopes after all.

It was pouring rain the afternoon the marquee went up at the Barrymore Theatre on West 47th Street. This was the theater where Noel Coward and the Lunts romped in *Design for Living*, Marlon Brando played in *A Streetcar Named Desire*, and the original production of *A Raisin in the Sun* made theater history. I stood on the right side of the marquee, the left side of the marquee, in front of the marquee, and was drenched to the bone but didn't care. My name was on a Broadway marquee. A mere torrential downpour wouldn't keep me away.

Screenplays

Psycho Beach Party

Die Mommie Die!

A Very Serious Person (with Carl Andress)

The Sixth Reel (with Carl Andress)

Novel

Whores of Lost Atlantis

Also by Charles Busch

Plays

Vampire Lesbians of Sodom

Theodora, She-Bitch of Byzantium

Times Square Angel

Pardon My Inquisition or Kiss the Blood Off My Castanets

Sleeping Beauty or Coma

The Lady in Question

Red Scare on Sunset

You Should Be So Lucky

Queen Amarantha

Shanghai Moon

Die Mommie Die!

The Tale of the Allergist's Wife

Our Leading Lady

The Third Story

The Divine Sister

Olive and the Bitter Herbs

The Tribute Artist

Judith of Bethulia

Cleopatra

The Confession of Lily Dare

Ibsen's Ghost

When I turned sixty, the photographer Michael Wakefield shot this brutally
realistic portrait to show one and all what the new sixty looks like.

My mother, Gertie, and her two older sisters, Belle and Lil.
By their names, you'd think they were saloon gals.

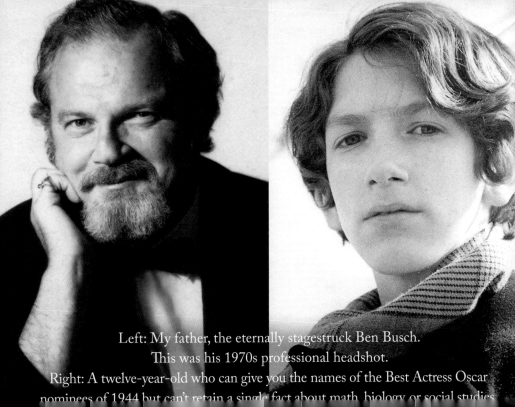

Left: My father, the eternally stagestruck Ben Busch.
This was his 1970s professional headshot.
Right: A twelve-year-old who can give you the names of the Best Actress Oscar
nominees of 1944 but can't retain a single fact about math, biology or social studies.

1973. My college roommate, Ed Taussig, and I never saw a photo booth we didn't want to jump into.

The faces that launched two hundred gasps: Ed Taussig and me in *Sister Act* in 1976. This was the photo that landed us on the front page of the Northwestern campus newspaper.

1977. A Windy City Sally Bowles living it up in Chicago post-graduation.

When I was starting out, outrageous bawdy drag held no allure. I preferred to explore the besmirched innocence of the silent film ingenue.

Although I stopped being a quick sketch portrait artist in 1984, occasionally I'll take out the pastels for my own pleasure, such as this 2014 portrait of my friend the beloved cabaret chanteuse Julie Wilson.

1984. My shabby portrait artist booth at the New York Renaissance Faire made my lane seem like Drifter's Row.

Alone With a Cast of Thousands was the title of my first two-act solo show. From 1978 to 1984, I was truly alone performing in Washington, DC, Chicago, San Francisco, and other burgs and hamlets.

Aunt Lil in late bloom. A mix of Auntie Mame, Helen Keller's
Annie Sullivan, and David Copperfield's Aunt Betsey Trotwood,
she has been the most influential person in my life.

In April 1984, I was temping as a receptionist at Robert Redford's Wildwood Productions. When his assistants weren't looking, as in a scene out of *Three Days of the Condor*, I took over the copy room and stealthily ran off these flyers.

1984. Plunging a dagger into Bobby Carey in *Theodora, She-Bitch of Byzantium*. An art gallery/bar on the Lower East Side gave me my chance to finally be Sarah Bernhardt.

Ken Elliott and me, Ma and Pa of Theater-in-Limbo, ready to hit the stage in 1984 as rival 1960s British fashion designers in *Sleeping Beauty or Coma*.

Dining after a show at McBells with Kathie Carr, stage manager, wig designer extraordinaire, and trusted accomplice.

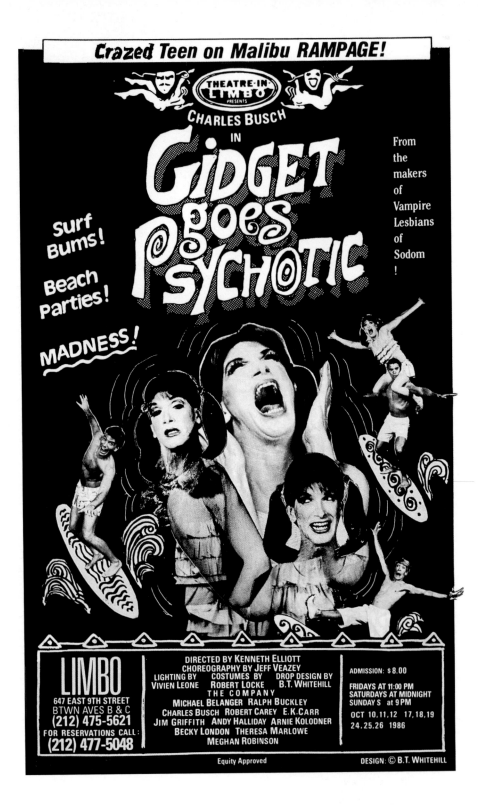

The original Limbo Lounge flyer for *Gidget Goes Psychotic*, later
retitled *Psycho Beach Party* for the Off-Broadway production.

Meghan Robinson and me in our splendid new costumes for the Off-Broadway transfer of *Vampire Lesbians of Sodom*. Definitely an upgrade from our Limbo Lounge thrift shop kimonos and sequined tube tops.

In full evening regalia, making an entrance at
a theater gala with Eric Myers. We look like a
prosperous orthodontist and his self-satisfied wife.

Theater-in-Limbo's finest moment. The 1989 New York production of
The Lady in Question. Top row left to right: Arnie Kolodner, Kenneth
Elliott, Mark Hamilton, Robert Carey. Front row left to right: Meghan
Robinson, Julie Halston, me, Theresa Marlowe, Andy Halliday.

My great stage buddy Julie Halston and me in a 2007 revival of *The Lady in Question* at the Bay Street Theater in Sag Harbor, New York. Over the past four decades, I've written thirteen roles for my dear friend.

Left: 1985. The marquee of the Provincetown Playhouse on MacDougal Street. I've been told that for many young gay people, this was the first show they insisted on seeing in New York.
Right: The Desert Inn, Las Vegas. 1990. Drinking in every delicious word uttered by MGM survivors June Allyson, Debbie Reynolds, and Ann Miller.

1987. It was a lucky break when my sister Margaret gave birth to Jimmy Stull, a most witty and caring nephew who appreciates Billy Wilder and Garbo.

1999. Playing ex-songstress Angela Arden for the first time in the premiere I
production of *Die Mommie Die!* with Carl Andress as my troubled son, Lanc

Left: Linda Lavin and Tony Roberts in *The Tale of the Allergist's Wife*. Lynne
Meadow directed a wonderful production with a perfect cast including Michele
Lee, Shirl Bernheim, and Anil Kumar.
Right: Playing death row inmate Nat Ginzburg on HBO's *Oz*.
The producers accepted my scathingly brilliant idea that Nat goes
to his execution garbed as Susan Hayward in *I Want to Live!*

Left: Captain Monica Stark comes to the rescue in the climax of the film *Psycho Beach Party*. I hope this wasn't my first and last experience as an action star. Right: Julie Halston and I had a chance to play antic Hollywood nuns in my 2010 play, *The Divine Sister*. With us, in the role of an imperious atheist dowager, is my other beloved muse, Jennifer Van Dyck.

My musical director, Tom Judson, and I have performed our cabaret show in four countries and more than thirty cities. After about five years, I removed the drag element from the act. I must confess, however, that at times I miss the glamour of being the lady at the mic.

Life is a banquet. Having grown up with my own Auntie Mame, it was a fantasy come true to play Auntie Mame in a summer theater tour in 2004.

Judith of Bethulia at Theater for the New City in 2012. Here I am as the courageous Judith, decapitating the evil Holofernes (John Wojda), with Mary Testa as my faithful handmaiden and wisecracking sidekick, Arga.

Taking a photo with Liza Minnelli after *The Divine Sister* and twisting my head toward my good side. Exceedingly painful in a nun's wimple. Don't try this at home.

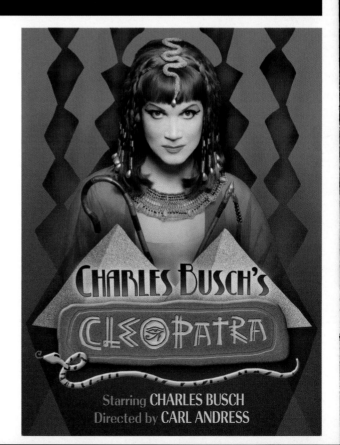

CHARLES BUSCH'S
CLEOPATRA

Starring CHARLES BUSCH
Directed by CARL ANDRESS

Every few years I seek refuge at the raffish and inspiring Theater for the New City in the East Village, as in this 2016 production of *Cleopatra*.

Cleopatra presented me as a redheaded Queen of the Nile (the ancient Egyptians did, after all, invent henna) and Andy Halliday as an overtaxed soothsayer.

Charles BUSCH

THE Confession of LILY DARE

Starring CHARLES BUSCH
Directed by CARL ANDRESS

My 2019 play, *The Confession of Lily Dare*, was an homage to the Hollywood mother-love tearjerkers of the early thirties. We had better luck than the tragic Lily. Thankfully, our limited engagement ended a week before the Covid pandemic lockdown.

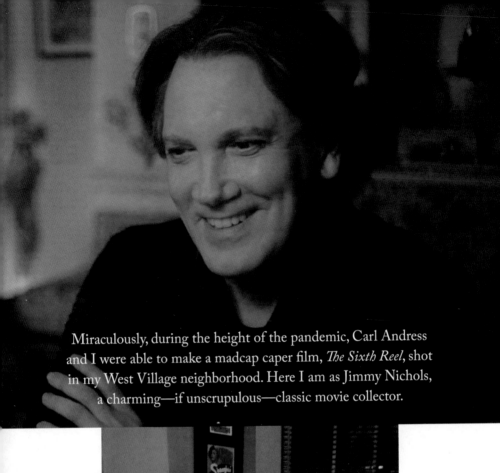

Miraculously, during the height of the pandemic, Carl Andress and I were able to make a madcap caper film, *The Sixth Reel*, shot in my West Village neighborhood. Here I am as Jimmy Nichols, a charming—if unscrupulous—classic movie collector.

Nearly everyone on the planet has a selfie with Joan Rivers. At my Christmas open house, leery about hanging her luxurious fur coat in my hall closet, Joan stuffed it in the bathroom hamper where I store my towels.

This study shot in Jackie Gleason's restored home in Miami Beach accurately conveys the poignant sensitivity behind the hard shell of glamour.

With My Tuchus on the Edge of My Seat

There was the aura of a hit about *The Tale of the Allergist's Wife* from the start and the previews were sold out. The box office was undoubtedly helped by a quote from Stephen Sondheim in a *New York Times* profile in which he stated that *The Tale of the Allergist's Wife* was the funniest play he'd ever seen. At the first preview at the Barrymore Theatre, the only seat available for me was in a box near the right side of the stage. It was an obstructed view seat, from which the back of the set was not fully visible, but I could see most of the orchestra seating and the entire balcony. I felt overwhelmed by the strangeness of my role—important yet invisible, elated, proud, vulnerable, scared, and a trifle mad, as if at any second I might have a giddy urge to climb over the railing and plunge into the audience below. It was an odd sensation hearing twelve hundred people laughing at lines of dialogue that I came up with alone in my apartment. After a long career in small Off-Broadway houses and viewing my talent as a decadent amuse-bouche, I'd never thought I could please so many people.

The afternoon of my opening night on Broadway, I received a telegram. A telegram? Who'd send me a telegram? It was from Stephen Sondheim. The telegram read, *Welcome to the big time.*

Though I was loving every minute of being the author of a hit Broadway show, it was a novel experience not having an ongoing function in the production. The cast of *The Tale of the Allergist's Wife* were fond of me and appreciated my occasional backstage visits, but it was a place of work, and I had the good sense to limit my appearances in the dressing rooms. I do recall

a turning point in my detachment. It was a Wednesday night, and I was lying on my sofa watching *Survivor*. During a commercial break, I noticed the digital clock on the TV read 8:30 and it occurred to me that Linda was just finishing the second scene of the first act. She still had a long way to go and here I was, lounging comfortably, munching on chocolate-covered pretzels, passively earning my 10 percent of the gross.

The Tale of the Allergist's Wife received three Tony nominations, including Linda for Best Actress in a leading role, Michele for Featured Actress, and Best Play. None of us won. I knew I didn't stand a chance against August Wilson, Tom Stoppard, and the deserving winner, David Auburn for *Proof*. I took my partner, Eric, to the Tonys. Eric appreciated the circus quality of the event, and, as an experienced film publicist, he made sure I was seen in the right places at the right times. I suppose it's human nature that in the final seconds before the winner's name was announced, the thought flashed through my head, *What if they all cancel each other out?* They didn't. Watching award shows, I never understand it when the winner babbles, "I don't have any speech prepared." Is it really possible that during the month between the nomination announcement and the actual show, they never, ever stood in front of the bathroom mirror and tried out a few ideas? I don't know about you, but I've been rehearsing acceptance speeches since I was ten years old.

After playing the taxing role of Marjorie for nine months, an exhausted Linda left the show and was replaced by Valerie Harper. In theory, Valerie seemed to be the perfect choice to replace Linda. They'd regularly circled each other in their careers, and in some people's eyes they were interchangeable. Lynne Meadow rehearsed Valerie for several weeks and saw to it that the show was in good shape to continue with its new star. Then, Lynne had to move on with her responsibilities as artistic director of Manhattan Theatre Club.

I slipped into the theater to catch Valerie's performance during the second week of her run. I noticed that, although Valerie was missing laughs, the

audience seemed content to spend two hours with TV's Rhoda. Linda and Valerie were different kinds of actresses. Unlike Linda, who revels in playing foolish pretention, Val looked uncomfortable with the negative aspects of Marjorie's character. Valerie, both offstage and as Rhoda, was the opposite of pretentious. Rhoda continually deflates people who put on airs.

I went backstage afterwards to offer a playwright's vote of confidence. It was not my place to give any kind of critique. Valerie greeted me warmly and I told her that she was marvelous, and the show was in good hands. Before I could exit the dressing room, she pulled me aside and in an exaggerated stage whisper (we were the only ones in the room) confided, "I'm having a terrible time landing the laugh on your wonderful line 'Don't say that to me now when the creative juices are flowing.' I remember Linda getting a big laugh. What am I doing wrong?" She was putting me on the spot. My impulse was to tell her to phone Lynne Meadow, but I knew exactly where the problem lay. Looking around as if the KGB were stationed outside the dressing room, I explained sotto voce that it was as simple as putting the emphasis on the last syllable of the last word. More importantly, Marjorie longs to view herself as an artist and she's continually stymied by all these small, unimaginative people. They keep poking at her until she can't take any more and then she says the line.

Valerie nodded her head and said I'd given her something to chew on, but would I please return and see the show again the next night? I felt guilty encroaching on Lynne's territory, but the following night I returned to the Barrymore in the role of undercover drama coach. Valerie took my suggestion and, sure enough, she got a laugh on the line. I've never considered myself a stage director, but I felt a jolt of pride that I'd made a difference.

After the show, I snuck into Val's dressing room to find her elated and practically leaping into the air. "Didja hear that laugh? I got it! *I got it!*" I praised her delivery and told her that she was on the right path, but before

I could leave, she asked, "What am I doing wrong when I walk in and catch Lee kneeling down tying Frieda's shoe? It's obviously a laugh but I'm not getting it." We sat down and I explained that it wasn't about the lines—the audience is reading Marjorie's unspoken thought. If she paused for a slow count of five before she screamed "Mother!" I was sure she'd get the laugh. Valerie nodded. "Yes, yes, I see. I'm gonna do that. I can't wait to try it tomorrow night. Will you come back again?"

This was making me nervous. If Lynne got wind of my secret coaching, it could get ugly. I should've phoned Lynne and told her that Valerie required some fine tuning, but I was getting such a kick out of playing Lee Strasberg to her Marilyn. After a year of feeling detached from the production, it was lovely to be needed. I returned the next night and, sure enough, Valerie got the laugh. She was in a state of ebullience as she saw her performance improving with each show.

Val asked me about several other key moments she felt weren't working. This time, it wasn't enough for me to simply give her feedback in the dressing room. She wanted to rehearse. Valerie was such a high-energy presence it was impossible to say no to her. We agreed that I would sneak out of the Barrymore and meet up with her half an hour later in the empty third-floor dining room of the theater hangout Angus McIndoe.

I felt as if I were in the throes of a clandestine affair with Valerie Harper. For the next three nights, I attended the show, took notes, and then furtively met her afterwards to rehearse in that empty upstairs dining room. I played the scenes with her and gave her every bit of insight I had at my disposal. After nearly a week of this, we both felt she was nailing all the laughs and had figured out a way for no-nonsense Val to portray a woman who sees herself as a tortured operatic heroine. I was both relieved and saddened when our forbidden affair came to an end, but our secret rehearsals became the bedrock of a dear friendship.

The *Allergist's Wife* company was fortunate to have Valerie at the helm during the nightmare of 9/11. The theaters were closed for forty-eight hours. Never before had Broadway shut down. (It seemed unthinkable then and yet in 2020, because of the Covid pandemic, the theaters went dark for well over a year.) In those first few traumatic days after 9/11, Valerie seemed to be everywhere promoting New York and the need to combat fear and return to normal life. She asked me to write her a short speech to give during the curtain call on the show's first night back. I felt a responsibility to give Valerie Harper/Rhoda Morgenstern, the quintessential New Yorker, an appropriately down-to-earth message of hope. Valerie's costar, Michele Lee, also wished to say a few inspirational words during the curtain call but was told that, magnanimous as that gesture was, it might be best for there to be only one speech.

I can't recall exactly what I wrote for Val, but I won't forget the emotional and grateful response of the audience. Neither will I forget how, as the ovation crested, Michele raised her hand to quell the applause. Placing her arm around a puzzled Shirl Bernheim, Michele shouted exuberantly to one and all, "And today is Shirl Bernheim's eighty-first birthday!" Michele's irrepressible bit of classic showbiz one-upmanship moved me as much as Valerie's curtain speech. Nothing can keep those gals down! Nothing! It gave me faith that we were going to be all right.

I suppose it's only natural, given my career as a leading lady, that I've often been asked if I ever wanted to play the role of Marjorie. Honestly, I never have. My goal was to write a tour de force role for an older actress. My province as a male actress has been theatrical parody and *The Tale of the Allergist's Wife* requires a realistic acting style that's not my forte.

In 2019, Linda Lavin approached me with an idea to celebrate the twentieth anniversary of the original production and raise money for the Actors Fund of America. She proposed that we do a one-night staged reading of

the play. Linda looks fantastic and is extremely active professionally, so I assumed that she'd re-create her original role. Nope. Her idea was that I play Marjorie, and since Shirl Bernheim had died several years before, Linda would take on the role of Frieda. The opportunity to be at the center of that play for one night was irresistible. Linda put on her producer's hat and contacted everyone connected to the original production. She got Michele Lee, Tony Roberts, and Anil Kumar to revisit their roles. Linda spoke to Lynne Meadow, who not only directed the event but was able to give us MTC's Broadway house, the Friedman.

At eighty-eight years old, Ann Roth returned to supervise our wardrobe choices, even though she was involved in about thirty-seven other projects in stage and film. Her frenetic schedule made it difficult to arrange a time for us to get together. On the phone, she croaked, "I'm taking the train in from my farm in Pennsylvania. Can you meet me at Penn Station at 8:30 AM and we can find some place there to talk?" I told her I didn't think that was such a great idea. We found a better time and place on another day at the design studio she was working out of.

Sitting somewhat collapsed on a folding chair, she looked at me and asked in all seriousness, "So, what do we do about the pee pee?" I explained that an over-blouse or sweater would solve the issue of any unsightly bulge. Following her specific directive, she had her assistant shop for an array of tops. Ann then chose for me a perfect striped velour sweater that managed to say about three different things about the character, and I had an inkling of what it was like to be costumed by Ann Roth.

The one-night event sold out quickly. We only rehearsed twice and, ironically, my first impulse was to play the role in a safe, tremulous manner. Lynne had to remind me of the offstage drama we'd gone through with Linda in 1999. The only way to play Marjorie is one step short of grand opera. I was thrilled to act with Linda. One never knows how she'll play a

specific moment, but it always seems right. I wanted to see if I could match her in spontaneity.

I tend to work out my interpretation and delivery while I'm writing a play and stick with those choices. I took this opportunity to ride a theatrical roller coaster with Linda and allowed each line reading to spring forth from listening to the other actors. It felt dangerous and very satisfying. Marjorie is a killer part. After huffing and puffing to get through it, I marveled at how those dames played it for so many months. Without a doubt, it was one of the great nights of my acting life, and a perfect capper to the entire *Allergist's Wife* tale.

This Heart of Mine

A little less than a year into the Broadway run of *The Allergist's Wife*, I woke up one morning with the most intense pain I've ever experienced. It felt as if I had been hit by a tsunami, the force of which almost propelled me out of bed. Twenty minutes later, when it subsided, I assumed that I'd twisted some muscle in my sleep. I made an immediate appointment with a chiropractor whose office was only a few blocks away. I hobbled over there and told him of the pain that went across my back and then down my arm. He proceeded to crack me in several places and sent me on my way.

Three months went by, during which I was struck with terribly unglamorous intestinal issues. I began steadily losing weight and feeling weaker and weaker. I was seeing a psychiatrist at the time, and when I'd tell him about

my physical problems, he'd always suggest that I get checked out by a physician. Of course he was right, but I was terrified, sure it was some form of terminal cancer. My health continued its downward spiral, until there were no more holes in my belts to keep my pants up, and my life was reduced to okay days and bad days.

One morning, I woke up so drained that I phoned my friend the allergist, Dr. Barry Kohn. Whatever I told him prompted him to put me on hold while he phoned his colleague, a gastroenterologist named Dr. Paulo Pacheco at Weill Cornell Medical Center, who agreed to see me as soon as I could get there. I filled Paulo in on what was ailing me, and he decided to start by giving me a general checkup.

As Paulo listened to my heart, a weird look spread over his face. "You have quite a pronounced heart murmur. You know that, right?" "Um, I think so. I always forget whether it's my sister or me who has the heart murmur." He insisted that I head straight to the fourth floor and have an EKG. I got to the fourth floor, and despite the waiting room being crowded, they rushed me through. I naturally assumed it was because I was a celebrity. Having a hit Broadway show brings that out in one. They hooked me up to the EKG machine, and soon the small room became filled with medical personnel, all focused on the screen and conferring with each other. Keenly attuned to the mood of my audience, I could see that I was in big trouble.

After I got dressed again, a doctor asked if I had a close relative who could join me. Ordinarily, I would've phoned Eric. He's the world's number one foul weather friend. Eric's been the chief caregiver for numerous elderly friends in need as well as young friends who have died of AIDS. In his apartment, he has a gallery of photos of his dearly departed. It looked like he'd soon be taking my eight-by-ten to the framers.

Unfortunately, Eric was out of town promoting the biography he'd written of the author Patrick Dennis. My sister Betsy was in her home in Brittany.

I hesitated before calling Margaret. My sister and I are empaths—we can often sense the other's emotions and physical condition from across long distances and I didn't want to frighten her. When she picked up the phone, I tried to counteract the unsettling news I was about to throw at her with a cheery opening line. "Margaret, the kookiest thing just happened." Later, she told me that her own heart skipped a beat as soon as I uttered those words.

Margaret raced across town and met me in the doctor's office. The cardiologist was Dr. Erica Jones, a warm Katie Couric type, and she was joined by a handsome surgeon, Dr. Girardi, still in his green scrubs. With everyone on staff at Weill Cornell so camera-ready, it's hard not to feel like you're doing a guest spot on a TV medical series. The two doctors stood side by side facing Margaret and me on the sofa. They began shooting all sorts of questions at us. "Has anyone in your family had heart issues?" We filled them in on Mommy's early death. "Have you experienced any sort of intense pain recently?" I didn't think so, but then I remembered my tsunami-like experience from three months before. When I told them about it in such terms as "And I had this pain down my arm and across my back," the two doctors exchanged looks that said "we have a character here."

The gist was that I'd miraculously survived an aortic dissection caused by an aortic aneurysm. More often than not, this kind of rupture of a major blood vessel kills you within an hour; I'd lasted for three months, during which I took a trip to the Caribbean, modeled a fifty-pound Follies headdress in a charity fashion show, and was nominated for and lost a Tony Award. If I had dropped dead on the stage of Radio City Music Hall, I would've made Tony history. Dr. Jones, in her most sympathetic manner, explained that I couldn't go home. I had to check into the hospital that minute and be prepped for open-heart surgery within the next forty-eight hours. Dr. Girardi, scuttling any notion I might've had of seeking a second opinion or getting the hell out of there, fixed me in the eye with a stony stare. "Mr. Busch, 90 percent of the

people in your condition die within an hour. You were lucky once. You will not be lucky again."

I phoned Carl Andress, who had a key to my apartment. I was surprisingly coolheaded for a performer specializing in melodrama and now on the brink of death. "Carl, I need my toothbrush, bedroom slippers, address book, the biography I'm reading of Alla Nazimova that's next to my bed, and, most importantly, go to a drugstore and get me no fewer than ten ChapSticks. Plain. No fewer than ten. This is not the time for me to go cold turkey."

Carl showed up at my hospital room just as I was being wheeled out on a gurney for some tests. He claims that as I was whisked off down the corridor, my departing words were, "I've made you my health care proxy, so if the plug needs to be pulled, it's up to you, kid. Go sign the paper. I'll be back soon."

Eric arrived from Arizona before the day was over, and except for the few hours when I slept, he never left my side. He was with me right up till the moment I was wheeled through the metal doors into the operating theater. Scared as hell, I assumed the air of Sarah Bernhardt bravely having her leg cut off.

The seven-hour surgery included the insertion of a metal valve, a Dacron graft, and a bypass. I have no recollection of my first few days in the ICU. My memories only begin after I was moved to a private room. What remains most vivid in my mind is the sickening medicinal smell of the antiseptic that surrounded the portals connecting the tubes to my chest—that and the alarmed beeping that sounds every time you shift your ass in the hospital bed. When Eric, Kathie, and Margaret were present, I was a docile if not quite cogent patient. Carl always seemed to show up when everyone had left for the day, the drugs had worn off, and the pain had me foaming at the mouth with unfocused fear and anger.

On the fifth day of my hospital stay, Carl arrived not long after I'd dragged myself to the bathroom trailing the tubes still attached to me and

wheeling the metal pole holding my IV bag. I ended up on the bathroom floor sobbing, and Carl had to lift me up and help me back into bed. I was sunk into a post-operative depression as deep as the lowest platform to the L train.

As a child, confronted with the death of so many close relatives, I retreated into a state of anemic sickliness. Nothing was physically wrong with me, and indeed I was never taken to a doctor, but it was accepted that "Chuck is fragile." When I developed into a sexualized being at the age of sixteen, a grey world became suffused with light and color. I became a corporeal presence with skin, blood, and muscle. Overnight I went from identifying as a mournful Oliver Twist to fully inhabiting my role as a cute teenage boy in tight jeans. I never drank to excess or experimented with drugs because I didn't want to alter this novel state of feeling good.

My aortic aneurysm at the age of forty-seven plunged me back into that dark childhood place of fragility.

In my room at Weill Cornell hospital, Greenberg Pavilion, what could possibly break through this wall of despondency? One day, treading carefully, Carl ventured, "I think you and Julie Halston should emcee a fundraiser for my new theater company." I shot him a dangerous "Lizzie Borden cracking her knuckles before reaching for the ax" look. He continued at his own peril. "And we'll have your costume designers, Bottari and Case, design you a gorgeous floating caftan that won't require you to wear any constricting foundation garment that might touch your surgical scar. It'll be the most fabulous gown you've ever worn." The tragic diva rose to the bait. In a diminished whisper recalling Garbo in the final scene of *Camille*, I uttered, "Carl, bring me that sketchpad and pencil. Chiffon. Yards and yards of orange Popsicle-colored silk chiffon."

Once home, I received a few select visitors, among them Julie Halston. In the years just before my surgery, we had been on the outs. She was finding

her way as a comic solo performer, and at times it went to her head. I grew jealous of the opportunities coming to her and, like a panther, I lay in wait for her to express any kind of puffed-up behavior, then pounced. After about four years of foolishness, we came to our senses and patched things up.

When she paid me a visit during my recovery, I was delighted to see her. Lynne Meadow had given me Deepak Chopra's book *The Seven Spiritual Laws of Success* as a tool to get over my post-surgical depression. An important part of the book was Chopra's advice to stop passing judgment on people and events. I found the book enlightening and tried to apply his teachings. Within twenty minutes of entering my apartment, Julie passed judgment on about thirty-seven people. "He's terrible. He's a comedy killer." "That movie career's gonna last as long as a holiday weekend." "Who the hell was her plastic surgeon?" Naturally, I couldn't help but chime in with a few comments of my own, but I finally had to put a stop to this orgy of harsh criticism.

"I was doing so well not passing judgment! You've set my serenity back three weeks." Julie, flipping through the pages of a magazine, shrugged. "But don't you feel purged?" Regaining some of my sizzle, I decided to pull a prank on my beloved comic muse.

"Julie, I should confess that a few years ago when we were at the peak of our feud, I had my lawyer, Glick, add a codicil to my will. It's so silly, and really kind of funny in retrospect. It says, 'Upon my death, at my memorial service, if Julie Halston attempts to speak, she must be forcibly and summarily ejected from said premises.'" Julie blanched. "Chawlz, you gotta change it. You gotta remove that codicil." It was hard to stifle my laugh—luckily, I am a professional. "Julie, I wish I could, but Glick charges by the hour. It would be very costly." Julie grew frantic and deadly serious. "Chawlz, you don't understand. I must speak at your service. I don't even have to be the last slot. I'll go second to last, but as your muse I must speak! You gotta call Glick! You gotta call Glick! I *must speak*!" Julie, if you're reading this book, I never put in that

codicil. I was just pulling your leg. By all means, when the time comes—and I hope it doesn't come for a long time—you *must* speak.

I'd like to say that I gleaned some insight from my experience. After the surgery I learned to avoid situations that would cause me unnecessary stress. I found it easier to say no, rather than reflexively saying yes. And that isn't always a good thing. Fortunately, I did still say yes to some terrific opportunities, such as the chance to play the title role in a summer stock tour of *Auntie Mame.* To be on the safe side, at my cardiology checkup, I asked Dr. Erica Jones if she thought I had the endurance to undertake the physically demanding role of Mame. Not in the least showbiz savvy, she leaned in with a concerned look. "Will you be lifting anything heavy?" To which I replied, "Well, I'll be carrying the plot."

Pictures That Talk

It was 2020. Carl and I were in a small screening room watching a rough assemblage of our new movie, *The Sixth Reel.* Nearly as miraculous as water springing forth in the grotto at Lourdes, we co-directed a feature film during the first year of the Covid pandemic before a vaccine was available. It had been fourteen years since my previous movie, *A Very Serious Person,* and it was looking like I'd never again have a chance to cavort in front of the motion picture camera.

A long unrealized wish was to star with Julie Halston in a caper comedy shot in my neighborhood, the two of us careening about in wacky disguises.

Carl wanted to direct a film that would preserve on celluloid (or digitally) the chemistry Julie and I had shared in over a dozen theatrical productions. Locked down in our respective abodes, Carl in Connecticut and me in Greenwich Village, we co-wrote the movie via Skype.

When you get to a certain advanced age, you assume your intimate circle of friends is complete and will only grow smaller with the meddling of the grim reaper. It ain't so. There's always room for someone smart, sweet, and fun. A few years ago, a talented young actor named Doug Plaut found his way in. I'm so glad he swam the castle's moat, for he's become a cherished friend. Doug, reed thin and with the physicality of the Scarecrow of Oz and the face of a silent film ingénue, gets pointed at by small children who ask their parents, "Is he real?"

Doug was determined to help Carl and me get our movie made. Let's not make him out to be St. Francis of Assisi in grease paint—we wrote him a swell part in the picture. Doug introduced us to Ash Christian, a prolific producer of small indie films, who agreed to take on the project. With the members of the Screen Actors Guild and Actor's Equity cooling their heels indefinitely, we were able to assemble a suddenly available and eager cast that included Margaret Cho, Tim Daly, André De Shields, Patrick Page, and a galaxy of veteran Tony Award winners.

My role in the film was that of Jimmy Nichols, an adorably disreputable collector and dealer in classic film memorabilia. Julie played Helen, a recent widow from Boca Raton, who finds herself caught up in my questionable shenanigans. Filming in the West Village, Julie and I were in the middle of a comic scene when an old man walked right between us and, jabbing his finger barely an inch from my face, shouted, "Mask!" I suppose I should take it as a compliment that the old grump was unable to tell I was acting.

Except for five days of location work in Manhattan, we shot the rest of the film on a sound stage in Newburgh, New York. The most important person on

the set was our newly assigned health and safety supervisor, Jason. A spry, elfin figure with his hair in a pixie's topknot, Jason did not take his duties lightly. He was unyielding in his insistence that we always be a safe several feet apart when off camera. It was perplexing on Tim Daly's first day on the film, when we sat on the bed double-masked going over our dialogue and then removed our masks to get under the sheets and play our love scene. Jason and his team did their job and did it very well. At the end of the three-week shoot, we could boast that not one of the eighty members of the cast and crew got sick.

In the screening room, watching the jigsaw puzzle of multiple camera angles assembled for the first time, I assessed my own performance. The plot had me not getting into drag until the final third of the movie. I'd wondered if I'd like myself in a male role. I never have before. I can enjoy seeing the "leading lady" on film, but I'm brutally critical of the "actor." It's always that gay kid within, told by society that his effeminacy was something to be eradicated.

Watching myself as Jimmy in *The Sixth Reel*, plotting, scheming, and running through the streets with Julie, I thought, *Hmmm, I'm okay with this fellow—a bit girly, a tad butch, whimsical, sharp, yet vulnerable*. That affirmation, however, didn't stop me from jotting down about ninety-seven notes on lines to be redubbed and unflattering shots removed.

What Price Hollywood

2002. I never thought *Psycho Beach Party* was a good idea for a movie—it seemed so rooted in the theater. My longtime manager Jeff

Melnick thought differently and for eight years wouldn't stop pursuing it. At last, Jeff managed to set it up with Strand Releasing as producers and an up-and-coming director named Robert Lee King at the helm. I'd never written a screenplay, and Bob, though much younger than I was, gave me a crash course in screenwriting. He turned the play into a movie, guiding me into layering in an entirely new thriller plot.

Bob and Strand wanted me in the movie, but at the age of forty-eight my days of playing a teenage girl on film, no matter how camp, were long past. But . . . if there was now a killer in the plot, then there should be a detective. I'd play the invincible Captain Monica Stark of the LAPD. Bob King has a great eye for casting. For my old role of Chicklet, he found Lauren Ambrose, who had played key supporting roles in a few big commercial movies but never a lead. Bob was stuck on the image of blonde Sandra Dee in the original *Gidget*, and worried that Lauren's natural red hair might be a distraction. He wondered if she should dye it blonde. "No!" I told him. "There's a great tradition of redheaded funny ladies. Y'ever heard of a woman named Lucy?" Lauren remained a redhead.

For the role of the mean girl Marvel Ann we cast a young actress who'd only appeared in one previous film. Her name was Amy Adams. In the climactic luau scene, there was a dance-off between Marvel Ann and the Marilyn Monroe–like movie star on the lam, Bettina Barnes. Bettina wins. Well, she's supposed to win. The problem was that Kimberley Davies, who played Bettina, was an actress who could move a little and Amy was a talented musical theater performer. When Bob called "Action," Amy went wild. Hips and legs and shoulders rocking and rolling and about 137 teeth flashing; no matter how Bob edited the sequence, Amy Adams was the victor.

Ken Elliott had moved to LA a few years before to pursue a career in TV directing—not an easy racket to break into. He phoned me with the idea that, since I'd be in LA filming *Psycho Beach Party*, perhaps we could

put on a play at the same time. The exposure might help him find TV work. Rehearsing and performing in a play and making a movie at the same time didn't strike me as impossible. The supporting role I'd written for myself in the movie would require me to work only ten out of the twenty-two shooting days.

Ken advised that in coming up with a play I should keep it to a budget-friendly single set and simple costumes. I needed a flashy star vehicle with the bawdiness of *Vampire Lesbians of Sodom*, the specific movie parody of *The Lady in Question*, and the social commentary of *Red Scare on Sunset*. Carl thought perhaps a myth or fairy tale might be a source of inspiration. Racking our brains, Carl suggested Queen Clytemnestra, who kills her husband and whose children are intent on proving her guilt.

Instantly, I saw the play in the style of a 1960s Ross Hunter melodrama starring Lana Turner. The mid-sixties marked the twilight of the Goddesses. Hollywood was in a time of flux; the studio contract system had ended, and the great stars of the past were desperately trying to extend their careers in a rapidly changing world centered on youthful rebellion. The studios made awkward attempts to refurbish their old genre formulas with the new hip sensibility, and almost always failed. This play would allow me to have fun with the aspirations and tawdriness of those films while also commenting on the period of change in which they were produced. Once again, I turned to my college friend Ed Taussig for a title, and he came up with *Die Mommie Die!*.

The plot and dialogue came easily. The play required no research since the movies it evoked (*The Big Cube*, *Dead Ringer*, *Portrait in Black*, *Where Love Has Gone*, *Picture Mommy Dead*, and *Imitation of Life*) were all familiar to me. My role was that of Angela Arden, a former singing sensation now married to a movie producer, Sol Sussman, who finds his liberal message movies hopelessly out of date in the new Hollywood of the sixties. Angela's

marriage has become a battleground and she's turned to the erotic ministrations of a handsome former TV star turned tennis pro, Tony Parker.

ANGELA
You ask me to throw away everything safe and secure for a man whose reputation is that of a highly paid gigolo.

TONY
I've always been the sort of guy people spread rumors about. Hell, there was a certain "big" rumor about me that made you reach for the phone in the first place.

ANGELA
Who are you, Tony Parker? You've slipped into my life as easily as vermouth into a glass of gin. Quickly and just a bit too smooth. Your life is a locked file cabinet of dark ugly secrets.

(He grabs her violently)

TONY
What have you heard?

ANGELA
I have it on excellent authority by way of every hair-burner in West Hollywood that the favors you've received were not only courtesy of the ladies but les garçons as well.

The plot adhered closely to the *Oresteia*, with a few minor changes. In my play, Angela (Clytemnestra) dispatches her husband, Sol (Agamemnon), not

by stabbing, but through the insertion of a poisoned suppository. Basically, the same idea. Carl, who'd be playing my troubled son, Lance, and I flew out to LA. The following Monday I began filming my role in *Psycho Beach Party*, and a few days later started rehearsing *Die Mommie Die!*. The schedule was working out surprisingly well, as I was rarely called to the movie set. We were booked to do the play at the Coast Playhouse on Santa Monica Boulevard in the heart of West Hollywood.

Upon arrival, our producer/theater manager informed us that he was having difficulty raising money for the show. Rather an understatement. During our first week of rehearsal, Ken and I learned that the producer hadn't in fact raised a penny. Ken was forced to take on the role of producer as well as director.

Ken, Carl, and I would show up at cocktail parties at the homes of various wealthy gay men. Carl and I would perform a fifteen-minute floor show of fragments from the play while Ken worked the crowd for investors. I felt foolish arriving at these magnificent LA homes, including that of *Will & Grace* creator Max Mutchnick, wearing a black sleeveless shift, red wig, and open toe black pumps. I looked like I was doing a door-to-door tour of *Sweet Charity*. Our act got laughs but Ken, dignified and scrupulously honest, had in him nothing of the huckster. The three of us left every home empty-handed.

Ken had to miss entire days of rehearsal while he worked the phone trying to rustle up investors. We were moving into the final week of our rehearsal period with still not a *centime* of capitalization. The unpaid designers were doing their work based on our past histories with them. A decision was going to have to be made soon to cancel the production. On the movie set, I confided in Victor Talbot, one of the producers of the *Psycho Beach Party* movie, and upon hearing our tale of woe, he picked up the tab for the entire stage production on the spot. I suppose I should've gone to him

sooner, but foolishly I thought it necessary to keep the projects independent of each other.

We shot most of the movie down the coast in Zuma Beach in the exact location where the original Beach Party movies had been made. Despite the distance of the location, the mad schedule of rehearsing a play and shooting a movie simultaneously continued without a hitch until the week we were to begin previews. The shooting schedule changed at the last minute, and on the day of my first performance of *Die Mommie Die!*, I was filming in Santa Clarita.

It was a forty-five-minute drive from West Hollywood, and the scene was a short one. As Detective Monica Stark, I had to step out of my squad car and engage in a brief bit of dialogue with Chicklet and her friend Berdine. Then Chicklet's mother pulls up in her car, and we have a short introductory scene. How long could that take? There were all sorts of production issues that I wasn't privy to, and after sitting around in costume and makeup for hours, we finally began filming shortly after 4:00 PM. My friend Beth Broderick was playing Meghan's old role of Chicklet's mother, Mrs. Forrest, and we'd periodically exchange looks expressing doubts about how long we had before we'd lose the light. We were still shooting at six o'clock, and my curtain was at eight. The director, Bob King, shook his head. "There's no way we'll be done."

As I had no understudy in the play, I was in the hideous position of having to phone Ken, after all the effort he'd gone to, and tell him that we'd have to cancel our sold-out first performance. Ken took the news with as much grace as was possible. The next day we were back in Santa Clarita, and the exact same scenario came to pass. Bob handed me the verdict: "You're going to have to make that phone call again, and you may be making that call tomorrow night as well." He was correct. Three days in a row I had to tell Ken to give the audience their money back and send them home. Ken is a

gentleman, but I could sense the fierce annoyance under his stoic acceptance. I'm sure it only added to his aggravation that the film causing all this trouble was based on a play he'd successfully produced and directed.

Die Mommie Die! finally opened at the Coast Playhouse and quickly found its audience. I've always enjoyed performing in LA, whether I'm in a play or doing my cabaret act. It's basically a New York audience transplanted west. It's also such a film and television industry town that they get every pop culture reference thrown at them. We played *Die Mommie Die!* for about three months, during which time I finished shooting my scenes for the movie without missing any more performances.

Unbeknownst to me, several years earlier, the West Coast–based stage director Mark Rucker was studying filmmaking at UCLA. After a screening of the 1942 movie *Now, Voyager*, Mark confided to his lover, the film producer Dante Di Loreto, "Someday I want to direct a classic women's picture starring Charles Busch." Fade out, fade in, while I was in LA performing in *Die Mommie Die!*, Dante and his producing partner, Anthony Edwards, contacted me about writing a screen adaptation of a novel they'd optioned. After a few meetings, we concluded that we wanted to work together, but not on that project. Quick on the draw, I invited them to see *Die Mommie Die!*.

Dante, on the lookout for a movie for Mark Rucker to direct, optioned the rights to the play and commissioned a screenplay. Within a few months, I'd pounded out a screen adaptation of *Die Mommie Die!*. It was accepted with no demands for rewrites and a production date was set. Movies of any budget, large and small, usually take at least five years to set up. This movie was put together so quickly, you'd swear we were at Monogram Pictures in 1940.

I met with Mark, and since he was also from the theater, we spoke the same language. There was a soft-spoken but commanding strength about him that reminded me of Ken. Over the next few months, Mark called from LA to confer with me on the casting process. I was pleased with all

of his ideas. Jason Priestley, Natasha Lyonne, Frances Conroy, and Philip
Baker Hall were excellent, accomplished actors and perfectly cast. Mark also
showed me an audition tape of a young man who had never appeared in a
film, Stark Sands, and it was obvious that Stark was an ideal choice for the
role of my son. I'm not glossing over the rough patches because frankly there
were none. I was starring in a movie based on my own play helmed by a
theater director who held me in high regard and in a role that fit me like a
figure-hugging gown by Jean Louis. It was divine.

We filmed most of the movie at a magnificent Beverly Hills home
designed by the architect Paul Williams. It was owned by a man named Jeff
Quinn who lived there with his partner, a prominent lawyer. Jeff convinced
his doubting mate that letting Charles Busch film a movie in their house for
the next month was a monumental gift to the gay community. Acquiescing,
his partner promptly skipped town for an extended trip to Europe, leaving
Jeff and their King Charles Cavalier spaniel to deal with the film shoot.
What originally promised to be a temporary occupation of a few rooms
turned into our taking over the entire house and grounds, with Jeff and his
dog gradually exiled to a small attic space for the duration.

It may have been an ordeal for our host, but it was the most glorious
twenty days of my life. So often we don't appreciate an experience until it's
long over. Every single day, I was cognizant of my good fortune. I had the
opportunity to play a love scene with my leading man, Jason Priestley, who
was a pleasure to work with. There's always choreography to be learned in
a movie love scene. Self-conscious that Jason might think I was *too* into it,
I became flustered and dithery. Jason, cool as a salad just out of the fridge,
taught me the technique necessary to make such a scene accessible to the
camera—how to angle my head, yet appear sexy and not stagy.

Playing a confrontation scene with the marvelous Frances Conroy was an
honor. In the scene, Angela drops her Beverly Hills pretensions and reveals

her hardscrabble roots. Barbara Stanwyck was my inspiration. Where many actresses chew the scenery to convey a hardboiled demeanor, Stanwyck goes deadpan. There's a lack of affect that's chilling, and in this scene with Franny, I enjoyed evoking that narrow-eyed inscrutable facade.

Angela had once been a celebrated singing star, and there was a musical number that required me to lip-synch. The woman who recorded the song sounded much too young and girlish for the character; I needed to be dubbed with an emotive Judy Garland–like belt. I recommended my friend Ruth Williamson, a Broadway musical theater actress who'd recently moved to LA. Ruth rerecorded the song "Why Not Me," and her gutsy emotional sound was a perfect match.

Natasha Lyonne played my daughter, and we established an immediate rapport rooted in our mutual love of classic film. In her early twenties when we made the movie, Natasha had the sardonic world-weariness of someone much older. Understandable, since she'd toiled in the salt mines of show business since childhood. She was entering a difficult chapter of her life, unsure of where she'd fit in as an adult actor and even of how her body might change with maturity. Despite these anxieties, Natasha was an excellent scene partner and she was genuinely enthusiastic about the project.

In the years following the movie, she sank deep into a morass of addiction and serious health issues. I recall one disturbing evening playing the tile game Rummikub at her dimly lit mausoleum of a home in the East Village. Under the influence, she kept furiously changing the rules of the game in a way that made the Mad Hatter seem reasonable. It's marvelous how she's since pulled herself together and risen like a flaming-haired phoenix as an actor, director, and producer of such highly regarded TV series as *Russian Doll, Loot,* and *Poker Face.*

One of the last scenes we shot was the ending of the movie in which Angela emerges from the gates of her estate and faces a battery of paparazzi

and reporters along with the waiting police squad car that will take her away to prison. I stepped back for a moment and was moved by the sight of Mark and the camera operator perched high up on a tall crane. All these actors and technicians striving to do their best—and it all sprang from a fantasy I once had of playing Clytemnestra.

The morning after we finished the last scene, I was on a flight back to Manhattan. For the next two weeks, still so connected to the project, I'd lie on the sofa with my eyes closed, assembling the film scene by scene and reliving every moment. The first time I saw the finished movie was months later when it was shown at the Sundance Film Festival in Utah. Mark had done a brilliant job capturing the precise tone of the sixties films we were aiming to mirror. He told me early in production that he wanted the movie to be a valentine to the work I'd done in the theater. It was a tremendous gift, a film that allowed me in every way to do what I do best, and for which I received the only acting award I've ever won—a jury prize at the Sundance Film Festival for Best Performance.

Die Mommie Die! was Mark Rucker's first and last movie. He became an associate director at San Francisco's American Conservatory Theater and was a much-loved artistic figure in that city. Suffering from an anxiety disorder, he died at the age of fifty-three of an accidental pill overdose. He was dear and quick to laugh, but there was also a remote, impenetrable quality to his personality. He's someone I wish I'd known better.

Taboo

One night in 2010, as I was leaving the theater with Carl Andress after a performance of my play *The Divine Sister*, a young man asked me to sign his Playbill from the 2003 Broadway musical *Taboo*. Over the years, he'd had it signed by almost everyone connected to the show; only my signature was missing. My spontaneous reaction was a full body shudder and the emission of a sound reminiscent of a rhinoceros hit by a stun gun. Composing myself, I queried, "You liked *Taboo*?" From my inflection, you might have thought I was asking, "You enjoy eating roadkill?"

The young man replied that he'd attended sixty-four of the show's one hundred performances on Broadway. After I signed his Playbill, Carl waited until we'd walked away down the block and then lit into me, "That was so rude. He loved that show. Why'd you have to spoil it by making him feel like an idiot? You should've just said, 'Thank you.'" Carl was right. I had imposed on that poor guy all my emotional debris from the *Taboo* experience. I've never behaved that way since.

A lot of people loved *Taboo*. There have been sold-out reunion concerts. The posters and original cast recording are collector's items. On Broadway-themed Facebook pages, discussion threads about notorious flops inevitably include comments that *Taboo* was unfairly maligned and a cherished theatrical experience. Unfortunately, another comment often appears as well: "despite the book by Charles Busch."

2003. It began with a phone call from my manager, Jeff Melnick, informing me that Rosie O'Donnell wanted to meet with me about an exciting project. I'd

only encountered Rosie a few brief times, when her support for *The Tale of the Allergist's Wife* led her to invite all our leading ladies to appear on her popular television talk show. Rosie's love of Broadway gave valuable television exposure to many shows and extended to her hosting the Tony Awards. She also created a foundation, Rosie's Theater Kids, that's provided arts education and changed lives for many young people. She'd recently ended her TV show, had finally come out as a lesbian (a cataclysmic shock to perhaps a few dense housewives in Albuquerque), and had cut her hair in a short, asymmetrical style that provoked more public furor than either of the other two developments.

Rosie is a performer, and like most of us theatrical folk, she slips easily into different skins to glide through uncomfortable situations. For our meeting, she not only borrowed the corporate boardroom we convened in, she also appropriated the persona of a hard-edged theatrical producer. She explained that on a recent trip to London, she'd seen a groundbreaking, sensational musical called *Taboo*. It was about the New Romantic movement in art and music in London in the early eighties. Boy George had written the music and lyrics and Rosie was planning to produce it on Broadway with Boy George in one of the leading roles. She felt, however, that the book didn't work, and she wanted me to write an entirely new one.

My immediate instinct was to flee. Writing a book to an existing score is rarely a good idea, for a musical should be a seamless synthesis of music, staging, plot, and dialogue. Rosie sensed that she was losing me and, skilled improvisational comic that she is, grabbed me back by suggesting I fly with her the following weekend on the Concorde to see the show. That, I could not resist. I wanted the experience of flying on the luxurious Concorde with a celebrity I admired. If nothing else, it would make for a nifty anecdote that I could dine out on for years.

Off we flew to London, not on the Concorde, but in first class in a Boeing 747. Within hours of landing, we were at the Venue Theatre, site of both

the show and the original eighties club Taboo, for which it was named. The show's co-creator and director was the Australian Christopher Renshaw. His career had mostly been in opera, but he had scored a success with a lavish revival of *The King and I*, which was a hit both in the West End and on Broadway. I knew Chris from his time in New York. He was smart and fun, with an appealing self-deprecating sense of humor.

The show was visually extravagant yet rough-edged, and Boy George was effective in his supporting role as the late performance artist/designer Leigh Bowery. In this original UK production, the character of Leigh Bowery was a musical role with no dialogue scenes. The music was tuneful but yes, the book was a problem. For a show celebrating the decadent, the plot was surprisingly old-fashioned and moralistic.

Despite my misgivings, I came away feeling that Rosie might be on to something. Perhaps the middle-aged New York theatergoing audience might be nostalgic about the '80s music of Boy George and Culture Club. I also could see why Rosie had thought of me; my experiences as a drag performer in the East Village of the mid-eighties mirrored the milieu of *Taboo*.

Rosie and I returned to our digs at the Covent Garden Hotel. I was still ambivalent about whether I wanted to get involved. I walked Rosie to her room and she invited me in for a postmortem of the evening. Prepared for a monologue, I was pleasantly surprised when we engaged in a genuine conversation. In an intimate setting, she exhibited an easygoing affability. We sat on the bed, and she expressed how meaningful it was for her to meet Boy George. When he first burst onto the scene, she'd been a lonely gay teenager in Commack, Long Island. His freedom of gender expression sent out a powerful message of self-acceptance. We sat on the bed for hours, going down a midnight rabbit hole that ended with us sharing that our mothers dying when we were children had, for both of us, informed every aspect of our adulthood.

After our marathon conversation, I felt that Rosie and I had forged a true connection. After a career in stand-up comedy and a long-running talk show, she longed to be in a room with artists. She grew up with an intense love for the theater and had a desire to be in a creative endeavor with people she admired. She'd met with her business manager and asked him if she could afford to lose ten million dollars. Wouldn't we all like to be able to pose such a question? He gave her the go-ahead and Rosie became *Taboo*'s sole producer and investor.

Jeff Melnick easily worked out a deal for my services. Rosie gave us what we asked for and her check arrived promptly. It was time to do some research. I read Boy George's memoir and a biography of Leigh Bowery, and found their stories so rich, it seemed unnecessary to create an original protagonist as Mark Davies had in the London version. Rosie and I were both impressed by the Scottish actor Euan Morton, who played the embryonic Boy George, and we agreed that the show should be built around him. This was an opportunity to create a Broadway musical about a free-spirited, highly sexual young gay man. It was the kind of role that so many of us growing up could only have dreamed of playing, a gay boy's *Funny Girl*.

In the British production, there was almost no interaction between the characters of Boy George and Leigh Bowery. Though George and Leigh were both active in the New Romantic movement, they didn't have much to do with each other. I felt their stories should be connected. In my first draft, I made Leigh a celebrity on the club scene who discovers and mentors the young George, giving the narrative an element of *A Star Is Born*. George refused to accept that story line, insisting he'd been successful before Leigh. My invented scenario would have worked theatrically and anchored the show, but George had script approval. I eliminated that concept and was never able to find an adequate substitute.

Rosie, impulsive by nature, wanted the show on Broadway in the following season. The Plymouth Theatre was booked with a scheduled opening only a few months ahead. To say this was a massively abbreviated timeline for such a production would be rather an understatement. A full workshop of the show was planned for just a few weeks before actual rehearsals would begin, which didn't leave us much time to implement ideas that we might glean from the workshop. My growing interest in Leigh Bowery as well as George's star billing had inspired me to enlarge Bowery's presence in the show and give him comic and dramatic scenes to play.

Unfortunately, George's numerologist, a witch named Dragonah, was adamant that there could be fatal consequences if he traveled westward during the month of February. Therefore, he would not be participating in the workshop of his upcoming Broadway show. In his place, Telsey Casting sent us Ritchie Coster, a British actor and singer unknown to me.

The two-week workshop culminated in a performance attended by Rosie, the designers, the ad agency, the press reps, the theater owners, agents, managers—you name it. Euan Morton and the entire company were everything we'd hoped they'd be, and Ritchie Coster was beyond superb as Leigh. People were grabbing at any available Kleenex during his death scene, and he received a well-earned standing ovation at the end of the performance. The rehearsal room was abuzz with whispers. "It's a hit. It's a hit. My God! Ritchie Coster! Ritchie Coster!" The excitement over his multidimensional, daring performance was palpable—but, wait a second, Ritchie Coster wasn't going to be in our show.

A few weeks later, rehearsals began for the Broadway production. Some singers are natural actors: Barbra Streisand, Bette Midler, Diana Ross, Cher, Sting, Jennifer Lopez, Tom Waits. Sadly, George O'Dowd, aka Boy George, is not among them. Rosie brought in an acting teacher, Candy Trebuco, as George's personal coach. Candy tried everything in her Method arsenal to

no avail. George didn't seem concerned with his lack of dramatic ability. He never expressed to me any insecurity about appearing in a leading role in a Broadway show. With an air of authority, he'd object to a word choice in a speech or the rhythm of a comedy line.

Chris Renshaw and George had created the show together in London, where it had been a hit, and that bonded them as a team. They were extremely loyal to each other. That closeness made Chris protective of George and willfully blind to his deficiencies as an actor. Toward the end of one frustrating rehearsal, Chris asked me, "Wouldn't you call him a gifted amateur?"

Rosie had engaged an acclaimed young avant-garde choreographer, Mark Dendy. His work was noted for its theatricality and sense of narrative, but he had no experience choreographing a Broadway musical. After several weeks in the rehearsal hall, we moved into the Plymouth Theatre.

Seeing Mark's hip-hop-inflected choreography on a Broadway stage made Rosie nervous. She found it "angry." Mark's work on *Taboo* was ahead of its time, and only a few years later, nearly all Broadway choreography would be heavily influenced by hip-hop and street dancing. After rehearsal, we were summoned for a tribal council in the lower lounge of the Plymouth Theatre.

Rosie presided over the meeting and informed the entire company that she was bringing in Jeff Calhoun, a well-known choreographer/director who she'd worked with in a long-running revival of *Grease*. I could see that this move was painful for Rosie. Her eyes tearing, she turned to Mark. "I'd love for you to stay and assist Jeff, but if you do, it must be with an open heart." I assumed that he'd head for the hills or at least First Avenue, but Mark chose to remain in this awkward role. For one thing, he wanted to retain his future weekly box office percentage. Still, Mark Dendy ought to receive a Nobel Peace Prize for handling a humiliating situation with the utmost grace. Never did he criticize his successor's work. He was an astute second pair of

eyes for Jeff and continued to be a welcome collaborator in the show. And to Jeff Calhoun's credit, he never made Mark feel like a demoted employee.

During the final weeks when we were rehearsing in the theater, Rosie liked having me sit next to her in the fifth row. Sometimes Jeff, Mark, Chris, and John McDaniel, our musical director and Rosie's longtime television colleague, would ask me to join them in their seats, which were far away from Rosie. It was important for the creative team to watch the show together. But what was I to do? I was dealing with a producer who easily accessed her childhood feelings of being shut out.

I chose to remain by Rosie's side. I did enjoy her company, and I felt that I could do some good by keeping her in the loop on the show's creative decisions. An essential part of her desire to produce *Taboo* was her longing to be "in the room" and to participate in the process of developing the show. Rosie is a gifted visual artist and had always intended to create the poster art. Her paintings of George and Euan in their roles were boldly original with intense saturated colors, but the ad agency and press reps felt they were too "bizarre" to adequately promote the show. They were wrong. Rosie was right.

When asked by any reporter how the production was coming, Rosie would predict that *Taboo* was going to sweep the Tony Awards. I asked her, "Are you sure you should be doing that? You don't think the critics will pan us just out of pique?" Rosie shrugged and replied that she couldn't help it. That's how she felt. I began to see that she was truly uncensored. There was never anything underhanded or deceitful about her. If she liked you, you knew it—and if she was furious, you definitely knew it.

We were now at the point where the company had to perform two full run-throughs of the show with sets, lights, and costumes. Before the first afternoon run-through, the cast was instructed to keep going until the very end, even if there were wardrobe problems or other issues. It was important to get the precise timing for the set changes.

It had been clear from the first rehearsal that Raúl Esparza, playing the role of George's flamboyant friend Philip Sallon, was going to be a dynamic presence in the show. He was on the verge of Broadway stardom due to his performances as a replacement in the role of the Emcee in *Cabaret* and as Riff Raff in a revival of *The Rocky Horror Picture Show*. He was also gaining a reputation as a fine interpreter of the work of Stephen Sondheim thanks to his participation in the Kennedy Center's 2002 Sondheim celebration.

During the first act of *Taboo*, Raúl had an impossibly fast costume change, causing him to make an entrance during the run-through with his shirt half on and his pants unbuttoned. He stopped the run-through to protest that the costume wasn't adequately rigged for a quick change. Rosie took it upon herself to grab a hand mic and remind him that we had to keep going—the costume issue would be taken up later. Tensions were high and Raúl would not be dismissed. He began shouting at Rosie that the actors' problems were constantly being ignored and that his costume problem had to be addressed now, whereupon Rosie countered that the show wasn't just about his costumes. Within seconds their confrontation escalated a hundred decibels. Raúl bellowed that he'd had it, and he was "fucking quitting." To which Rosie shouted back, "Then quit! We'll put on the understudy!"

Raúl stormed off the stage and out of the theater. I turned to Rosie. "Um, I . . . I think you need to get him back. We have another run-through tonight." "Let him quit," she said. "I'm not gonna apologize." Surely, she wasn't serious. I moved over to our embattled director, who looked like he'd just been taken out of a washing machine in the middle of the spin cycle. "Chris, I think you need to find Raúl." He threw up his hands and implored me to do something about it. Was it really up to me, the book writer, to bring Raúl back? I threw on my coat and went in search of Raúl Esparza. I recalled that he lived only a few blocks away, next door to the French bistro Cafe Un Deux Trois.

I reached 44th Street and found Raúl sitting on his front stoop, sobbing to his agent on his cell phone. I sat down beside him. He put down the phone and poured out his feelings: his initial excitement over creating his first original role on Broadway and how disappointing the entire experience had been. He was done. He was finished. He didn't care if he was blacklisted on Broadway.

I tried calming him down, pulling out every variation of "The show must go on." Nothing was working. Then I remembered a line of dialogue from Judy Garland's final movie, *I Could Go On Singing*. In it, Judy played an auto-biographical role as a famous singer who at the end of the film is fed up with the emotional sacrifices she's made throughout her career. Her former lover, played by Dirk Bogarde, must pull her together so that she'll go onstage at the London Palladium and perform before the impatiently waiting sold-out audience.

He has since come out in public, but at the time Raúl had only recently come out privately as bisexual. I crossed my fingers and prayed that Raúl, as a newly out bisexual, might not have seen *I Could Go On Singing*. *A Star Is Born* or *Meet Me in St. Louis*, perhaps. I mean, those films are Gay 101. *I Could Go On Singing* was more graduate-level Judy-ism.

I took a chance and, evoking Dirk Bogarde's quietly empathetic tone, I quoted from the film verbatim, "I don't give a damn who you let down, but you're not going to let you down." As Raúl let my purloined words sink in, there was a kind of spark in his dark eyes. He took a dramatic pause and said, "Thank you. That's something I need to think about." He was coming around, but I had yet to seal the deal. "Raúl, let's go into Un Deux Trois and have a cocktail. I think we both deserve it. C'mon."

We entered the restaurant, which was nearly empty in late afternoon. I say nearly, because sitting at a table by herself was the veteran singing actress Polly Bergen. She was appearing next door at the Belasco Theatre in

a play called *Six Dance Lessons in Six Weeks*. Raúl had worked with her in the Broadway revival of *Cabaret*. At this time, I knew Polly only slightly. (A few years later, I would direct her in my film *A Very Serious Person*.)

Joining her at her table, we filled Polly in on the fraught situation over at *Taboo*. Raúl was still torn as to what his next move should be. Polly, a wise old bird with a half-century of showbiz experience behind her, had seen it all. She advised Raúl to get his keister back to the Plymouth Theatre. "Kid, you have two options in this business: be a known kook or be a professional. You're much too talented for the first option." Raúl downed his drink and returned with me to the theater for the second run-through.

Michael Riedel's latest column in the *New York Post* documenting the show's trials and tribulations revealed that *Taboo*'s poor timid book writer, Charles Busch, was being forced to cannibalize his own work. It was true that I was editing out quite a bit of dialogue. For one thing, I was new to musical theater and learning on the job to allow the songs to tell as much of the story as possible. What made my task daunting was that George had written songs that were melodic but had lyrics full of ambiguous poetic imagery that could've been sung by any of the characters at any point in the plot. It was up to me to construct a dramatic context for the song and make the lyrics appear to illuminate the situation of whatever character I chose to sing them. All of this was to be achieved in at most a page and a half of dialogue—and one of my two leads was not an actor.

I thought it best to protect George by simplifying his dialogue and allowing his excellent scene partners, Sarah Uriarte Berry and Liz McCartney, to handle the dramatic heavy lifting. The problem with gossip columnists is that they frequently get the facts right, but very rarely the background motivations.

We were nearing our final week of previews and the critics, tongues hanging out, were poised to pounce. The rules of Actors' Equity allowed us only ten more hours of rehearsal to be parceled out over those last few

days. We still had the ending of the show to restage along with some other important cleanup. Rosie urgently called me over for a private conference. George had just informed her that he despised the end of Act One. Why hadn't George expressed his dissatisfaction earlier?

I will concede that one part was a bit wonky. I'd felt we needed an example of Leigh Bowery as an audacious performance artist. During the brief period he spent living in New York, Leigh made a memorable appearance at the annual East Village drag festival, Wigstock. Wearing a voluminous two-piece maternity outfit, he began groaning in agony. From underneath his skirt, his wife, Nicola, emerged nude from a fake vagina, slathered in gooey placenta and afterbirth. Find the clip on YouTube. It really is hilarious, transgressive, and perversely beautiful.

We couldn't adequately re-create that comic grotesque routine. George's back was unable to support the harnessed Sarah as Nicola, and for the sake of stage safety, we had to eliminate the slippery afterbirth. A few years ago, a producer in LA phoned me inquiring about the *Taboo* production rights. He said, "I think the book is fine, except for that awful scene where Leigh gives birth to Nicola. I guess that was a leftover from the original British script." "Um . . . No. That awful idea was mine."

However, other than that miscalculation, the end of the act was working well. I was juggling three story lines with seven principal characters and leading them all to a temporary resolution with an element of suspense to lure the audience into Act Two. Rosie showed me George's handwritten notes for a suggested revision. We'd all worked particularly hard to protect Euan from being perceived as simply a Boy George impersonator. George's new scenario stripped away all the plot threads we'd built throughout the first act and replaced its culmination with a mini concert of Euan performing a medley of Culture Club's greatest hits, with the real George as Leigh Bowery bopping blissfully along to the music. End of Act One.

I didn't soft-pedal how appalling I found it. Rosie agreed, "I know. But what are we gonna do? He won't go onstage." "I'll do my best, but you're not going to like it," I warned her. "And there'll be no time to change it back." I returned to my desktop computer and attempted to make dramatic sense of George's outline.

I handed in the new material two days later. George said nothing to me, so I assumed he was pleased. Jeff and Chris quickly staged it and thereby used up the rest of our union-allotted rehearsal time. The new material went into the show for the first time at the soonest possible preview performance, and I sat with Rosie to watch. It was as egregious as I'd expected. When the lights went up for intermission, Rosie turned to me: "I haaaaate it! I *haaaate* it!"

It was difficult not to appear smug. "I told you it was gonna be awful. I did the best I could." "Well, it's got to be changed back." "That would be impossible. We have no more rehearsal time." "Well, it can't stay this way!" Never one to resist a snappy retort, I was compelled to reply, "Rosie, I don't like the MetLife Building on 45th Street. Can you tear it down for me tomorrow?" The show's general manager, Charlotte Wilcox, overhearing us, suggested we move the conversation out into the alley. Once there, we were quickly joined by my collaborators. Rosie was beside herself at the desecration of her show. Members of the audience began to create a circle around our beleaguered group. Charlotte whispered for us to laugh so that it would appear as if Rosie were putting on a comic performance.

There was nothing to be done. George's version was performed for the critics and for the rest of the run.

The show opened to nearly unanimous scathing reviews, although George came out of it smelling like a rose. Ben Brantley in the *New York Times* praised his tuneful score and "vaudevillian" performance. Most of the reviews placed the bulk of the blame on Rosie's hubris at thinking she could be a producer. These were the same critics who'd often bemoaned the trend of

Broadway shows having a consortium of forty impersonal corporate producers. Here was Rosie, a sole producer, investing her own money in this highly personal project, and they ripped her apart for her arrogance.

My book didn't escape the critical onslaught. I was painted as a mainstream Broadway pro who had vulgarly commercialized an entertaining London fringe production.

The entire experience had been so miserable that once the show opened, I rarely stopped by. At one of my few visits, I ran into Stephen Sondheim as he was leaving the theater. He congratulated me and said he found himself tearing up at the end of the show. This I was unprepared for. "Why? Were you weeping for the state of the musical theater?" Sondheim was on the level. "I really liked it. The show was *about* something. It's not music I would normally respond to, but I liked it a lot."

He was not alone in his praise for *Taboo*. Over the next few weeks, I was amazed to hear that Tony Kushner, John Weidman, and Susan Stroman had also admired the show. I couldn't get past the compromises and backstage drama. Since that experience, I've stayed as far as away from the musical theater as row H in the mezzanine. Time hasn't mellowed my feelings for *Taboo*, but I can understand the enthusiasm for its melodic score, the colorful costumes, the exciting performances from our excellent cast, and the daring subject matter.

Taboo received four Tony nominations: George and his musical associate Kevan Frost for Best Score, Mike Nichols and Bobby Pearce for their costume design, Raúl Esparza for Featured Actor in a Musical, and Euan Morton for Leading Actor in a Musical. They had to be content with a nomination because none of them won. Rosie, out of loyalty to the cast, kept the show running for a hundred performances until her business manager convinced her to cut her losses and call it a wrap.

It was several years before I saw Rosie again. My cardiologist was briefly sharing office space with the Iris Cantor Women's Health Clinic. As I was

leaving the building, I ran into Rosie on her way for a checkup. I accompanied her to her doctor's office on an upper floor and sat with her in the waiting room where we had a chance to catch up. There were a few other women seated in the room, several wearing scarves covering their hair loss from chemotherapy. I gathered one of the doctors sharing the waiting room was an oncologist. Rosie shifted her attention from me to these other women and began asking them questions about their lives and their children.

On our first night in London, she had confided to me that the title "The Queen of Nice" bestowed on her by the press during her talk show reign had been a burden. In truth, she had always been an edgy outsider, she told me. She was Ro to her family and friends—the cuddlier name "Rosie" was forced on her by an agent wanting her to appear more accessible. Observing her in that waiting room, she became the sweet, gregarious personality familiar from her TV show, and, though she may disagree, I believe that person is the true Ro. She had me take photos of her with each of the ladies using their cell phones, and gave those frightened, anxious women a warm, amusing anecdote to share with their families. I could imagine them saying, "You won't believe who I met today."

The Seventh Veil

2018. My friend the music journalist/biographer James Gavin once said when he was in a sour apple mood, "Cabaret is what you do when you're on your way up or on your way down." There's some truth to that statement,

but I refuse to believe it applies to me as I've dipped my feet into that particular pool at various times during my career. For the past decade, my pianist/arranger/duet partner Tom Judson and I have peddled our musical wares in four countries and over thirty cities. We would've made our long-awaited Columbus, Ohio, debut if we weren't waylaid by a worldwide pandemic.

When Tom and I began this latest foray into cabaret in 2011, I assumed I'd be performing in drag. A friend once told me that if he came to see my act and I wasn't in drag, it would be like going to Disneyland and finding that Space Mountain was closed. I'm eager to please, so I got out the wig, rhinestones, and feathers.

After a few years as a flame-tressed chanteuse, however, I had a gnawing suspicion that my drag appearance was at odds with the cabaret act I was presenting. After all, I wasn't appearing as a character in a play. I was introduced as "Charles Busch." Our shows centered on my sharing anecdotes from my life along with interpreting songs by the likes of Michel Legrand, Jimmy Webb, and Henry Mancini.

My advice to those starting out in cabaret has always been to strive to present onstage as authentic a version of oneself as possible. If I intended to grow as a cabaret performer, it might be necessary to strip off that final veil of self-protection. I aspire to embody British theater critic Kenneth Tynan's description of Marlene Dietrich: "She has sex without gender."

My gifted costume-designing friend Jimmy Johansmeyer offered to make me a suit that would traverse the narrow isthmus where Bruno Mars meets Judy Garland at the Palace. Picture if you will a slim boyish figure in a perfectly fitted narrow suit of emerald-green paisley brocade with rhinestone buttons. Instead of a formal button-down, I wore a simple black T-shirt underneath. To dial up the theatricality, I donned a single strand choker of small black jet beads that skimmed the edge of the T-shirt's masculine neckline. Continuing the 1960s Judy theme, I gelled and fluffed up my own short

brown hair and darkened my eyes with copious amounts of eyeliner and mascara. I thought the look exceedingly stylish, and in it I felt at ease performing without relying on a specifically female appearance. Interestingly, I also sang with increased breath control. Well, that might've been because I wasn't encased in a torturous tight-laced corset.

I posted a performance photo on Facebook and shortly afterward received a personal message from Michaele Vollbracht. A renowned fashion designer and illustrator from the seventies, the striking celebrity portraits he painted became frequent covers of Andy Warhol's *Interview* magazine. He also created notable logos for Broadway shows and book jackets and was a Coty Award–winning designer of women's evening wear. It all somehow fell apart, but years after he'd been exiled to the panhandle of Florida, he popped up on social media.

I was a longtime admirer, and over the previous few months we'd cultivated a Facebook "friendship." Once I mentioned to him that I'd always longed for a Michaele Vollbracht portrait, and a short time later a stunning four-by-four-foot painting of me arrived in the mail. When I posted the photo of myself in my new paisley suit, Michaele's message was a request for my phone number, which I immediately sent.

Within minutes the phone rang. The first thing I heard upon answering was Michaele Vollbracht's gruff voice growling, "That photo! You looked terrible! Dreadful!" How does one respond to such invective? "You didn't like the suit?" I asked. "The suit's fine, but that silly necklace couldn't be more wrong. Tacky!" I explained that with the green paisley being so flamboyant, I wanted something minimalist with just a hint of sparkle to border the neck of the T-shirt. Michaele Vollbracht refused to listen. "Charles, you need to fill in the entire space from your neck down to the first button of the suit with *beads*. Beads of every kind, of every color, glass beads, rhinestone beads, tribal beads, barbaric beads, violent beads, beads, beads, *beads*."

I tried to explain that it was important that it not seem as though I was in full drag. I was walking a tightrope between male and female and I didn't want to fall off on either side. He wasn't interested. "I'm telling you, Charles, the black T-shirt with that dime store necklace looked stupid. I've gotta go." And with that, he hung up.

I was left holding the phone, thinking, "That old man just doesn't get it." Half an hour later, I was in a bead store on West 38th Street filling up a basket with glass beads, rhinestone beads, tribal beads, barbaric beads, and violent beads, beads, beads, *beads*. I sank about eighty bucks into them beads.

Well, Michaele Vollbracht knew his business. All the disparate strands of beads melded together into one opulent fashion art piece that went beyond gender. I emailed him a photo of me wearing the suit with the beads. He emailed me back: "Perfect."

That was the last I heard from him. A few weeks later, his niece posted on his Facebook page that Uncle Mike had died from a long illness. How odd to feel a sense of loss for someone I'd never met in person. Wearing my green paisley suit with that abundant array of beads has granted me a visa to travel to new and more interesting territories in honest storytelling.

However, I didn't give up on drag in the theater. Far from it. In my near future lay such lavishly costumed leading roles as Judith of Bethulia, Cleopatra, and Lily Dare, the heroine of my 2018 mother love saga that had me age from innocent girlhood to majestic middle age to alcoholic hag in a parade of fashion-worthy frocks.

A Woman's Face

2005. The phone rang, and it was Joan Rivers. We'd seen each other over the years mostly when she'd come to my shows, or when we'd appear together at benefits such as *Joan Rivers' Funny Gay Friends* or the staged reading of *Caged* put on at Town Hall. It was a surprise that she still had my phone number, and an even bigger surprise that the first words out of her mouth were not "Hello, this is Joan," but "I'm working on a performance art piece. Wanna write it with me?" Joan Rivers? *Performance art?*

As much as I was starstruck at the notion of being involved with this legendary woman of comedy, I had projects of my own, and this sounded to me like something that would take up a lot of time and then never see the light of day. I replied, "Um . . . uh . . . no, I just don't see how I could, um . . . to be fair to you . . . I . . . um . . . no." Ignoring my eloquent attempt to decline, she proceeded to share her vague objective: to do something in a theater space, autobiographical but not exactly, not stand-up but funny, maybe not even that funny, perhaps with other people in the cast or perhaps not.

It's impossible for me to refrain from cranking out ideas. Over the phone I began tossing Joan potential concepts, including a Ruth Draper–type monologue that had her presiding over a dinner table of eclectic celebrity guests. I couldn't tell if she was responding or not. After a while, we bid each other goodbye.

Four years later, the phone rang again. When I picked it up, the first words I heard were, "So I took your advice." "Hello? Who's this?" Again, Joan asked me to work with her on this "performance art piece." It had

evolved into a play starring her as herself with an ensemble of actors playing her assistant and makeup artist and television producer. The plot was the behind-the-scenes drama of her reporting on the red carpet. Occasionally, she wanted to stop the action and reminisce about her life in a spotlit reverie. I couldn't dismiss Joan Rivers. I'd grown up loving her on *The Ed Sullivan Show* and then on *The Tonight Show.* "Joan, let me look at the script. I'd be happy to give you any ideas that might come to me, gratis." That seemed the most respectful yet noncommittal way of handling a comedy icon.

The manuscript was messengered over the next day. I read the play as soon as it arrived, then I phoned Joan. As I discovered over the next few years, for a workaholic jetting back and forth every week from New York to LA and often to London, Joan Rivers was one of the easiest people to reach of anyone I knew. I told her that the play was very funny, but that I didn't think she'd achieved her goal. There wasn't anything in those spotlit reveries I hadn't heard her reveal on a television talk show.

I still wasn't keen on rewriting it, but the possibility of getting to know Joan Rivers better was irresistible. In truth, at this time I didn't have much going on, and by Joan's standards, neither did she. For her, a dry spell was performing several out-of-town comedy gigs a week, running a home shopping clothing and jewelry empire on QVC, reporting on award shows for the E! channel, and being the subject of an ongoing documentary film.

I proposed that I come over to her apartment every day for a week and interview her. She could have the tapes transcribed and I'd shape the interviews into monologues. She warmed to the idea and insisted that I ought to be paid. I declined. It seemed important to me that this be less a professional collaboration than an act of friendship.

Every day that following week I showed up at noon at her place on 62nd Street, just off Fifth Avenue. Joan had bought her spectacular duplex apartment for a relatively low price after her husband's death and her move

to New York from Beverly Hills. The building had originally been built by the turn-of-the-previous-century millionaire J. P. Morgan as a private residence for his daughter. Years of neglect had left it something of a ruin. Joan's apartment had once been the magnificent gilded beaux arts ballroom and the rooms adjoining it, including the original orchestra's cloak room and servants' quarters. Joan retained the ballroom as her main salon and turned the other rooms into a library and master and guest bedroom suites. In her comedy act, she said that this was how Marie Antoinette would live if she had the money.

Having been in therapy for many years, I simply pretended that Joan was my patient. I asked her every possible intimate question on a wide variety of topics. Of course, she held all the cards. The tapes belonged to her. If she felt she'd gone too far, she could toss out whatever disturbed her. Still, she was incredibly candid and emotionally available—tears, rage, laughter, sentiment, bitterness, gratitude. We explored her complex relationships with her parents and her daughter, her disastrous late-night talk show, and Johnny Carson banishing her from late-night television, an event that led to her husband-manager Edgar's suicide. The threatened loss of her career induced the most intense emotion. She began to relive the anguish of Carson's revenge. She sobbed, her hands reaching out like claws. "He was unrelenting! It was like he had these tentacles trying to strangle me! To *destroy* me."

Over and over, she'd been screwed by producers, executives, and managers. Betrayed, fired, and ruined, she crawled back from the abyss time and again. Hers was an ugly world I'd chosen to avoid. As an Off-Broadway actor/playwright collaborating with longtime friends, mine was a gentler one. I said to her, "Joan, after all you've been through, I would think you'd hate show business." She looked at me dumbfounded. Was I insane? "*Hate show business?*"

Ruthlessness was a game both sides could play. When I asked her opinion on any extras I should put in writing for a cabaret contract, she advised, "Always ask for something difficult. They'll respect you more."

One morning she answered the door, her face covered with black scabs. I gasped. "What happened?" She made a dismissive gesture. "Oh, I had a little facial peel. I can only work two hours today because I'm doing a show tonight in Connecticut." She looked hideous. "But . . . but . . . but your face?" "Oh, I cover it with makeup." Bob Mackie once told me, "I love Joan. She shows up at fittings with blood still in her hair."

When I watch TV clips of Joan from the sixties and seventies, I don't recognize the person in them. I only got to really know her with her final face, and it bore as little resemblance to her early self as her renovated apartment would have to J. P. Morgan's daughter's original digs.

In the soft light of her home, Joan's surgically transformed visage reminded me of a porcelain doll. When you saw her in the harsh glare of an elevator, she could look a mite strange. We once attended an LGBT Kol Nidre service. As I escorted her down the aisle to our reserved seats, I overheard a woman rudely commenting, "Can you believe what she's done to her *face?*" I saw Joan as she wanted to see herself, so I thought she was beautiful. I should add that when the service was over, I commented to Joan that I'd been deeply moved when the elderly grey-haired lesbian sitting in front of us joined the men of the congregation in carrying the Torah down the aisle. Joan, who'd stood in rapt concentration throughout the service, replied, "It would've been more moving if she'd washed her hair."

At the end of our week of interviews, Graham, one of Joan's assistants, transcribed the tapes and I edited them into monologues. Joan put some of that material into her play, which she went on to perform in limited engagements in San Francisco, LA, and London. Again, Joan insisted that I be

compensated for my work. "Darling, you put the time in. You must get paid, and you must get a credit." I again refused, but she wouldn't relent. "Okay," I finally told her. "Whatever you think is appropriate." My manager, Jeff Melnick, got in touch with her notoriously combative lawyer, John Breglio. Within five minutes the negotiation grew ugly. "So, what did your client do? He wrote a few monologues. For that he should get a percentage of the gross?" When Jeff reported back to me, I reiterated what I'd said all along. "I don't want credit. I don't want money. I've established a friendship with Joan. That's all I hoped for."

Shortly afterwards, Joan invited Eric, Margaret, and me to her apartment for Thanksgiving. Thanksgiving at Maison Joan was a lavish affair; there was a long, magnificently appointed table seating up to forty people, rather like the dining table on *Downton Abbey*. I was honored that she had me seated next to her. Joan was so easy to talk to. As funny as she was onstage, she was also a great listener. One never felt as though she was marking time until it was her turn to speak, or that someone more interesting might just be over your shoulder.

We were in the middle of dinner when I felt Joan lightly touching my thigh. *What the hell is she . . . ?* Oh dear, were we moving into *Sunset Boulevard* territory? I looked down and found her slipping me an envelope. "Shhhh," she whispered. I surreptitiously opened it. Inside was five thousand dollars in cash. Unofficial payment for my work on the play. It would've been déclassé to refuse her munificent gesture of gratitude. I gently whispered in her ear, "Thank you. But you know, I would've fucked you anyway." To which the lady replied, "That's what they all say."

Our friendship grew. Is there anything that strengthens a bond like seeing a rare 1940s Andrews Sisters musical together at a revival cinema on a rainy Sunday afternoon? Big celebrities can suck all the oxygen from the room—not Joan. When Joan and Eric and I went to dinner after a critic's preview of my

play *The Third Story*, she wouldn't let the conversation drift away from what I was experiencing. She wanted to know how I felt the performance went. What was the genesis of the play? How were the rehearsals? What were my future hopes for the production? If I attempted to change the subject to something about her, she brought it right back to me. This was my night.

For the next few years, Joan attended my annual Christmas Day open house party. One year, she was accompanied by a glamorous friend, the much-married Countess Sondes. Joan had been to my building several times, but on this day, she crossed to the elevator on the right side of the lobby instead of the left side, which services the part of the building where I live. Exiting on the second floor, Joan rang the doorbell of an older gay man named Anthony. He was watching TV in his underwear and was annoyed that someone would have the nerve to ring his bell on Christmas Day. Thinking the hell with them, he opened the door to the intruders without throwing on so much as a robe. Imagine his surprise to find Joan Rivers and the Countess! Joan asked if this was Charles Busch's party. Seriously, what sort of party did she think I'd invited her to? A gay orgy? After they'd straightened things out, she commanded, "Anthony, put on your pants. You're coming with us!"

The Leading Ladies

When a simple exploratory throat procedure plunged Joan into a coma, it didn't seem possible that this was the end. Although she

was eighty-one, she was so vital, so full of plans. The night before, she'd done a full comedy set at a midtown cabaret room.

During the week that she lay in a coma, I debated whether I should visit the hospital. Aunt Lil had instilled in me the habit of analyzing my motives. She'd always prompt me to ask myself whether I was acting out of ego gratification.

My relationship with Joan's daughter, Melissa, was a casual one. We'd only met a few times at Joan's Thanksgiving dinners, since Melissa and her son, Cooper, lived in Los Angeles. I knew Melissa would be surrounded at this sad time by her close friends and her mother's most intimate circle. Would my appearance be appreciated or seem like a desire to consolidate my place in the mythology of her mother's life? Joan was reported as brain dead. If she'd been in any way conscious, I would've been there.

I took it badly when the news of Joan's death was confirmed. Tom Judson and I had a cabaret show that night up in Hudson, New York, and I could hear Joan's voice commanding me to pull myself together. "You put on your makeup, you go out there and make 'em laugh. This is what we do." And so I did.

My sister Margaret, Eric, and I attended Joan's funeral at Temple Emanu-El in Manhattan. Melissa delivered a service that was funny, honest, touching, and elegant, but with show business flair. As the ceremony drew to a close and Hugh Jackman sang the stirring Peter Allen song "Quiet Please, There's a Lady on Stage," I clung to the hope that the massive bronze doors of the temple would be flung open and there would be Joan, surrounded by a camera crew, and we'd see that this was all part of a surprise season finale for her reality series. Alas, the funeral concluded with a medley of Broadway hits sung by the New York City Gay Men's Chorus.

I was reminded of another celebrity funeral held a few blocks away in June 1969. Judy Garland had died in London at the age of forty-seven and her

body was brought back to New York to lie on view at Frank E. Campbell's funeral home before burial at Ferncliff Cemetery in Hartsdale, the same cemetery where my mother's ashes are interred. I wasn't allowed to attend my mother's funeral at Ferncliff in June 1962. Being seven years old, it was felt that I was too young. Margaret told me that she's been forever haunted by the sight of Mommy lying in her open casket.

Around the time of my mother's death, my father told me that the neurasthenic lady with the thrilling singing voice we were watching on television was Dorothy from *The Wizard of Oz* all grown up. From that point on, Judy Garland became a mother figure to me—she even had a son, Joey, who was exactly my age. The image of Judy hugging and kissing her little boy was a powerful one. When she died, there was no question that I'd cut school and join the throng bidding Judy farewell. I hadn't been at my mother's funeral, but I would see Judy lying in state.

Eighty-first Street between Fifth Avenue and Madison was packed with more than a thousand people as the line of mourners outside Frank E. Campbell's snaked around and around in concentric circles. I caught the eye of a gentleman in a belted trench coat and foulard, standing about fifty feet from the entrance. Picking up on my distress at the prospect of starting at the back of the line, he gave a quick nod and allowed me to cut in front of him. He confided that he was able to get away from work because he was a hairdresser with his own salon on 57th Street and he'd left his ladies in good hands.

We were ushered into the chapel, where we saw Judy lying in a glass-covered white coffin, a soft pin spot providing illumination. It was difficult accepting that the doll-like figure on display was Judy Garland. She held a slim prayer book in her hands. I remember thinking that a hand mic would've been more appropriate and somehow less kitschy. My companion muttered, "They've got her hair all wrong." Her hair was teased and sprayed,

similar to how she'd appeared on her 1963-1964 CBS TV series, not the casual contemporary style we'd seen in her last photos in London. How odd that after a lifetime of tour de force performances and volcanic offstage emotions, she was now an inanimate object to be studied with cool objectivity.

A few years ago, I was invited to teach a master class at the University of Western Michigan in Kalamazoo. They put me up in a meticulously restored 1869 Italianate villa on campus, replete with a winding staircase and furnished with museum-like accuracy. It was rumored to be haunted by the original owner, Mr. Babcock, and his wife, as well as several other generations of deceased midwestern academics. Except for a mysterious never-seen caretaker, I was alone in the twenty-three-room mansion.

Lying in the four-poster bed in the master bedroom, I welcomed all ghosts. If the joint was haunted, might the local ectoplasm of Kalamazoo invite my personal ghosts to join in their nocturnal meet and greet? How divine it would be to catch up with Meghan and Bobby! We'd reminisce about the performance of *Vampire Lesbians of Sodom* when my waist-length wig got caught on Bobby's spiked armband. When I tried to pull away, the wig shifted and created a solid curtain of auburn synthetic hair over my face. Meghan, in the wings, was shouting out what she hoped were helpful directions as I stumbled blind across the stage. At the time I'd wanted to murder Bobby, refusing to see the slapstick humor in the situation, but now the three of us could share a good laugh.

I could only hope that the Kalamazoo ghosts would extend an invitation to Joan. I could see her being intrigued by these early twentieth-century phantoms. In her refined "Mrs. Rosenberg from Fifth Avenue" mode, I could easily imagine her asking the shade of the school's first woman mathematics instructor, Laura Mickey, about her experiences navigating the all-male department. What if Miss Mickey inquired of Joan whether she'd enjoyed a

smooth transition after death? Joan, slipping into her stage persona, might reply, "I was waiting for the golden light I'd heard so much about. Nobody warns you that first you're plunged into total darkness. It was so dark. It was darker than my friend Claudia's crack before her anal bleaching."

I leave Joan and the speechless Miss Mickey in search of Aunt Lil. If there was ever a spirit strong enough to rip aside the veil of death, it would be hers. Yes. I see her standing by the tall window. Our eyes meet. No longer racked with pain, she's returned to her original erect posture. There's no melodramatic embrace. I take her hand in mine and I'm struck by how much my aging hand with its long fingers resembles hers. We're so connected that we pick up right where we left off. She needs to know how my sisters are and if I'm financially secure. I fill her in on the success of *The Tale of the Allergist's Wife*. She's impressed. "It ran two years? I hope you managed to hold onto some of that dough."

Though the role of the aged mother in that play was based on Aunt Belle, I tell Aunt Lil that I once wrote a TV sitcom pilot for CBS about her called *Lillian!* It was one of eight pilots I sold to CBS, HBO, and Showtime, with none ever produced. I wasn't temperamentally suited to pleasing a squadron of corporate vice presidents. It always felt like a form of highly paid office temp work. Aunt Lil is relieved to learn that I nevertheless receive a nice pension from the Writers Guild of America from writing the pilots.

I take out my phone and show her photos of my apartment. "Aunt Lil, doesn't this remind you of your decor, just dialed up a notch?" She laughs. "A notch? The walls are bright red. It looks like a whorehouse."

"Well . . . yes, but a high-class one."

"It *is* elegant. Ever since you were a little boy, you were fascinated by whorehouses. You must've been ten years old and still living out in Hartsdale. You drew this large drawing of a cross section of a Parisian bordello. You'd worked out the interiors of every room on three floors, and even the attic,

with the girls lounging on the sofas and against the doorways. The drawing was magnificent, so creative, but your fifth-grade teacher refused to hang it up on the wall with the other students' work. I went out to the school to speak to her, but there was nothing I could do."

Aunt Lil always knew when to step aside, and she's aware that there's someone else present I've been waiting a long time to see. Her eyes begin to tear up. Tough-minded and scientific, Aunt Lil is also deeply sentimental.

"She's in the library. She wants to be alone with you. Go."

A wave of insecurity passes through my body. What if she doesn't approve of me? What if I've turned into a grave disappointment for her? She hasn't seen me since I was seven years old. Is she still in the world of 1962 or has she kept up with the times? I move through the main salon and gesture to departed buddies such as Marian Seldes, Julie Wilson, and Tammy Grimes to please wait; I must speak with them before they vanish.

I find the library. It appears to be empty, but it's not.

My mother is seated in a Queen Anne chair. She's forty-one years old and looks more than ever like the actress Teresa Wright. Too shy and reserved to engage in conversation with strangers, her face lights up as she instantly recognizes the adult me. I kneel on the floor by her chair and at long last can place my head in her lap. *Ahhhhh.* It's as if I've been holding my breath for nearly sixty years. As I write these words, I hear Aunt Lil warning me, "Be careful. You don't want to get maudlin. You'll lose them."

The following day in Kalamazoo, I was asked by the theater department to perform in a reading of my latest stage vehicle, *The Confession of Lily Dare.* With less than an hour to rehearse the student supporting cast before the arrival of the audience, all I could do was impress upon the young actors the importance of playing in a highly energized but truthful style. The reading went well. The kids threw themselves into the play with gusto.

Afterward, my friend Greg, a New Yorker transplanted to Kalamazoo, asked what I was whispering to one of the boys in the cast during the last scene. There was nothing mysterious about it. I'd simply murmured, "We're at the end. Goose it up, kid. You don't want to lose them."

Acknowledgments

Acknowledging people at the end of a memoir puts one in the same self-aggrandizing situation as thanking the deceased at a memorial service for having had the profound insight to recognize your brilliance. I shall endeavor to steer clear of that trap. It's not easy.

An early attempt at putting my memories on paper was interviewing my comic muse Julie Halston on a newfangled mini-recording device that would also transcribe our ramblings. That proved disastrous when Julie's Commack, Long Island, accent and my high-falutin' verbal quirks emerged in print as indecipherable gibberish. Thank you, Julie, for submitting to that amusing failed experiment. Carl Andress, my longtime collaborator, who has an endless fascination in rehashing my worst professional disasters, was always on call to provide the correct details and sequence of events. I also benefited from excellent literary, publishing, and editorial advice and notes from Robb Pearlman (who acquired this book for publication), John Campbell, Victoria Wilson, Tom Judson, Nancy Balbirer, David Noh, Eric Myers, and my attorney Stephen Breimer. Jeffry Melnick, my late and deeply missed manager of thirty years, kept after me to write a book. I wish he were alive to see the finished memoir and how often he was mentioned. I was touched that my friends Chris Smith, De De Deville, Vince Sestito, Doug Plaut, and Matthew Ryan, and my nephew James Stull, asked to read early drafts of the manuscript and actually did read the whole thing.

Facebook has given me an invaluable forum to try out stories and receive immediate feedback. I have the best Facebook friends. Almost never indulging in easy snarky comments, they've greeted each of my long reminiscences with enthusiasm and affection during times when I was ready to delete all my files.

My friend since teenage years Andy Halliday and my sister Margaret Busch shared painful memories that provided me with insights into our shared pasts. My thanks as well to Amy Rose Marsh and Abby Von Nostram at Concord Theatricals for clearing the path for me to quote directly from my published plays.

The photographers whose work is represented in this book couldn't have been more accommodating. Thank you, Michael Wakefield, Joan Marcus, Jim Cox, Victor Mascaro, Ron Case, Walter McBride, and the estates of George Dudley, Marc Raboy, T. L. Boston, and Gene Bagnato. Thank you, B.T. Whitehill, for granting permission to display your poster art. You've provided the visual vocabulary for so much of my career. Marcus Hu and Jay Hartmann of Strand Releasing were wonderfully helpful in excavating a photo of Captain Monica Stark in *Psycho Beach Party* and Evan Schwartz at Wolfe Releasing for the use of the photo from *The Sixth Reel*. A special thank-you to David Rodgers for providing the glorious cover image and for the wonderful memories of our many photo sessions.

I'd like to thank Glenn Yeffeth, Leah Wilson, Claire Schulz, and Brigid Pearson at BenBella for their enthusiastic support and shepherding of this memoir. Arriving toward the end of a long creative journey was my editor, Alexa Stevenson, whose insight and intelligent questioning and problem solving led us through a lovely collaboration.

The book is dedicated to Katherine Carr, but that may not express enough gratitude for someone who's put so many hours, nay years, into this project, and more importantly, who is a true loving sister to me. I'm fortunate

to have as my agent Tom Miller, who, along with his vast knowledge of the ins and outs of publishing, brings to his clients his expertise as an editor and his gift for friendship.

In writing this memoir and diving into the past, I expected to be filled with renewed anger as I remembered the actions of the villains in my life. Upon reflection, however, I realize there were no real villains—just complicated people, all with a point of view. And I certainly see that there were heroes. I hope these pages have revealed the extent of the major roles that Ed Taussig, Ken Elliott, and Carl Andress have played in my life. It's an honor to have been a character in their lives.

The leading lady of this book is Lillian Blum. I wanted to create a full portrait of Aunt Lil. I never grew tired of listening to her repertoire of stories about her past and our shared experiences. I've derived great pleasure from retelling those stories and all the stories that I've shaped from the experiences of my nearly seventy years.

From early childhood on, I have viewed my life as a movie while I was living it. This may be the credit crawl, but I'm already filming the sequel.

Photography Credits

Photo Insert

Page 1   Photo of Charles in pink by Michael Wakefield

Page 2   Family photos courtesy of Charles Busch

Page 3   Photos of Charles and Ed courtesy of Charles Busch

Page 4   Photograph of Charles in 1977 courtesy of Charles Busch

Photo of Charles as ingénue by Gene Bagnato

Page 5   Julie Wilson portrait courtesy of Charles Busch

Page 6   Personal photos courtesy of Charles Busch

Page 7   Studio portrait of Aunt Lil with color restoration by Victor
Mascaro

Page 8   *Vampire Lesbians of Sodom* flyer courtesy of Charles Busch

Page 9   Photo of Charles and Bobby in Theodora by George Dudley

Page 10   Personal photos courtesy of Charles Busch

Page 11   *Gidget Goes Psychotic* flyer, graphic design by B.T. Whitehill

Page 12   Photo courtesy of the Estate of Marc Raboy

Page 13   Photo of Charles and Eric courtesy of Charles Busch

The Lady in Question cast photo by T. L. Boston

Page 14   Photo by David Rodgers

Page 15   Photos courtesy of Charles Busch

Page 16   Photo of Charles and Carl in *Die Mommie Die!* courtesy of
          Charles Busch

          Photo of Linda and Tony in *The Allergist's Wife* copyright Joan
          Marcus

          Photo of Charles on *Oz* courtesy of Charles Busch

Page 17   Photo of Charles in *Psycho Beach Party* courtesy of Strand
          Releasing

          Photo of Julie, Charles, and Jennifer in *The Divine Sister* by
          David Rodgers

          Photo of Charles and Tom at piano courtesy of Charles Busch

Page 18   Photo by Bottari & Case

Page 19   Photo by David Rodgers

Page 20   Photo of Charles and Liza Minnelli courtesy of Walter McBride
          Photography

          Cleopatra postcard – Photo by Michael Wakefield, graphic
          design by B.T. Whitehill

Page 21   Photo by David Rodgers

Page 22   Photo by Michael Wakefield, graphic design by B.T. Whitehill

Page 23   Photo of Charles in *The Sixth Reel* courtesy of Wolfe Video

          Photo of Charles and Joan Rivers courtesy of Charles Busch

Page 24   Photo by Jim Cox

Front Cover

Photo by David Rodgers

Jacket Back Flap

Photo by Michael Wakefield

About the Author

CHARLES BUSCH is an actor, playwright, and drag legend. He is the author and star of many plays, including *Vampire Lesbians of Sodom*, one of the longest-running plays in Off-Broadway history. His play *The Tale of the Allergist's Wife* played 777 performances on Broadway and received a Tony nomination for Best Play. Busch wrote and starred in the film versions of his plays *Psycho Beach Party* and *Die Mommie Die!*, the latter of which won him the Best Performance Award at the Sundance Film Festival. He has been honored with a special Drama Desk Award for career achievement as both performer and playwright and he also received the Flora Roberts Award for Sustained Achievement in the Theater by the Dramatist's Guild. For more about the author, please visit CharlesBusch.com.